"A masterpiece of Christ
tion's most thoughtful hist.........
universities should rush to share *Christian Historiography* with their history students. Jay Green leaves no stone unturned in his introduction to the way historians of faith understand the past."

—JOHN FEA, Chair of the History Department and
Professor of American History, Messiah College,
and author of *Why Study History?*
Reflecting on the Importance of the Past

"*Christian Historiography* is an excellent introduction to the state of the arguments regarding the relationship of Christian faith to historical writing. It should be required reading for Christian historians who want to understand how their faith should relate to their vocation. Green offers lucid summaries and gentle critiques of a wide range of approaches."

—GEORGE MARSDEN, author of *The Outrageous Idea
of Christian Scholarship*

"The faithful Christian life requires obedience to one's calling. But what is the specific nature of that calling, for those who have been called to write, think, and teach about the past? As Jay Green stresses in this thought-provoking book, there is more than one way to answer that question; but there are criteria that may help us discover which of those ways are the best and most fruitful. I predict that Green's fivefold taxonomy of Christian historiographical models will form an essential part of our discussions of these matters for years to come."

—WILFRED MCCLAY, G.T. and Libby Blankenship Chair
in the History of Liberty, and Director, Center for the
History of Liberty, University of Oklahoma

"In this learned and tremendously useful book, Jay Green describes five recent and remarkably varied approaches to the study of the past by Christian, primarily Protestant evangelical, scholars. In the end, his measured analysis offers an eloquent and passionate defense of the importance of historical reflection. This is the indispensable foundation for a new generation's questions about faith and history."

—BETH SCHWEIGER, Department of History,
University of Arkansas

CHRISTIAN HISTORIOGRAPHY

CHRISTIAN HISTORIOGRAPHY
Five Rival Versions

Jay D. Green

BAYLOR UNIVERSITY PRESS

Unless otherwise stated, Scripture quotations are from the New Revised
Standard Version Bible, copyright 1989, Division of Christian Education
of the National Council of the Churches of Christ in the United States
of America. Used by permission. All rights reserved.

Cover Design by Stephanie Milanowski

Library of Congress Cataloging-in-Publication Data

Green, Jay (Jay D.)
Christian historiography : five rival versions / Jay D. Green.
252 pages cm
Includes bibliographical references and index.
ISBN 978-1-4813-0263-0 (pbk. : alk. paper)
1. Christianity—Historiography. I. Title.
BR138.G685 2015
230.007—dc23
2015005076

Printed in the United States of America on acid-free paper with a
minimum of 30 percent post-consumer waste recycled content.

For Beth Ann

CONTENTS

ACKNOWLEDGMENTS

Perhaps the greatest pleasure of finishing a book is the opportunity it affords to celebrate the many relationships and acts of generosity that made it possible. I have been thinking about the book's subject for so long that it makes no sense to distinguish assistance offered on this specific project from the more general kinds of encouragement and support I've been receiving from dozens of mentors, friends, colleagues, students, and family members over the past twenty-five years. The book's many flaws reflect on no one but me. But if its pages bear any insights at all, significant credit must go to those who have supported my endeavors, listened to my ideas (many of them half-baked), challenged my assumptions (a lot of them confused), and sharpened my thinking during that span.

Questions about faith and history have occupied my attention since at least my freshman year at Taylor University. My history professors—Bill Ringenberg, Alan Winquist, Tom Jones, and Steve Messer—first introduced me to "the integration of faith and learning," and I continue to draw personal and professional strength from their uncommon winsomeness and grace. My first serious conversations about Christian historiography, though, took place in the office of John Woodbridge at Trinity Evangelical Divinity School. John both imbued the subject with intellectual excitement and persuaded me to believe that my own voice might count for something. As a doctoral student at Kent State University, I had the privilege of studying under an advisor with a national reputation for historical scholarship that was both brilliant and clearly informed by Christian faith. Bob Swierenga remains a helpful critic, a model, a mentor, and a dear friend.

The greatest portion of my energies devoted to this subject has been spent in the good company of my peers. And Eric Miller and John Fea have proved my most enduring and durable conversation partners. From our heady M.A. days at Trinity, to the ups and downs of our respective Ph.D. programs, to the stresses of the job search, and finally to landing in our posts teaching history at Christian liberal arts colleges, we have remained in steady conversation surrounding our personal and professional struggles to relate faith to history. Whether in challenging one another to read yet another "latest" article, essay, or monograph, or in talking through the very real struggles of family, professional, and church life, I have relied heavily on the rare empathy and insight of these friends. I am ever in their debt.

A great many other friends and colleagues have lent me their listening ears and challenging perspectives, each significantly expanding my understanding of issues covered in this volume. Some of the most formative of these have included Fred Beuttler, Jon Boyd, Lendol Calder, Rob Caldwell, Eric Carlsson, Joel Carpenter, Jay Case, Colin Chapell, John Green, Brad Gundlach, Tim Hall, Mike Hamilton, Darryl Hart, Kenn Hermann, Will Katerberg, Hubert Krygsman, Mike Kugler, Tom Mach, George Marsden, Bill McClay, Tom Okie, Paul Otto, Dick Pierard, Russ Reeves, Beth Barton Schweiger, Chris Shannon, and Ron Wells. I am especially indebted to Jamie Smith for helping me refine the initial framework for the book, and to Barry Hankins, Sarah Huffines, Rick Kennedy, Jim LaGrand, Tracy McKenzie, Doug Sweeney, Bill Trollinger, Kent Woodrow, and Don Yerxa for taking time to read and comment on portions of the manuscript at various stages.

Being part of the Covenant College community during the past seventeen years has molded and formed me in more ways than I can count. And the impact my faithful and deeply learned colleagues have had on my understanding of Christianity and scholarship is beyond description; counting myself among this group is a singular honor. I am especially grateful to the members of my department: Richard Follett, Cale Horne, Alicia Jackson, and Paul Morton. Their good humor and unflagging support through the years—especially through the process of writing this book—has been remarkable. Many other Covenant colleagues have goaded, challenged, encouraged, and inspired me to think more carefully about our common task of doing faith-informed scholarship. Here, I am especially indebted to Nick Barker, Bill Davis, Bill Dennison, Chris Dodson, Rebecca Dodson, Kevin Eames, Jack Fennema, Brian Fikkert, Christiana Fitzpatrick, Cliff Foreman, Daphne Haddad, Russ Heddendorf, Paul Hesselink, Scott Jones, Steve Kaufmann, Ed Kellogg, Roger Lambert, Gwen Macallister, Dan MacDougall, Hans Madueme, Russ Mask, Reg McLelland, Tim Morris, Jack Muller, Tom Neiles, Richard Nelson, Becky Pennington, Don Petcher, Scott Quatro, Tim Steele, Ken Stewart, Bill Tate, Matt Vos, Elissa Weichbrodt, Lance Wescher, Jim Wildeman, John Wingard, and Dan Zuidema.

Two Covenant colleagues warrant a special mention. Kelly Kapic and Jeffrey Morton have been more like brothers to me than friends or coworkers. Their serious-minded dedication to their work, their students, their families, their churches, and their faith encourages and grounds me almost every day, and reminds me that the task of "faith and history" is anything but theoretical or merely academic. I am grateful to them for their kind encouragement and their grace.

Some of my richest "faith and history" conversations at Covenant have bubbled up through the years in the classroom. It's been an extraordinary privilege to teach (especially) Introduction to History and Historiography to hundreds of the brightest, most thoughtful Christian students I can imagine. The genesis of the book emerged amid years of lively discussion with them, and their amazing questions nourished almost every decision I made from beginning to end. I thank them for their openness, patience, hard work, and their trust.

I have received tremendous support—both moral and financial—from the Covenant administration. I am especially indebted here to Frank Brock, Troy Duble, Jeff Hall, Derek Halvorson, and Niel Nielson. I would also like to thank Billie and Norris Little for their generous support that stood behind some of my research, along with Covenant's many other faithful supporters who make our work in and outside the classroom possible. I'm also thankful for Covenant librarians Tom Horner, Tad Mindeman, John Holberg, and Barbara

Beckman, who kept me flush with interlibrary loan books and many other hard-to-find materials.

I owe an extraordinary debt of gratitude to one Covenant colleague, conspicuously absent from the lists above. The opportunities I've been given to engage students and colleagues at Covenant are really inconceivable apart from the great legacy of my dear friend Lou Voskuil. Lou taught history at the college level for well over forty years, nearly thirty of those at Covenant. There he helped build a rigorous and theologically astute culture of learning that my students and I benefit from every day. Among his many contributions to the college, Lou developed an upper-division survey of historiography that quickly became a "must-take" course for majors and non-majors alike. His unassuming brilliance as a scholar, his bravery as a colleague, his grace and humility as a teacher, and his kindness as a friend continue to shape me in large ways and small. The endless generosity and plodding faithfulness displayed by him and his extraordinary wife, Audrey, function as an enduring model for our whole community. A simple "thank you" seems inadequate. But it will have to do for now.

I am humbled by the unfaltering support I have received from the members and regular attenders at two churches: Akron Christian Reformed Church and Saint Elmo Presbyterian, and my pastors at each: Harry Winters and Cal Boroughs. They have always taken a genuine interest in my studies, but they also taught me that the value of historical learning should never be confined to college classrooms or professional conference sessions.

Two members at Saint Elmo played a critical role in making this book possible. Herb and Susan Lea graciously made their beautiful sixty-acre farm in Henagar, Alabama, available to me for several extended periods of writing. "Leahaven" became my refuge and my muse where close to 75 percent of this manuscript was written. I will always associate this book with that special place and those very dear friends.

Many thanks also go to Carey Newman and his staff at Baylor University Press for affirming and supporting the project from the beginning, and for providing so much support and encouragement along the way.

My parents, Jerry and Judy Green, and my in-laws, Bill and Mary Hoover, were loving and steadfast supporters of all my ambitions long before I had the foggiest notion of studying history, much less taking up this subject. Their deep and abiding faith in God sustained me from childhood, rooted me in the church, and helped me understand that any vocation I pursued could only matter to the extent that I envisioned it as part of God's kingdom.

My children are the joy of my life. Lucy, Matilda, and Charlie have not only shown me great patience—especially when my writing took me away from home—but have taken a surprisingly keen interest in this project. I can't imagine a greater delight than watching each of them grow in their knowledge of God and its wondrous implications for how they see and experience the world. The rock of my life and the center of our home is my amazing wife, Beth Ann. At every turn in our almost three decades together, she has shown me unflinching support, unselfish commitment, and unconditional love. She has created a home that bears witness to Christ's unearned grace and peace, and, in her own work teaching struggling young readers, she embodies everything good that Christian education might possibly mean. She is for me the most powerful demonstration of the ways that faith richly informs all aspects of life, and I gratefully dedicate this book to her.

INTRODUCTION
How Faith Matters to Historical Study

No stable meaning has ever attached itself to the idea of "Christian history."[1] Both through the centuries and more recently, Christian writers have explored and debated innumerable questions bearing on the relationship of faith to historical study. But these discussions have largely failed to form any clear consensus about what it means to think about and "do" history in a *Christian* way. I have grown convinced that there really can be no such thing as a single or definitive *Christian understanding of history*. And, as far as I'm concerned, this should be no cause for anxiety.

Christianity can never be reduced to just one of its many dimensions. As a religious—but also a political, social, and cultural— tradition with deep roots, countless branches, and a transnational presence, the faith takes many different forms and has played an almost infinite variety of roles in human civilization. It is formal dogma, institutional governance, canon law, moral statute, mediating social structure, cultic liturgy, and personal experience. It is speculative philosophy, supernatural revelation, existential belief, and an embodied community—living and dead—with a continuous witness to the life and significance of Jesus Christ stretching back to the first century, or, according the Paul's letter to the Colossians, to the very foundations of creation itself. It stands to reason that Christian believers have read and interpreted the significance of faith for historical understanding in many different ways.

Philosophers and theologians have long reflected on the grand and underlying meaning of history with God's creative acts at its

1

foundations, the fall of humankind as its definitive first act, the cross of Christ at its redemptive center, the persistence of God's people as one of its chief themes, and the eschatological hope of divine renewal as its climax.[2] But such philosophical and theological discourse, while interesting and valuable, offers precious little practical guidance to the working Christian historian of, say, nineteenth-century Belgian colonialism. Such a scholar may be comforted by the fact that the structures of time and eternity are underwritten with meaning and informed by various Christian axioms and truths. But said historian is likely to feel somewhat baffled when trying to apply such abstractions to Leopold II's misadventures in the Congo.

This book is *not* an attempt to produce a Christian philosophy (or theology) of history, nor even a history of Christian philosophies of history. The following survey is less concerned with trying to understand *the theological meaning* of history than with attempting to address the more concrete question of *how faith has mattered* among Christian authors doing the labor-intensive work of reconstructing the past. It offers a general overview covering the range of ways that contemporary Christians have applied faith-based priorities to historical thinking, research, writing, and teaching. In short, this study considers the various ways that formal and informal Christian historiography might be considered "Christian." Again, I do not believe there is any such thing as a single, universally applicable *Christian approach to history*. There are only a variety of commonly used, sometimes overlapping, often contradictory *models* for thinking and writing about the past in deliberately Christian ways. The task of this book will be to identify five such models or versions of Christian historiography, devoting a chapter to describing and evaluating each.[3]

To further clarify, when I refer to *versions*, I do not mean to denote competing Christian 'schools of interpretation' or 'philosophies history,' but rather the varied ways that faith is exercised, reflected, or demonstrated amid efforts to reconstruct the past. So when different Christian historians work within the same basic "version" of Christian historiography, they may well differ in specific ways when they put that model into practice, and will very often arrive at radically different conclusions. What participants within each version of Christian historiography share is instead a common understanding of *how* faith is exercised in pursuit of reading and interpreting the past.

Importantly, the boundaries that divide one version of Christian historiography from another are regularly and inevitably permeable; in other words, examples used to illustrate these approaches may occasionally reflect characteristics found in more than one model. It also bears noting that a specific historian may find herself applying faith commitments to history one way within a certain setting but differently someplace else. So it's likely that readers will find particular historians referenced in more than one chapter, expressing different but often overlapping strategies of faith-oriented history in each case. This cannot be helped. The purpose of this system of classification is not fine-grade exactitude. What it promises is order and explanatory efficiency in the service of understanding some semblance of a larger picture.

I do not pretend that this catalog provides an exhaustive account of every contemporary strategy for doing "Christian history" ever imagined or tried, nor would I ever say that mine is the only or even the best way of arranging this material.[4] As with any attempt at typology, this one is surely flawed. In any event, I believe this framework productively accounts for the *dominant pathways* that most self-consciously Christian students of the past have followed in bringing insights of faith to bear on their topics of inquiry. And, as a result, I believe it provides a useful guide to understanding the contemporary conversation about faith and history.

An overview like this one is intended to be helpful to fellow Christian historians and students of history who are interested in making sense of the varied ways their own faith commitments might shape their understanding of the past. I am inclined to believe that the challenge of Christian historiography is the business of every believing historian. But I would imagine that other nonbelieving students of historiography and intellectual history might also have an interest in this survey both as it sheds light on various knotty theoretical and methodological questions common to all modern historical endeavors, and as it reveals at least some of the intramural discussions and debates that have animated certain quarters of Christian intellectual life during the past few generations.

While my aim is not to advance or defend any particular model or approach to Christian historiography, I make no attempt to hide some of my own predilections. It would be dishonest of me to deny that, as a relatively traditional Christian myself, and an academic historian of somewhat conventional training, I find some of the models presented here more promising than others; this will become clear in due course. Nevertheless, this study is meant to be primarily descriptive and evaluative. While I don't believe the Christian tradition either offers or intends to provide a *single* or *clearly elucidated* vision of history, I hope to demonstrate that every model described here contains both faithful insights and troubling blind spots. In order for students and teachers to begin their own efforts at cultivating a more nuanced and sophisticated Christian understanding of the past—and for interested, nonreligious bystanders to begin making sense of this discourse—I believe they must start by understanding the variety of Christian options that have been tried. Toward this end, I hope this survey provides a useful starting point.

By way of introduction, it will be helpful to sketch a summative review of *how* faith has been said *to matter* for historical study to many believing historians. In doing so, the broad outline of these rival versions of Christian historiography (and the book generally) will come into focus. But before doing that, some of the chief objections and sources of indifference to the "faith/history conversation" among believing historians need to be considered.

How Is Christian Historiography "Christian"?

It would be nice at the outset to declare that faith plays an evident, indispensable role in the working lives of all believing historians. But the truth is more complicated. Many who fit this description simply don't see it that way at all. In fact, it is plausible to surmise that most Christian historians working today are largely indifferent to the question of "faith and history." This is partly explained by the fact that, as a subset of the general population, historians are famously oblivious to—even somewhat suspicious of—philosophical thinking. Thus for many students of history, contemplating such questions probably qualifies as at least a broadly *theoretical* concern.

Such believing historians are not necessarily hostile to questions of faith's place in historical writing; it just doesn't necessarily seem all that relevant to them.[5]

As an act of observing, reconstructing, interpreting, and writing (or teaching) about the past, history has been governed since the end of the nineteenth century by a fairly sturdy set of procedural norms that make its habits comparable more to the laboratory scientist than to the speculative philosopher or systematic theologian. In practice, if not in theory, traditional historical study is an enterprise that honors the careful, orderly, and fair-minded reading of primary sources, and prizes interpretations crafted without bias or ideological color. Most historians who have attended graduate school will be familiar with contentious debates over postmodern theory and the accompanying crises that have at times seemed bound to topple the entire profession.[6] But the world of critical theory has had surprisingly little influence on the workaday lives of most practicing history teachers and scholars.[7] Most hold to the ideal that their states of mind, political persuasions, and religious beliefs should have as little impact on their work as possible. To make matters of faith consciously applicable to one's choice of topics, selection of source materials, or interpretive decisions is to contaminate and undermine the results. Many would echo the sentiments of the avowed Roman Catholic historian Leslie Woodcock Tentler, when she admitted that, "save for my interest in matters religious, I can see no obvious ways in which my written work betrays a Christian author."[8]

Historian D. G. Hart has more recently expressed overt hostility to the idea that personal insights derived from biblical revelation or Christian theology should influence the way Christians think about activities *outside the church*. "Secular" vocations like scholarship (or law, or medicine, or horticulture, etc.) require nothing more of their Christian practitioners than to abide by the standards established by their respective guilds. To look for distinctively Christian ways of "doing" such vocations is to misunderstand the intent and even to distort the meaning of Christianity. Attempting to "redeem" or "Christianize" scholarship by applying faith-based strategies to it, concludes Hart, will only produce bad scholarship and, worse, wrongheaded notions of faith.[9]

The lack of interest in—or antagonism toward—questions of faith and history may also stem from an assumption that religion is chiefly a private matter whose bearing on public discourse is tenuous at best. It doesn't seem the least bit obvious to many historians that weekly participation in Mass or a small group Bible study could make a plausible difference in tomorrow's lecture on the New Deal or for an ongoing research project on labor conflict in nineteenth-century Dublin. Aside from a general commitment to producing quality work, treating sources honestly, and acting charitably toward students and colleagues (all generically professional rather than uniquely religious values), matters of faith seem little relevant to the working lives of many believers who teach and write history.[10]

Other historians are skeptical of mixing their religious faith with their craft because they assume that doing so will create more problems than it solves. A recent discussion among Christian historians revealed broad sympathy for the practice of "bracketing faith and historical practice." Within the pages of a journal dedicated to exploring the ways that faith informs historical scholarship, the distinguished intellectual historian Jon H. Roberts confessed a complete lack of interest in doing so. To lean on insights derived from faith was, for Roberts, tantamount to "a Christian arson inspector who ascribes a fire to the work of God and chooses to leave it at that or that of a physician who diagnoses a recurrent headache to divine punishment and opts not to call for x-rays." Instead, as a Christian, Roberts has elected to follow the widely accepted "common rules" of the discipline known as methodological naturalism, which, he contends, "involves no metaphysical claims at all."[11] Roberts spoke for many Christian historians who see the profession's religiously "neutral" norms as perfectly adequate and well suited to the practice of their trade. Nothing could be gained—and much lost—by drawing on the personal insights of religious devotion.

If believing historians like Roberts feel skittish about bringing faith into discussions about historical practice, it's often because they strongly associate Christian historiography with providentialism, or the aspiration to identify and narrate the role of God in the affairs of past human civilizations. While the centrality of divine providence in Christian teaching and writing is rarely questioned, few professionally trained Christian historians give this approach much credence, and even fewer attempt it themselves. However, among many ordinary Christians, pastors, and popular writers, there is a remarkable desire to see "God's hand" in human history revealed and explained (and its absence within secular textbooks and other monographs is taken as proof of the books' anti-Christian bias). Many Christian school and homeschool history curricula take the role of God in the past as foundational, making their study of history a natural extension of their study of Scripture. This, for many, constitutes the plainest meaning of Christian historiography.

While resisting talk of God in the past, many professionally trained historians who study religion found an alternate way to regard their work as "Christian." Christians who pursue church and religious history are naturally interested in questions of faith as a matter of research and teaching, if nothing else. It's likely what drew them to their topics in the first place. But the experiences and sensibilities Christians bring to their study of religion are arguably distinct from those of nonbelievers. In the wake of twentieth-century secularization, scholars regularly treated religion as an illusion or a symbolic expression of more "real" material factors. Amid a broader reaction that endeavored to "take religion seriously" within scholarship, it was frequently persons of faith who led this charge. This sense of empathy for religion—and the scholarship it produced—would come to constitute an important expression of faith-informed historiography.

For some Christian historians, though, simply taking religion more seriously has never been sufficient. A movement of "Christian worldview thinking" emerging in the late 1960s made it clear that Christian historiography could be far more than "history written by Christians" or "historical studies of the church and theology." These worldview advocates urged the study of all dimensions of past human life from a distinctively "Christian frame of reference," sparking a debate about whether Christians in fact *do* see the world in fundamentally different ways "through the eyes of faith." They called on Christians to "enter into the study of history in such a way that it may lead to an analysis and account of the historical process that is true, insightful, and revealing of the human condition."[12] This highly influential conception of Christian historiography was at least initially the province of Reformed Christians who maintained that one's background faith commitments determined one's overall vision for life.[13] But this "integrationist model" ultimately spread to become, at least until recently, the reigning paradigm for Christian college and university research and teaching.

Other believing historians have been similarly interested in breaking "scientific" history's hold over the study of the past. But they have been more interested in seeing history return to its ancient status as a branch of moral philosophy. Faith has mattered for them, not in the work of "technical history" but rather in a secondary maneuver through which Christian values are used to evaluate the actions and decisions of past actors, and in the ways that offer moral guidance and a variety of "useable pasts" that can guide right moral action in the present. Filled with a storehouse of "lessons" that will lead to better lives and improved social arrangements for those who learn from its wisdom, they argue that history should function as a kind of exercise in applied Christian ethics. Of course, the peculiar lessons it teaches differ depending on the particular Christian concerns various writers bring with them to the past. "Conservative" and "liberal" Christians have each come to this task with competing and often irreconcilable priorities, but members of both factions stand on common ground in viewing history as a useful and reliable moral tutor.

Still other Christians have been drawn to history because of its value in demonstrating that the claims of Christianity are actually true. This apologetic or evangelistic sense of history sometimes sets out to resolve questions of the Bible's historicity. Writers in this tradition have often held that a straightforward, objective reading of past facts is the best means of defending Christianity's truth. The life, death, and resurrection of Jesus are true, authentic, historically verifiable facts, and the honest observer of these unassailable facts will have no choice but to submit to Christ's claims. These writers rely not on a "distinctively Christian" sense of history but, rather, on an unbridled confidence that history is objective and accessible to anyone.[14]

Other adherents of historical apologetics assert that, if Christianity is true, then its benefits to humankind will have been manifested in its impact on human cultures. Various Christian historians and "public intellectuals" have set out to describe the enormous number of social, intellectual, and cultural benefits that Christianity has bestowed on human civilization (including but not limited to science, democracy, capitalism, and the eradication of slavery). Others have attempted to show the consequences of abandoning faith by looking at stories of decline in cultures and civilizations that have forsaken the insights of Christian faith. These histories are often written in reply to those who reject Christianity due to its purported record of violence, abuse, and social harm.

These five broad versions of Christian historiography—as taking religion seriously, as application of background faith commitments, as applied Christian ethics, as Christian apologetics, or as a search for God—provide a window into the conversation among contemporary Christians both inside and outside the academy on how faith-based insights might matter to historical study. Much of the writing generated by these approaches has produced thoughtful, nuanced knowledge about the past. Much of it has not. But if the witness of Christians studying the past in these ways has taught us anything, it is that the Christian tradition offers us a sumptuous buffet of options for applying Christian faith to this endlessly interesting and infinitely complex craft. Sampling, reviewing, and better understanding the various courses in this feast is the challenge of this study.

1

HISTORICAL STUDY THAT TAKES RELIGION SERIOUSLY

Among Christians who pursue graduate study in history, a disproportionate number seem to gravitate toward religious topics. Their reasons for doing so are almost certainly autobiographical: "Write what you know!" A quest for self-understanding among historians is an undeniable factor in developing and shaping their research interests. There are similarly lopsided percentages of African Americans doing history and race, women studying gender, and gay and lesbian scholars working on LGBT topics. Believing historians are no different: they often enter graduate school with an unsurprising curiosity about religious themes. This is not a trivial observation. Regardless of their convictions about personal faith and history, the mere fact of their own religious identities inclines these scholars to engage their subjects with a measure of built-in empathy. This fact doesn't mean they will inevitably endorse their subjects' beliefs, choices, or actions, or always assess their fates with a "rooting interest." Sometimes they will; other times, not. But, consciously or unconsciously, historians who experience faith as a central feature of their personal lives are more prone to treat past religious beliefs and experiences as also something real, knowing that reality consists of far more than the observable, material world.

The massive corpus of historical scholarship on religious themes produced by believing historians is a testament to one of the important ways that *faith matters* to historical study. The natural empathy believers have toward their subjects has been instrumental in raising the banner of religion's importance in human history and played a decisive role in producing a renaissance in modern religious historiography. But the unique challenges of studying religion in the modern academy have also brought these scholars into conflict with some of professional scholarship's reigning orthodoxies, and inspired them to forge new and innovative ways to be part of the intellectual discourse about the religious past.

The Problem of Religion in Twentieth-Century Historiography

Modern Western history has been a story of declining religious power, and nowhere has this been more evident than within the academy. That American and European universities have undergone an intense process of secularization since the late nineteenth century seems such an unassailable fact that a detailed analysis of this plotline is unnecessary.[1] But the implications of this process for the status of religion as a subject of inquiry bears closer inspection. Since at least the early twentieth century, the academic study of religion has been highly contested within the human sciences, history included. Academic treatments of religion for well over a hundred years have been shaped chiefly by secular "scientific" biases that encouraged scholars to treat religious ideas, experiences, and motives as something less than what *religious people* imagined them to be. Religion seemed too subjective, too medieval, and ultimately too unscientific to analyze in a straightforward fashion. Rather than genuine experiences of the divine or normative descriptions of transcendent truth, the scientific ethos tended to treat religion as an epiphenomenon that reflected deeper, more empirically discernible psychological experiences (e.g., Freud and James) or socioeconomic interests (e.g., Weber and Marx).

Historian Brad Gregory contends that the professional standards governing the academic study of religion have long been imbued with *metaphysical commitments* that make it impossible for scholars to take the beliefs and practices of their subjects seriously. In the interest of promoting objective analysis, the "scientific" study of religion has adopted a form of dogmatic naturalism whose roots can be traced at least back to David Hume.[2] "On this view," writes Gregory, "religion must be reducible to something social, political, economic, cultural, psychological, or natural, because by definition there is nothing ✗ more for it to be." This "secular confessionalism" has so thoroughly woven itself into the discourse of modern scholarship that it is simply regarded as a "method" rather than the fully operative system of belief that it is.[3]

Already by the final decades of the nineteenth century, historian Bruce Kuklick observes, "there was a revolution in the way reflective Americans came to understand the world. Instead of serving as an assumption underlying one's knowledge, Protestant theism itself became a subject for study and analysis." Unable any longer to envision theological dogma as a legitimate foundation for learning, scholarship began gradually to turn its attention to religious themes only as they "manifested struggles for power, worldly perquisites, and psychic gratification."[4] Religion could no longer be believed, as such, but that didn't mean it couldn't be dissected scientifically. Such dissection became an important aspect of academic inquiry.

Kuklick contends that the advent of biblical higher criticism was a major turning point in Western intellectual life. Beginning in the 1870s, students of the Scriptures were invited to measure stories of virgin births, bodily resurrections, and divine interventions against their own experiences informed by decidedly modern notions of scientific cause and effect. "What investigators believed could possibly happen in the contemporary period," argues Kuklick, "was a measure of what was acceptable as what could have happened in the past—no matter what the Bible or other venerated sources told us." Those who wrote these sacred texts may have earnestly believed in the supernatural stories they described, but modern authors simply could not. Such impulses, Kuklick concludes, were instrumental "in reordering the worldview of twentieth-century thinkers, more crucial I think than Darwin." This scientific ethos ushered in a new morality for historians in which they could no longer establish their beliefs upon their hopes or wishes, nor simply give intellectual assent to one or another established authority. The only ground for historical truth available to the historian was scientific verification. Summarizing the central argument of Van A. Harvey's influential book, *The Historian and the Believer*, Robert Handy writes that scholars at the beginning of the twentieth century had imbibed an entirely "new morality of historical judgment, one that celebrates methodological skepticism and that proceeds by raising doubts at every juncture."[5]

While new attitudes toward sacred texts may have helped usher in this critically minded ethic, it was the newly emerging social sciences that provided historians with methods and paradigms they would need to make it operative. Early twentieth-century psychologists such as William James, Stanley Clark, and James Leuba were hard at work in universities across the country, developing research programs that aimed to understand religious experience through the empirical lenses of personality development, feelings, and "inner experience." Meanwhile, Franz Boas was beginning to apply the insights of anthropology to religious practices by making use of ethnographic assessments of folklore, ritual, and myth. Soon, the social theories of German thinkers like Max Weber and Emile Durkheim were beginning to make their way into American universities, encouraging scholars to think about religious institutions and beliefs in relationship to the rise of capitalism or as little more than a potent social glue. What participants in this social scientific ethos shared was a general commitment to exploring the structural underpinnings of religious phenomena because such constructions were empirically knowable and measurable. "Accepting a broadly naturalistic world view," observes historian Edward Purcell, led this early generation of social scientists to conclude "that the only real knowledge available about both man and society was empirical and experimental. Theological dogmas and philosophical absolutes," Purcell notes, "were at worst totally fraudulent and at best merely symbolic of deep human aspirations. Metaphysical questions, dealing with such nonempirical concepts as essence or soul, were simply meaningless."[6]

Of course, this modern social scientific study of religion—along with scholarship more generally—wasn't interested in dispassionate study or the pursuit of knowledge as an end in itself. These research programs were accompanied by an ascendant confidence in the power of science to serve humanity and to solve long-standing social problems. Indeed, the academic vocation during the first two or three decades of the century was shaped by an imperative of social reform and human improvement, ever confident that an empirically verified account of the social order might lead to the eradication of vexing problems such as poverty, ignorance, and political corruption.

A related set of developments within American Protestantism emerged right alongside the academy's reconsideration of religion. Theological modernists like Shailer Mathews and advocates of the "Social Gospel" like Walter Rauschenbusch hoped to make Christianity more fully adapted to science, and to harness the power of socially engaged, scientifically informed churches to "Christianize the social order."[7] They also aimed to modulate the supernatural and confessional baggage associated with traditional Christianity, but, unlike many within the academy, they believed it was important to maintain the institutions, the language, and even the values of faith. Many of them firmly believed that such adaptations were an antidote that would *preserve* rather than *extinguish* Christianity in the modern age. What they shared with their counterparts in the social sciences was a belief in the power of science to advance humankind. Mathews thought of himself as a Christian "who implicitly trusts the historical method of an approach to Christian truth" and who was capable of using "the methods of modern science to find, state and use the permanent values of inherited orthodoxy in meeting the needs of the modern world."[8]

The mood among religious thinkers by the late 1920s was well reflected in H. Richard Niebuhr's *Social Sources of Denominationalism* (1929).[9] Though he was a theologian with a heart for serving the contemporary church, Niebuhr's book suggested that Christians were guided much less by their theological commitments than by their respective social-structural, psychological, political, and economic contexts. In fact, Niebuhr argued, theological formulations of all kinds in every age have been shaped by "the demands of the national psychology, the effect of social tradition, the influence of cultural heritage, and the weight of economic interest."[10] While revealing Christianity's "social sources" did not lead Niebuhr to abandon his personal connection to the faith, the theologian conceded that the social sciences should play an essential role in defining and framing what constitutes religion.

Progressive historians during these same years would have had little understanding or use for the balance Mathews or Niebuhr were attempting to strike between the virtues of modern science and the ongoing value of religious practices.[11] Emerging proponents of a "new history," including James Harvey Robinson and Charles Beard, began applying the insights of social science to their work and called for the abandonment of all historical explanations that weren't clearly grounded within the social environment. According to Robert Skotheim, Robinson thought of ideas as "ultimately creatures, rather than creators, of the environment. Human thought was a tool which was fashioned by an environmental crucible to help man adjust to his changing environment."[12] Using the techniques of social science (most importantly psychology and economics), Robinson called on fellow historians to push back against the "conservative" idea that human nature is fixed and static, and to demonstrate the good prospect of radically reforming human nature by altering the human environment.[13]

While the vogue of Robinson's more progressive ambitions for history as a tool for social reform faded rather quickly, his vision of framing all features of human development within the strict scaffolding of past social environments would become an article of professional orthodoxy. And religion as a subject of inquiry, when it was considered at all, was consistently treated as an epiphenomenon. Most historical study of religion was relegated to ecclesiastical history, and, even here, the methods of a strict socio-historical method guided most interpretations. In his *Christian Philosophy of History* (1943), distinguished University of Chicago church historian Shirley Jackson Case argued that the Christian past needed to be subjected to unrelenting, rigorous, and complete social analysis because, he argued, there is no reality outside of strict historical cause and effect.[14]

More aggressive brands of materialism—Marxism most importantly—were adopted by a growing number of historians by midcentury, and studies informed by these theories were (not surprisingly) unsympathetic to religion as a genuine feature of human life. British historians such as Christopher Hill and E. P. Thompson led the way in subjecting various topics in English religious history to withering Marxian analysis. Hill's many books on seventeenth-century Britain envisioned the Puritan movement as an emerging bourgeoisie, experimenting with new and progressive forms of economic interchange. "His Marxist views," according to David Bebbington, "induced him to see the intellectual dimension of religion as a product of the fundamental economic processes that determined the course of history."[15] In his masterwork, *The Making of an English Working Class* (1963), Thompson arrived at many similarly reductionist conclusions about nineteenth-century British Methodism.

By the 1950s and 1960s, even many social theorists who dismissed Marxism also dismissed religion as an illusory category that masked deeper material factors. They confidently held that the incontestable forces of modernization would in all likelihood bring about the eradication of religion in Western life during their own lifetimes. The ascendant "secularization thesis" was often employed not merely as a useful theory that explained the shrinking authority of religious institutions and ideas but an iron law of modern development going forward. Many of them would have assented to Emile Durkheim's remarkable assertion: "If there is one truth that history teaches us beyond doubt, it is that religion tends to embrace a smaller and smaller portion of social life."[16] To the degree that social theorists remained generally committed to assessing and resolving *contemporary* social challenges, it made little sense for them to focus much attention on what amounted to an illusory set of social formations that were not long for this world.

Throughout the balance of the century, among most rank-and-file scholars, religion as a serious category of historical analysis largely fell under the precepts of what Wilfred McClay has called "a soft, cautious, inoffensive secularism that omits rather than debunks."[17] With some notable exceptions, religion held little standing as an explanatory category in human history. But in the undercurrent, while most assumed genuine religion was being written out of human life—past and present—at least a few diligent scholars were conspiring to preserve its status as a meaningful force in historical development. This so-called "return of religion" to both social theory and historiography would be one of the more notable and surprising features of academic life during the 1960s and beyond.

The "Return of Religion" in Historiography and Social Theory

There were currents of discourse at midcentury on both sides of the Atlantic that not only questioned the secularizing reduction of religion *in scholarship* but also recognized such reductionism as merely symptomatic of the larger, far more worrisome disintegration of religion itself *as human civilization's vital force.* Having just endured the bludgeoning devastation of Nazism, and now being confronted by the rising threat of Stalinist totalitarianism, many in and outside the academy were calling for a restoration of religion's humanizing and civilizing power. Writing in the *Journal of Higher Education* in 1947, the University of Chicago's president Robert Maynard Hutchins lamented, "Civilization is doomed unless the hearts and minds of men can be changed, and unless we can bring about a moral, intellectual and spiritual reformation."[18] The problem wasn't simply located in the ways academic scholarship conceived of religion. Many worried that the institutions of religion and their animating ideas were losing their capacity to speak to a culture under threat. Some of these scholars began to address what they saw as a cataclysmic decline in their historical assessments of the West. And many of them struck a notably countercultural tone by asserting religion not merely as an independent variable, which was controversial enough, but as the beating heart of human civilization.

No one embodied this impulse better than H. Christopher Dawson (1889–1970). As scholars go, it would be hard to surpass Dawson's status as an academic outsider. A British Roman Catholic and cultural conservative who never held a regular university appointment, Dawson nevertheless managed to forge a commanding and consequential voice in the discourse of Western intellectual and cultural history that won him praise across the spectrum. Between the 1920s and the 1960s, he wrote dozens of books—displaying deep erudition and masterful synthesis in history, economics, sociology, and anthropology—delivered hundreds of lectures and addresses, and held a number of temporary prestigious academic posts, including a four-year stint at Harvard near the end of his life. *Time* magazine named him one of the greatest historians of the 1950s, and his friend, playwright and poet T. S. Eliot, regarded him as his generation's finest thinker.[19] An unabashed advocate of a "Christian view of history" at a time when such talk had grown quaint, Dawson endeavored nothing less than the recovery of the Christian mind and the cultural renewal of Western civilization.

In delivering the University of Edinburgh's prestigious Gifford Lectures in 1947, Dawson made plain his contention that religion had been the central and defining feature of human history. The reconstruction of the past is impossible without considering its power. Social groupings are formless without culture, which, in the end, is entirely dependent on a common view of life. And religion has always been the source of any coherent culture's common view of life. "Now it is easy for a modern man living in a highly secularized society to conceive of this common view of life as a purely secular thing which has no necessary connection with religious beliefs," wrote Dawson. "But in the past, it was not so. From the beginning man has already regarded his life and the life of society as intimately dependent on forces that lie outside his own control—on superhuman powers which rule both the world and the life of man."[20] Dawson was sure that nothing in any society was knowable or understandable without accounting for the religion on which it was built.

But Dawson well understood the challenges social theory had posed to the scholarly study of religion. In an essay for *The Sociological Review* in 1934, he recalled the damage done by Auguste Comte (whom he called "a sociological Moses"), whose logical positivism endeavored to expel all appeals to metaphysics or theology in building the foundations of modern social theory, convinced that he had harmed sociology as much as theology. Not only had Comte " 'sociologized' theology," but he also " 'theologized' sociology," imbuing social theory with an outrageous level of all-knowing, all-seeing authority. He implored sociologists to recognize that religion could only be understood properly as "an autonomous activity which has its own independent principle and laws." Never should it be treated as a "function of society" or *merely* "a factor in the social process." He believed that the sociology of religion had a valuable role to play in the study of religion but hoped that its practitioners would be careful to work more narrowly within the confines of what sociological insights can tell them, and to rely on the normative insights of philosophy and theology where appropriate.[21]

There were other evidences in the postwar years of a renewed willingness to think about religion as a serious and genuine feature of intellectual life. In 1948 the American Historical Association (AHA) elected as its president the devout Protestant historian of Christian missions at Yale (and former Baptist missionary), Kenneth Scott Latourette (1884–1968). More revealing still was his presidential address, "The Christian Understanding of History," which C. T. McIntire has described as "plainly, but politely, evangelistic."[22] Here, Latourette did not revert to the use of vague Christian principles with generic implications for historical practice. He proclaimed the Christian gospel quite baldly, describing in some detail the historical origins of Jesus Christ—his life, teachings, death, and resurrection—and its cosmic, transformative significance for Christian faith and world history.

Latourette admitted that the "historian as historian can neither refute nor demonstrate the Christian thesis, but he can detect evidence which suggests a strong probability for the truth of the Christian understanding." Although he claimed that he was spelling these ideas out at the AHA annual meeting because this Christian understanding might offer a useful "framework" for thinking about meaning in history, Latourette seemed more interested in urging his colleagues to consider their own mortality and existential standing. He also hoped they would see in this challenge the limits of their craft. Man, Latourette argued, is "obviously incomplete within history. He has longings which cannot be satisfied in the brief span of the existence of individuals in this flesh. The Christian view of history regards what occurs beyond physical death as essential to the realization of man's capacities and holds out confident hope of that fulfillment."[23] In short, the mystery of human existence, and its salve provided by religious faith, is beyond what historical study can understand. In fact, Latourette concluded, the operations of human reason should open the door broadly to Christianity's proposals.

> The historian, be he Christian or non-Christian, may not know whether God will fully triumph within history. He cannot conclusively demonstrate the validity of the Christian understanding of history. Yet he can establish a strong probability for the dependability of its insights. That is the most, which can be expected of human reason in any of the realms of knowledge.[24]

While there is little evidence that an evangelical revival in the AHA followed Latourette's address, the very fact that he delivered the speech at all reveals that authentically religious themes then held at least a modest presence within the university, and, in this postwar moment, the academy had developed some appetite for the transcendent meaning that religion could offer.[25]

Princeton University historian E. Harris Harbison (1907–1964) stated years later that Latourette's AHA address helped allay some of the loneliness that so many believing historians working in the profession had long felt.[26] Late in his career, the scholar of sixteenth-century Europe observed what he took to be a growing trend among scholars who were more sympathetic both to Christian themes and faith-informed voices. As a believer himself with a long-standing interest in promoting a Christian approach to historical understanding, Harbison had spent most of his career watching as religion was squeezed out of scholarly discourse. Near the end of his life, he expectantly observed, "I think it can be shown that the treatment of Christianity by historians who are not believers is becoming somewhat more sympathetic than it was, say a generation ago." Comparing histories of Western thought written in the 1920s—condescending and contemptuous of Christian belief—versus those that had begun to appear in the 1950s, Harbison wrote, "The trust in science is chastened and disillusioned, and the treatment of Christianity begins significantly with a statement to the effect that although the writer is not a professing Christian, he will do his best to be fair."[27]

Harbison believed he was witnessing "the revival of a Christian understanding of history," evidenced not only by what he saw as a growing sympathy for Christianity among nonbelievers but also in greater attention to the history of Christian historiography, the emergence of specifically theological insights (namely those of neoorthodoxy) in historical scholarship, and the increasing presence of "professing Christians" among scholars who are keen on making "Christian presuppositions more explicit" in their historical writing. He believed these trends offered a positive opening not only for Christians working in the academy, but might also supply more general benefits even to nonbelievers such as sensitizing "historians to moral and spiritual values in reaction against moral relativism" and renewing "the search for . . . eternal greatness incarnate in events."[28] In a world that seemed always on the verge of crisis and conflict, Harbison believed that such a Christian understanding of history offered unique insights to those seeking meaning in the contexts of tragedy.

Though not personally committed to any religious faith, historian Henry May had been writing sympathetically about religion in American history since the 1940s. In an important 1964 essay, "The Recovery of American Religious History," published in *The American Historical Review*, May aimed to help his contemporaries understand that religion remained a vital scholarly concern, and, contrary to the assumptions of some, it had not disappeared from formal historical scholarship. It was alive and well! He notably traced this "recovery" back to the 1930s, when a series of cultural shifts along with a compendium of works on religion began to loosen the hold that the dominant progressive paradigm had had on the study of religious topics.[29] He provided a long litany of books and articles about religion that laid some of the foundations for what writers by the end of the century would describe as the "return of religion" in Western historiography. But May's essay has more often been cited in subsequent decades as, itself, an important sign to emerging scholars that the icy grip of secularization and reductionist thinking about religion was perhaps beginning to thaw, and most who have cited his pivotal essay since consider, in retrospect, that it marked more of a beginning—some would even say a catalyst—than an end.[30]

It's important here to observe that whatever "return of religion" occurred during the postwar years happened amid a variety of other divergent impulses that were, if anything, pushing academic scholarship in ever more secular directions. The postwar era remained, in the words of John Coffey and Alister Chapman, "a self-confidently secular age."[31] This observation serves as a helpful reminder that the story of academic scholarship during these years is best understood as one of pluralistic splintering rather than a movement toward or away from tolerance for religious faith. It is also helpful to remember that, for the most part, whatever advocacy for religion developed in the second half of the century was nearly always pushing back against larger consensuses within the disciplines that were, by turns, hostile or mostly indifferent to religion as a valid category of human life. But the larger world of scholarship was at least beginning by the 1960s to carve out important spaces in which religion was taken seriously, and faith-informed people were beginning to join formal scholarly discussions in greater numbers.

The Importance of "Taking Religion Seriously"

By the 1960s, religious believers and others sympathetic to religious themes were quietly beginning to protest the long-standing practice of ignoring or marginalizing religion and religious perspectives in historical study. But they were not alone in their dissatisfaction with the profession and its priorities. In fact, they were the beneficiaries of some significant, though somewhat surprising tailwinds. In 1967, Irwin Unger described a rising backlash in American historiography against what John Higham eight years earlier had called "the cult of the 'American Consensus,'" a culture in the profession that had rendered American history "almost sedate." "The postwar generation of American historians had concluded," wrote Unger, "that continuity, contentment, and 'consensus' characterized the history of the nation; all else was either the illusion of the historian or that of his protagonists."[32] In response, a rising generation of young "New Left" historians were entering the profession and challenging the status quo with renewed attention to past "conflicts," reminiscent of Progressive historians like Charles Beard. In doing so, they drew attention to weaker, marginalized, and less well-represented voices in the past, laying the groundwork for a wide variety of new research agendas that would in the following decade begin to give a host of such groups (e.g., ethnic and racial minorities, wage laborers, and women) their due.

As marginalized scholars keen on studying less-than-popular topics, New Left radicals inspired a rising generation of Christian writers to begin speaking out. A young assistant professor in 1962, Jeffrey Burton Russell lamented the secular assault that he and other believing historians faced in attempting to build an academic career. "Some such men have found it difficult to secure appointment or advancement in universities and colleges where faculties by and large subscribe to the secular ethos," wrote Russell. He found the general refusal within the discipline to countenance religious views ironic in light of the fact that the academy maintained its own intractable orthodoxies that were, if anything, even more dogmatic and unyielding. Russell did not believe his religious faith gave him license to engage in biased special pleading, or to violate the canons of evidence and interpretation. "Bias, clearly, is undesirable, even immoral," wrote Russell. "But point of view is desirable as it builds facts and evidence into a meaningful construction. And it is desirable because it is by opposition of view to view that we can best weigh, evaluate, and proceed."[33]

Religiously committed historians, in Russell's view, were left with one of two options. They could, as the profession seemed to demand, segregate their beliefs from their work. "If you must hold such absurdly outmoded ideas, they say, at least do us the courtesy of keeping them out of your professional life." Or, as an alternative, such historians could take both their faith and their scholarship seriously. "Here the historian's religious opinions are a historical point of view," insisted Russell, "and he should write history from this point of view without the least qualification or apology." To embrace this latter option, which Russell clearly did, was for him a simple matter of intellectual honesty. There was no need to sacrifice either personal or professional integrity within an environment that claims to value genuine intellectual give and take.[34]

Russell was not alone in his feelings of loneliness and frustration on the academic margins. Sentiments like his helped to bring energy to the founding of a new professional organization dedicated to these very concerns. The Conference on Faith and History (CFH), according to D. G. Hart, traces its genesis back either to a breakfast fellowship group of Christian historians who met at the 1959 Chicago meeting of the AHA, or to a 1967 conference for Christian historians on American Protestantism held at Greenville College.[35] In either case, the CFH was formalized in 1967 as a gathering point for historians of evangelical conviction who wished to find fellowship and discuss connections between "faith and history." As it happens, most of those linked to the organization's origins were studying religious and church history. And, while the organization's eclectic purposes make it difficult to understand all it hoped to achieve, the CFH has most consistently functioned as a venue for encouraging and publishing historical scholarship about religion.[36]

Though the evangelical historians who founded the CFH did not reliably share any of the same political leanings of the New Left, they benefited from the mood this younger generation helped sweep into the historical profession. Their interest in religion at the time reflected well the larger hunt for underrepresented "minority voices," rendered mute by academic elitism and the bland "cult" of consensus.[37] And, like Russell, many evangelicals by the 1960s had begun to think of themselves as something of a repressed minority.[38] Strangely enough, some of the same patterns of disaffection and marginalization from the "mainstream" that had fueled the identity politics of second-wave feminism, Black Nationalism, and youth rebellion on college campuses animated the political mobilization of the rising Christian Right.[39] In this way, the CFH owed some portion of its origins and growth to both the New Left and the Christian Right. From the New Left CFH members received a boldness to challenge the conventions of their guild, and, while decidedly nonpolitical in its purposes, the CFH joined the Christian Right in developing an emerging public voice on behalf of evangelical conviction.

The founding of the CFH was a forerunner and a catalyst to a dual resurgence in both evangelical scholarship and religious historiography in the 1970s and 1980s.[40] Arguably, religious history has been the discipline most altered in the last forty years by the swelling tide of Christian scholars. The rise and growing sophistication of CFH conferences and publications through the decades provide a barometer for this revitalization of religiously sympathetic scholarship.[41] An exhaustive accounting of religious historiography written by believing religious historians since this renaissance is obviously impossible, but a summative overview seems in order.[42]

Aside from Dawson, Latourette, and Harbison, whose careers were coming to an end by the 1960s, few distinguished religious historians of faith could be identified by the mid 1960s. A noted exception was Timothy L. Smith (1924–1997), a Nazarene who labored quietly on the faculty of Johns Hopkins University for over twenty years, but who also left a legacy of scholarship and graduate students that would reverberate much farther.[43] A student of Arthur Schlesinger Sr. at Harvard, Smith made his first and most enduring contribution to religious historiography with his book, *Revivalism and Social Reform:*

American Protestantism on the Eve of the Civil War (1957). Recognized as a truly original work, Smith demonstrated that profound movements of social reform that helped fan the flames to civil war had their origins in the revivalism of the American evangelical heartland. A longtime member of the Church of the Nazarene, Smith made no effort to hide his faith or sympathy for those he studied: "It happens that I hold deep affection for the faith of the revivalists whose labors this book recounts."[44]

A sizeable proportion of the CFH's founding generation would go on to distinguished careers writing and teaching religious history at public universities, and many would also take on graduate students who would do the same. Other believing scholars of religious history who were unaffiliated with the CFH likewise produced first-rate scholarship (often specifically related to their own confessional traditions) at major public and private universities.[45] Still others of this earlier era distinguished themselves working in theological seminaries.[46]

The most commonly cited group of self-conscious Christians to emerge from the 1970s' resurgence include Reformed Protestant historians George Marsden, Mark Noll, and Nathan Hatch.[47] Together they have not only produced a small mountain of fresh and probing scholarship—many of them prize-winning—covering a wide array of religious themes, they have left an indelible mark on the field of American religious history. Most notably, these three did more than any other to move the study of their own heritage of American evangelicalism to the center of scholarship on religion. But at least as significant as their scholarship has been their efforts at networking and encouraging fellow scholars, and in serving as graduate advisors.[48]

The same could be said for another equally distinguished trio of religious historians, David Edwin Harrell Jr., Wayne Flynt, and Samuel S. Hill. Although they have received fewer accolades than Marsden, Noll, and Hatch together, their impact on the religious historiography of the American South has been nothing short of monumental.[49] They rarely factor or even appear in faith-history conversation because they have written little about the role played by their Christian beliefs in their scholarship. Also, until recently, Reformed evangelicals from the North have dominated this conversation, and they are neither Northern nor Reformed. But the dignity they each have brought to their historical subjects—especially when looking at the religious underbelly of the impoverished South—reveals a rare level of compassion and understanding that is easy to trace to their own religious sensibilities.

Many of the first generation of the CFH who didn't secure high-profile positions at research universities toiled away in relative obscurity at small Christian colleges and universities (most of which have at least one religious historian on their faculties; in some cases more), burdened with heavy teaching loads and limited professional development support. Many of them stayed active by attending conferences, presenting papers, and, for at least some, writing scholarly articles and monographs. More recently, their second- and third-generation successors at such schools have had greater ambitions of maintaining their research agendas, and, often with greater support from their institutions, they have been more successful in producing significant scholarship, publishing in top journals and with university presses.[50]

In the same way, many private colleges and universities have proved highly supportive of ever more distinguished work produced by various top-notch historians of faith.[51] One of the most distinguished religious historians of his generation, Randall Balmer, has held endowed chairs at both Columbia and Dartmouth, and remains open about the ways his scholarship is informed by his Christian convictions. Recent years have likewise generated a relatively new cohort of religious historians populating the ranks of seminary faculties, which have proven increasingly strong locations for the production of first-rate scholarship,[52] while a second generation of Christian scholars is doing the same at various public universities.[53] Like many of these settings, these historians are in turn attracting their own (often religiously committed) graduate students.

Two private, religiously affiliated research universities have risen in recent decades to become premier programs in the United States for graduate study in religious history. And on the faculty of each are some religiously devout Christians who attract graduate students both by their first-rate scholarship and by their interest in approaching their subjects as people of faith. The presence of Marsden, Noll, and Hatch at the University of Notre Dame has made its history department an attractive place for those interested in the study of

American Protestantism, but the department obviously has a rich and much older tradition of Catholic historiography. For many years, Jay Dolan and Philip Gleason trained graduate students in the history of Catholicism as devout Catholics. More recently, students of faith (among many others) have been drawn to study the social and religious history of American Catholicism with John McGreevy and R. Scott Appleby, early modern European religious history with Brad Gregory, the intellectual history of American religion (and nonreligion) with James Turner, and a wide range of religious topics across the spectrum of American history with Thomas Tweed.

While Baylor University does not have the long tradition or the resources of Notre Dame, it has made great strides during the past two decades in developing both a solid research program in religious history and a higher profile in its ambition to examine the worlds of ideas through the lens of its Baptist and Christian heritage. Two of its historians who have been most keen on strengthening these bonds are Barry Hankins, who has written voluminously on many different aspects of American evangelicalism, and Thomas Kidd, who may be the most productive young scholar of American religion now working. A scholar of colonial American religious history, barely into his second decade of work, Kidd already has a curriculum vita that would be the envy of most emeritus professors.

The foregoing review is surely inadequate and incomplete, but it provides at least a small sense of how the landscape of religious historiography has changed over the past half century and highlights the role that self-consciously Christian writers have played in bringing it to pass. Although one does not have to be a religiously observant person to *take religion seriously*—as countless nonbelieving historians demonstrate—faith-oriented historians have had an especially strong reason for doing so.[54] I have suggested that believing historians who write about the religious past are inclined to do so in a way that reflects something of their own personal commitments. But simply enumerating the volume and accomplishments of religiously committed historians since 1970 does little to address questions about *how* faith has (or perhaps hasn't) informed their work. This question warrants closer consideration.

The Difference Faith Makes—The Hermeneutic of Affection

Questions about the relationship between personal identity and written history have been posed within many of history's subdisciplines. Do men write women's history differently than women do? How is race-themed history affected by the racial identities of its writers? Can a relatively affluent Anglo American legitimately write the history of India's urban poor? Is a historian who is a Marine combat veteran especially suited to write a history of the Battle of Iwo Jima? Or, for the sake of objectivity, should historians stick to topics outside of their spheres of experience?[55] Empathy is regularly touted as one of the great virtues that exemplifies the best kind of historical study. Indeed, R. G. Collingwood argued that the human capacity for imaginative sympathy with past human actors is one of the factors that enable the historian to practice her craft.[56] But at what point does empathy turn into partisanship and special pleading?

Questions of empathy have obvious relevance to the matter of religion in historiography. What kind of "belief" (if any) is needed in order to study and interpret the practices and traditions of belief? As someone with no formal religious commitments, Henry May recognized the necessity of empathy and makes a thoughtful case for it.

> To write excellent religious history, I believe, one must have something like religious sensibility or imagination. Obviously, one does not have to be a believer. It is possible to write well about something one totally disbelieves, fears, or hates. But it is really not possible to write excellent history about something one dismisses, however tacitly, as unimportant. Somehow one's definition of reality must be broad enough to include the religious stream as well as the social and intellectual banks between which it flows.[57]

The ambition of reconstructing the past in a manner faithful to the intentions and perspectives of past actors, even if (especially if) the historian entirely lacks any of the same shared outlooks of those actors, has remained a basic part of the "noble dream" of the modern historical profession.[58]

There may be something intrinsic to religion that demands a special kind of sensibility by those who aim to study it. Wilfred McClay observes, "Religion is the ultimate 'totalizing discourse,' the master narrative of master narratives. Hence," posits McClay, "students should come away from the study of religion with the feeling that they have passed through the eye of a massive storm, though a force of immense power for creation and destruction, and therefore of immense consequentiality, since every religion is in some way an attempt to take account of the ultimate and of our proper relationship to it."[59] Of course adopting such a stance would necessitate an assent to something genuinely ultimate that one might even describe as "religious." This surely raises as many new problems as it solves, but McClay believes that "students should learn to understand and accord basic respect to established faiths other than their own" not out of some "misplaced sense of relativism or multiculturalism" but because religion naturally commands such respect.[60]

But among those who already believe, what (if any) real difference does such belief make in writing religious history? Lutheran historian of the Protestant Reformation Lewis W. Spitz was convinced that "the churched church historian" had "certain advantages" in doing religious history that her secular counterparts lacked. The likelihood of having received some theological training from childhood and having experienced years of liturgies and feast days provide devout historians with a deeper awareness of the past religious worlds they are trying to explain. More significantly, Spitz argued, believing church historians are apt to feel "a special responsibility for the history of religions" that make them sensitive not only toward their own faith but toward the faiths of non-Christian religious believers. He suggested that the practices of faith shielded devout historians from captivity to ideologies that might lead other scholars to distort and retrofit facts into ready-made systems. Adopting, instead, a "theology of history" enabled devout historians to remain hopeful about the prospect of discovering truth, "to cultivate a sense of tragedy, or irony," and to envision the task of writing history as "a genuine vocation," as a significant dimension of their larger religious devotion.[61]

Fellow lifelong Lutheran church historian Martin E. Marty was not as convinced of faith's obvious benefits to religious scholarship.

Often described as "the dean of American church history," Marty thought the question merited greater scrutiny. He imagined two scholars of equal training—one a believer, the other an atheist—who are each given the same topic to explore, along with comparable working conditions, resources, and funding. Would there be any measurable difference in the resulting research projects? He observed that scholars with clear Marxist commitments could be distinguished easily from their non-Marxist counterparts. By the same token, he argued, most would allow that being a woman, an African American, or a "psycho-historian" would naturally inform what the practitioner "sees" when conducting research in areas related to the historian's personal identity. Why not Christian faith?[62]

In trying to answer this question, Marty drew a distinction between what he called "substantive philosophers of history" and ordinary historians who operate (usually unconsciously) according to more modest "analytic philosophies of history." The former group aims at the production of grand interpretations of "total" or "universal history" and its meaning. Some of the more notable among them have attempted such schemes as Christians, including Wolfhart Pannenberg, Karl Löwth, and Pierre Teilhard de Chardin. In seeking to understand world-historical developments—past, present, and future—such Christian substantive philosophers seek to understand history in a very Christian philosophical sense: as history writ large. Among these, Marty argued, a Christian orientation will make all the difference in the world.

The latter group, Marty suggested, is not on such a grand odyssey. Ordinary historians work within a comparatively narrow set of constraints, usually with quite different goals. They are using particular sources from the past to reconstruct specific events on the ground. They are limited by what their sources tell them by the tenets of "ordinary empirical verification," and they are loath to fit such events into schema that go well beyond the area under consideration. They may believe there is a larger or deeper meaning found in such ordinary events, but the protocols of their discipline usually requires that they suppress any metaphysical or normative assertions. Among these, Marty concluded that having particular Christian commitments makes little or no practical difference to the basic tasks of what these historians are called to do or their outcomes.[63]

Historian Harry S. Stout came to a different conclusion. In an effort to address this question more concretely, he decided to actually test the scenario on which Marty only speculated. In trying to discern how his own theological commitments might have informed his scholarship on the history of Puritan New England, he decided to compare his work with two of the most distinguished scholars in his field, both avowed atheists: Perry Miller and Edmund Morgan.[64]

Stout professed the deepest respect for these two titans of American historiography, who were together responsible for a genuine renaissance in American intellectual history, and a considerable rehabilitation of the Puritans in the American imagination.[65] Although neither shared any part of the Puritan worldview, they both managed to offer deep, searching, and fair-minded analyses of Puritan ideas, social organizations, and actions. As scholars, they are models of erudition and evenhandedness. Stout concluded that Miller's and Morgan's atheism had no bearing on their methods and was in no way an impediment to their capacities for understanding their subjects.[66] But that isn't to say that their lack of shared commitments with their subjects had no bearing on how they interpreted the Puritan experience.

Drawing on the insights of theologian and historian H. Richard Niebuhr, Stout observed that all writers inevitably develop a kind of existential relationship with their subjects, which creates a unique dialectic between "subject/actor" and "historian/observer." Niebuhr suggested that, for the nonbelieving historian writing about religion, this relationship can never be more than "external" or "outer" history.[67] "No matter how sympathetic the history might be in its identification with the believing community," wrote Stout, "it is still seen from the outside looking in. The atheistic observer, regretfully or not, turns down family membership in the community of faith he or she describes." The believing historian, however, has a special link to the religious past that is "internal," even autobiographical. In this instance, "story teller and historical subject are bound in a common kinship of shared spirituality that incorporates both into a 'community of selves' that is nothing less than the kingdom of God."[68]

Stout acknowledged that Miller and Morgan both found a sense of "community" with Puritans as a part of their shared *American* identity, but his difference with each of them, born of divergent ultimate commitments, is substantial, and leads him to some very different conclusions. For instance, Stout understood "church" rather than "mind" as the primary frame of interpretive reference for understanding the Puritans; he understood "faith" rather than "mind" as the most salient factor in explaining their story; he attends to matters of piety and theology as preeminent rather than politics and social status; and, where Miller and Morgan interpreted the Puritan idea of themselves as a "redeemer nation" as "an index of their Americanization," Stout felt that, as a fellow Christian, he should chasten this sentiment as a form of idolatry.[69] While taking nothing away from the excellent scholarship and storied legacies of these two scholars, Stout concluded that his own personal religious convictions proved formative—even transformative—to his work as a religious historian.[70]

The Catholic historian Philip Gleason shares Stout's sensibility about personal faith. He notes that holding personal convictions born of Christian faith "entails a lively awareness of the limitations of human possibility, and like sensitivity to the human capacity for evil." Personally mystified by those who trust in "the kind of millennial future promised by Marxism," Gleason writes that it had always seemed "to me that anyone not invincibly self-deceived could verify the doctrine of original sin by a few moments of introspection."[71] While he makes it clear that he had not pursued the study of Roman Catholic history out of a religious motivation, the fact of his own religious life made treating religion as anything other than an independent variable in human experience unthinkable. He harshly criticizes the common tendency to treat religion as an epiphenomenon, under the assumption that "considerations of ethnicity, race, class, gender, or power provide deeper insights into what was really going on." Gleason was convinced by his own experience "of the power of religious belief in shaping a person's view of life and giving direction to his or her actions."[72]

Another Catholic historian, David Emmons, agrees. "Historians who do not recognize [the irreducible authenticity of religious experience] miss half the fun and much of the significance of studying the people who lived before them." But he balks at any suggestion that his calling requires him to provide specifically Christian answers to historical questions. "It is one thing to believe that God created all things, visible and invisible," he insists, "and that God was thus an agent in human history, and quite another to write such into a historical narrative or to offer it up as a historical explanation." Emmons prefers instead to think of his personal task in studying history by distinguishing between *"asking Catholic questions"* (a project he finds inherently worthwhile) and *"offering Catholic answers"* (an agenda that he describes as "outrageous").[73]

An insight Emmons learned after the publication of his book *The Butte Irish* is the significance of having a "right relationship with the people whose lives I intrude upon and mean to study."[74] After the book appeared, he had been gently criticized for treating his subjects with a "hermeneutic of affection," and after thinking about it further, decided this was a charge he should happily embrace. He had come to believe that empathetic affection was the least he owed his subjects.[75] That non-Catholics find historical Catholic beliefs "silly and absurd—or sinister and subversive," Emmons argues, does not give them the right to tell those people how they should have believed or behaved. He calls such attitudes "academic imperialism," which he believes perpetrates nefarious forms of injustice on the peoples of the past. "It is no way to treat friends," he insists. "It is not a right relationship." He sees it as a necessary ethic for all historians, not just those who are personally informed by faith. But he wonders if Christians, in the end, might have an inside track in this endeavor. "That tradition of grace, faith, good works, justice, and right relationships," Emmons concedes, *"may give* Catholics a significant advantage in trying to find that compassionate ideal, may even make them more assiduous in the search."[76]

Conclusion

In the early 1970s, University of Iowa graduate student Stephen E. Berk was putting the finishing touches on a book manuscript based on his Ph.D. thesis about the great early nineteenth-century minister and Yale president Timothy Dwight, whose revival preaching and educational leadership helped spawn the Second Great Awakening. Along the way Berk had received able, thoughtful guidance from two of the finest, most well-regarded religious historians alive, Sydney

Ahlstrom (at Yale) and Sidney Mead (at Iowa). Though not a believer himself, Berk had learned from both of these sensitive scholars much about the necessity of critical judgment and personal empathy. The result was an excellent, well-regarded analysis of tensions existing in the young republic between Dwight's almost Puritan-styled Calvinist orthodoxy and the nation's rising democratic spirit.

In an astonishing note in the book's preface, Berk reported that after he submitted the book for publication, he "experienced conversion to evangelical Christianity," the result of what he describes as a "long search for inner peace." Though it isn't clear that Dwight's witness from the archives had been a precipitating factor in Berk's conversion—which would have won the great revivalist yet another convert—the author wanted to make it clear that he believed the "overall spiritual basis" of events described in the book was in fact genuine.[77] Berk's story reminds us that empathy for past religious lives is indeed possible for historians who have no religious faith. It is unclear whether the experience of faith would have made a material difference in the level and quality of his empathy. It's possible that he would have written his book the same way *as a Christian* as he did before his conversion. But Berk seems to have believed that a postconversion look at Dwight would have been very different. His personal embrace of his subject's faith led him to connect existentially to Dwight, after the fact, far more than he could have in the midst of his studies. As a believer, Berk suddenly shared a common life with the great evangelist, and now had a deeper reason to care for his mission, the fate of his ideas, and the spiritual state of those who heard him preach.

The Christian faith practiced by many religious historians does not confer upon them special powers or grant them access to secret methods unavailable to nonbelievers, nor does it make them better (or worse) historians. But it can incline them for personal reasons to muster an unusually strong kind of identification with their subjects, which both preserves religion's irreducible quality and, indirectly, bears witness to the faith they profess.

2

HISTORICAL STUDY THROUGH THE LENS OF CHRISTIAN FAITH COMMITMENTS

Conceiving Christianity as a full-orbed "way of knowing" or "way of seeing" played an important role in reenergizing conservative Christian engagement with politics, culture, and intellectual life in the United States during the second half of the twentieth century. The assumption that Christians had some "distinctive" contributions to make and very specific responsibilities in public life helped propel them into the fray in new ways. This seemingly simple insight, sometimes called "Christian worldview thinking," likewise stands behind a prevailing conception of Christian historiography that during this same period dominated the discourse on Christian historiography. It sees Christian faith as a unique interpretive framework through which believing historians see reality and make sense of the past.[1] Christianity serves here as a "worldview" or a set of "spectacles" that gives reality a peculiar texture and hue. Regardless of *what* is being studied—religion, politics, culture, social structures, or war— the Christian historian will see them in markedly Christian ways.[2] Christian historical scholarship is *Christian* because the scholar, as a committed believer, *sees differently.* She sees *Christianly.*

This account of Christian scholarship has become the standard strategy for thinking about the disciplines among many Christian colleges and universities over the past thirty or forty years. Those schools that have maintained a formal Christian orientation—most among the 115 member institutions of the Council of Christian Colleges and Universities (CCCU)—have aimed to provide a "distinctively

"Christian" education by practicing what has been commonly called "the integration of faith and learning," an approach that envisions academic learning through a Christian world and life view.[3] Although Christians from diverse traditions have adopted this language, this peculiar way of talking about faith and scholarship has been dominant among evangelical Protestants in the United States, and owes much of its intellectual energy to the Reformed theological tradition.

The Sources of the Integrationist Model

Evangelical academic life was significantly revitalized during the second half of the twentieth century in no small part due to the potent force of this "integrationist" model of learning.[4] Early last century, conservative Protestants largely retreated from mainstream academic life in the wake of what many at the time perceived as an assault on traditional beliefs and ideas from an increasingly secular academy that had little tolerance for traditionally Christian propositions. Christian fundamentalists were pegged as anti-intellectual and ill-suited for service in the human or natural sciences, and many of them spent the 1930s and 1940s building an "alternate academy" of Bible colleges and training schools that emphasized biblical study, personal faith, and evangelism.[5] But following World War II, many fundamentalists (who then began to refer to themselves as "evangelicals") made a concerted effort to reassert themselves in the academic disciplines, confident that they could think and produce scholarship on par with anyone in the world.

This rising generation of young evangelical scholars, though, did not abandon their sense that tensions continued to exist between their Christian commitments and the reigning norms of the academy. While they largely affirmed that truth is truth *wherever it is found* and that the university could be a legitimate sphere in which to pursue it, the first postwar generation of Christian scholars continued to think of themselves as aliens working in at least moderately hostile territory. As Douglas Jacobsen and Rhonda Hustedt Jacobsen observe, Christian scholars of this era viewed their task as having two dimensions: "(1) to critique the premises of modern learning when and where they directly conflicted with Christian truth, and (2) to discover the ways modern learning at its best might either reinforce or refine the truths of faith. This was and is the foundation of the integrationist model of Christian scholarship."[6]

This formula has afforded evangelical scholars an efficient way to participate actively within the academic world—achieving Ph.D.'s in every field from the top universities in the world and going on to thriving academic careers teaching at universities large and small—while simultaneously resisting the temptation to become coopted by the normative proposals advanced by the academy. It has functioned as an elegant version of the biblical injunction to be "in" but not "of" the world.

The intellectual resources that inspired and shaped the integrationist model are most commonly traced to the theological tradition of historic Calvinism, and, more specifically, to a smaller strain within it identified with the famed nineteenth-century Dutch statesman and scholar, Abraham Kuyper (1837–1921). Richard Mouw has labeled this subtradition "cultural Calvinism." The most notable architects of the integrationist model since the 1970s have been from this tradition: Nicholas Wolterstorff, James Sire, Arthur Holmes, Brian J. Walsh, and J. Richard Middleton, to name only a few.[7] Although many scholars and institutions have adopted the language and mannerisms of integration, fewer abide by (and are sometimes oblivious to) all of its specifically Reformed underpinnings.

Cultural Calvinists hold that God created the world as thoroughly good and intended it from the beginning to glorify him in every respect. Humans were created in God's image to be stewards of creation, to fill the earth, and to commune with him forever. But through Adam's rebellion in the garden of Eden, the whole world fell into corruption and thoroughgoing decay. Sin warped and twisted every feature of creation from the broken moral sensibilities of humankind to the death and rot experienced within the animal and plant kingdoms. While the human calling to care for the earth remains in play, this task was thereafter met with suffering and futility, and the nature of human dominion became fraught with corruption and abuse. God continues to exercise absolute sovereignty over his creation, and its fundamentally good structure remains intact, even as every part of it languished in rebellion and disarray.

The story of humankind traced throughout the balance of Scripture, according to this tradition, is one in which God is unfolding his plan to redeem and restore creation. The Scriptures bear witness to creation's yearning for wholeness and human flourishing, and the fulfillment of this longing is met in the cosmic redemption achieved in the life, death, and resurrection of Jesus Christ. The reign of God is confirmed in Christ, as he continues in his triumphant work of making all things new. The Reformed account of redemption argues that God is calling out a portion of sinful humanity to become the recipients of God's saving grace. All of humankind receives manifold blessings from God in the form of his common grace, which explains why hints of true knowledge, insight, creativity, and civil order are evident within every civilization in history. But an ongoing conflict, or "antithesis" between God's good purposes and human rebellion will continue until the consummation of God's redemptive plan is complete, when every knee will bow and every tongue confess that Jesus Christ is Lord.

"Within this scenario," according to Jacobsen and Jacobsen, "it makes sense for Christian faith to serve as a fulcrum of correction for humanity's sinful thought and action. And the integration model does exactly that, stressing the need to bring a distinctively Christian perspective to bear on all merely human efforts to understand the created order."[8] The starting point here presumes that academic learning has been tainted by human rebellion and sin. While the integrationist model presumes the overriding truth of Christianity, it acknowledges both that the ongoing stain of sin will keep even Christians from always getting it "right" (the antithesis runs through all people rather than neatly dividing them into sheep and goats) and that non-Christian thinkers are often more than capable of gaining true and authentic insights about the world (common grace).

So there is a vibrant, world-affirming sensibility that drives integrationist Christian scholarship into every area of creation to observe, interpret, write, paint, compose, and sing the praises of God as a part of his original design for humankind and as part of Christ's redemptive work of renewal. In what has become the most commonly quoted phrase meant to capture this spirit and ambition, Abraham Kuyper wrote, "There is not one square inch of the entire creation about which Jesus Christ does not cry out, 'This is mine! This belongs to me!' "[9] But there is also a world-hesitant dimension of the integrationist paradigm that acknowledges creation's continued brokenness and its desperate need of healing. Together these sensibilities have set an agenda for Christian scholarship that continues to define much of the work and teaching done within Christian colleges and universities.

The Epistemological Assumptions of American Evangelicalism

In order to make sense of the resurgence of American evangelical intellectual life after World War II, it is important to look more closely at the sources of its prior collapse. Historian George Marsden believes that evangelicals lost their way intellectually well before their storied retreat from mainstream culture after the fundamentalist-modernist controversies of the 1920s. He believes the decline can be traced back to the late nineteenth century as evangelicals wed themselves to an outmoded, unworkable epistemological framework.

Until the era of the American Civil War, academic life in the United States had been virtually synonymous with the Protestant establishment and cohered comfortably with generally evangelical sensibilities. Marsden argues that evangelicals operated with an epistemology of naïve realism and an unwarranted confidence in the enduring promise of "Baconian science," which assumed that, regardless of what kinds of advances developed in human knowledge—and within the sciences in particular—the results would always ultimately correspond with basic assumptions evangelicals held about God, the Bible, and the traditional accounts of Christian orthodoxy.

"This blanket endorsement of the Baconian-Newtonian scientific assumptions and method, shared by Christians and non-Christians," argues Marsden, "had the important implication that, outside of theology, Christians did not consider themselves to belong to any special school of thought." Evangelicals naïvely held that science, "built on firm foundations universally recognized, and proceeding to virtual certainty by careful Baconian principles of induction, would yield the same results to all inquirers." While Christians might understand a few additional insights—namely those derived from special revelation—that non-Christians would not affirm or understand, American evangelicals continued to assume that all humans see the same reality and draw the same basic conclusions about the natural world. Since "the Creator had built a definite set of laws into nature and provided laws of the human mind that guided our access to nature's laws," writes Marsden, "in almost all areas Christians and non-Christians stood on exactly the same footing."[10]

The epistemological assumptions that reigned within American evangelicalism, notes Marsden, held that all knowledge about the world had to be established on objective, evidentiary grounds and that starting "with the certainties of common sense and following the careful inductive methods of Baconian science, [these evangelicals] were confident one could reach sure conclusions, compelling to any unbiased observer, in almost every aspect of human inquiry."[11] The rise to prominence in the early twentieth century of Darwinian science, Marxian social theory, and Freudian psychology created a crisis of epic proportions for evangelicals working in the academy. It became apparent that Baconian induction would no longer dependably yield unified or consistently biblical results.

The lesson Marsden draws from the experience of past evangelical intellectual failures is to acknowledge that there can be no "wholly neutral epistemology" capable of solving disagreements in human inquiry. "Rather, a Christian epistemology must frankly begin . . . not only with common sense but also with data derived from revelation. Our understanding of something of the full range of human knowledge is in important ways derived from our belief in a Creator who communicates to his creatures both in nature and Scripture."[12] Marsden is here building a case for a central plank in the integrationist framework known as *reformed epistemology*.

Marsden finds the antidote to naïve epistemological realism of American evangelicalism in Kuyper's assent to the notion of "two sciences." Just as there are two kinds of people living in the world— regenerate and unregenerate—so Kuyper argued, there are also two kinds of science. Since Christians begin their exploration of the world with, in Alvin Plantinga's phrase, a "properly basic" belief in the God of the Bible, they will predictably arrive at some different conclusions than those who do not. Kuyper isn't saying that Christians and non-Christians will *always* produce divergent readings of the world. He concedes, "There is a very broad realm of investigation in which the difference between the two groups exerts *no* influence." Still, explains Marsden, "the differences in basic principles mean that the two sciences soon diverge, much as a branch of a fruit tree grafted beside the branch of a wild root . . . Ultimately the goal and direction of these two sciences are at odds with each other, even though in some respects they are alike."[13]

Beginning in the 1970s, evangelical scholars began to employ the notion of "worldview" to express Kuyper's idea of "two sciences," a move that enabled them to push past a simplistic epistemology. Acknowledging that everyone comes to the task of inquiry with prereflective assumptions that shape their conclusions meant that no one could any longer claim the status of neutrality and that evangelical thinking could claim to offer a "rational" option even when it conflicted with consensus views of the mainstream academy. Worldview thinking empowered the integrationist's dual tasks of (1) critically evaluating the reigning norms embedded within the secular academy, and (2) selectively making use of serviceable insights drawn from the secular academy.

History from a Christian Perspective

The idea of "faith-informed" scholarship came into its own during the 1970s with the rising prominence of Kuyperian thinking and the ascendency of Christian colleges that began to reform their teaching and scholarship in self-consciously "integrative" ways. For Christian historians, the 1967 founding of the CFH and the launch of its journal, *Fides et Historia*, marked a new departure for discussions about the integration of faith and history. As discussed in chapter 1, the CFH helped carve out an important social and scholarly niche for Christian historians to demonstrate their scholarly bona fides (mostly as religious historians) as explicitly committed believers. But the CFH also played a critical role in shifting discussions about history away from the presumption of neutrality and objectivity toward an embrace of worldview thinking.

Thanks in part to the cultural and academic ferment of the 1970s, the first fifteen years of the CFH's existence witnessed a kind of golden age for worldview thinking about Christian historiography. More than at any later point in its subsequent history, the CFH was animated during this time by a lively, sometimes combative discourse about the implications of Christian faith for historical study. And, while no single or clear consensus emerged about how a Christian worldview shapes historical study, there was demonstrable enthusiasm for exploring every facet of the question.[14] In addition to the heady thought-pieces published in *Fides et Historia*, this era witnessed the publication of two dynamic edited volumes of essays (many of them first appearing in *Fides*), notably dominated by Calvin College faculty and graduates: *A Christian View of History?* (1975) and *History and Historical Understanding* (1984).[15]

One of the first substantial attempts in *Fides et Historia* to explain how Christian faith shaped the ways believers approached historical study was C. T. McIntire's "The Ongoing Task of Christian Historiography" (1970). A committed Kuyperian working at the Institute for Christian Studies in Toronto (and son of the strict Fundamentalist Presbyterian firebrand, Carl McIntire), McIntire observed that mainstream professional historians stubbornly refused to acknowledge their own underlying philosophical assumptions. They instead presumed that their only values were neutrality, objectivity, and a pragmatic quest to uncover the past honestly. Neo-Marxists knew better. Marxists exhibited a refreshing willingness to speak openly about their own distinctive assumptions and likewise showed that "established positivist-liberal" historians were similarly brimming with rules, values, and assumptions that they had embedded within universities and historical associations. In fact, argued McIntire, "all historians function with pretheoretical commitments, however unselfconscious they may be, which shape their research, method, teaching, and writing."[16]

Since all historians operate with acknowledged and unacknowledged worldview commitments that have implications for their scholarship, McIntire urged believing historians to embrace and exercise their own "pretheoretical commitments" in the form of underlying Christian beliefs, values, and convictions. As much as Christian believers might learn from both positivist-liberal and neo-Marxist historians, McIntire insisted, "our Christian perceptions of things are radically different from both."[17] The anti-philosophical bias among modern historians led to widespread prejudice against "Christian historiography"—notably shared by many practicing Christians—assuming it to be either inappropriate or a narrow-minded brand of propaganda. Since everyone operates with embedded presuppositions, McIntire argued that dismissing or discounting a formal Christian historiography was no longer tenable.

Many of the essays published in *Fides et Historia* during its early years took up McIntire's challenge to articulate a Christian historiography. A key task in this effort involved revisiting some of the history produced by non-Christians that exhibited obviously biased assumptions inconsistent with a Christian worldview. One such assumption was <u>determinism</u>, or the belief that humans exercised no genuine agency but were rather pawns at the mercy of fixed and inexorable social forces. Another regularly cited assumption was <u>reductionism</u>, or the tendency to insist that all historical events could be sufficiently explained by purely naturalistic forces of cause and effect. And yet another questionable notion often embedded in traditional historical accounts was a <u>naïve confidence in human goodness.</u>

Distinctions between what Christians and non-Christians could claim as historical knowledge were sometimes taken to extremes. Some assumed that Christians had special access to the unseen world. Historian Janette Bohi argued that God never intended for his people to flounder about in doubt about his workings in the world. "Acting upon faith," she continued, "a Christian may safely assert that the God of eternity . . . has a definite program for this world and that he intends his people to understand it clearly enough to act upon it." She discerned that it was possible to know that God-honoring nations have been and will continue to be blessed, while those that have dishonored the Lord have and will continue to crumble. "As I see it," continued Bohi, "the Christian historian has a mandate from God which should make him the most optimistic, the most indefatigable, and the most accurately informed scholar on the market." Because they have "a personal relationship to the Fountainhead of all knowledge," Christian historians have "special insight into God's program for the world," and she believed this program could be summed up in his protection of the moral law, his sustenance of gospel preaching, and his preservation of the Jewish people.[18]

W. Stanford Reid seemed to agree that what gives a Christian historian the capacity for a "Christian interpretation of history" isn't merely a peculiar philosophical or historical outlook but the experience of supernatural regeneration. "Only when that takes place does one become a new creature in Christ and begin to see all things new, that is, in light of eternity (2 Cor 5:17). Therefore, to formulate a Christian interpretation of history," continued Reid, "the historian requires not only to know what Christianity is, but to have committed himself to the living Christ. Only then can he interpret history from a Christian perspective."[19] The existential commitment of the historian to the tenets of Christian belief, Reid further argued, couldn't help but lead the believing historian to recognize that all of historical development occurs under God's sovereign governance. But he carefully warned against overreaching to explaining exactly *how* divine providence was guiding the past. As a student of *human* actions and events, the historian must "content himself with studying and understanding secondary causes."[20]

While it seemed appropriate to expose non-Christian (sometimes called "anti-normative") assumptions rooted in secular historical method, an underlying question left many unsettled: how incommensurable are Christian and non-Christian ways of doing history? Put another way, given the widespread acceptance of "perspectivism," to what extent can anyone appeal to common ground or objectivity in reconstructing the past? M. Howard Rienstra recognized that worldview thinking could logically descend into radical subjectivism and relativism. A wholesale indulgence of presuppositionalism would ultimately topple the very pillars of historical study, shifting attention away from a meaningful engagement with the past toward a preoccupation with the present in which "one would read history only for its perspective. History is no longer good or bad, subjective or objective," noted Rienstra. "Rather, one history would be distinguished from another primarily by the political, religious, or sexual preferences of its author."[21]

Rienstra wasn't alone in arguing that any conception of Christian historical scholarship needed to preserve some significant account of objectivity. In fact, there were plenty of CFH members who believed that the entire descent into perspectivism was a dangerous and ill-conceived business. A significant number of articles and rebuttals published in *Fides* during those early years revolved around the proposals of John Warwick Montgomery (some of whose ideas are addressed in chapter 4). Montgomery, who primarily studied history as a way to establish the truth claims of Christianity in the Bible, argued that the epistemological realism that had long defined traditional historical methods remained valid and reliable. If Christians simply applied them with rigor and care, they would come to true and objective accounts of the past. *This* was a Christian view of history![22]

In one issue of *Fides*, Steven A. Hein replied to an earlier critique of Montgomery's methods by Ronald VanderMolen. A student of Montgomery, Hein insisted that, contrary to VanderMolen's criticisms, Montgomery *did* hold to several presuppositions but only those that underlie and support the "empirical method in historical study." Namely, Hein argued that his teacher firmly held "the assumption that knowledge is possible, the assumption that the universe is regular, and that the human senses can be trusted."[23] Hein argued that the most important facet in any Christian's investigation of the past involved preserving an ultimate commitment to the rigors of empiricism and the scientific method.

Some took the quest to develop a comprehensive Christian framework of knowledge to extremes. If Kuyper was the father of Christian worldview thinking, his student Herman Dooyeweerd (1894–1977) was among its most ambitious advocates. Dooyeweerd advanced the Kuyperian project to a new level by developing a program that attempted to revamp the entire structure of human knowledge and to place it within a complex and distinctively Christian framework. He set about unpacking the "creational norms" and "modal spheres" of reality in breathtaking detail, thereby providing a fully realized, manifestly Christian way of describing the world. Many hard-core presuppositionalists believed that the best pathway to developing a truly Christian understanding of human knowledge was found in following Dooyeweerd's complex and well-developed program.[24]

Even within the Kuyperian-friendly confines of Calvin College's history department, some believed Dooyeweerdians took this quest for worldview thinking to an unhealthy extreme. Calvin's Dale Van Kley spoke for many when he expressed skepticism about the whole project. Rather than lashing ourselves to a philosophically rigid "world-historical vision" of a Dooyeweerd (which he saw as little different to the rigid paradigm of someone like Karl Marx), Van Kley concluded that Christian historians would be better served playing "the gadfly in the historical profession, to abase academic history every time it is unduly exalted by reminding it unceasingly of what it cannot prove—or disprove—and of its severe limitations both in the kinds of evidence at its disposal and its all too blunt tools of analysis."[25] In short, the Christian historian would serve the cause of historical learning best not by attempting to build and impose a complex philosophical grid on the past but by monitoring an otherwise serviceable profession by keeping it honest and making sure its ambitions remained manageable and modest.

Most historians committed to the "integration project" would likely agree with Van Kley that the basic norms of professional history are worth preserving and that adopting a self-consciously "Christian perspective" need not require a radical overhaul of traditional history's methods or goals. Even so, most also believed that developing a distinctively "Christian perspective" on history is an important responsibility. A long-standing faculty development practice at many, if not most, CCCU schools is the production of some kind of "integration paper." This is often a condition of tenure. Usually by their third or fifth year of employment, faculty members are required to spell out the ways that Christian faith informs their teaching and scholarship.[26] These papers usually enumerate various biblical and theological insights that undergird and guide traditional disciplinary practices for the believer.[27]

Alongside their colleagues across the disciplines, history professors at CCCU schools have undoubtedly produced dozens—probably hundreds—of these integration papers over the years, each giving voice to the varied ways that biblical insights provide a foundation for historical knowing, thinking, teaching, and scholarly research for Christians. Though they usually reflect personal theological and tradition-specific peculiarities, they are typically committed to situating history within a broadly conceived Christian worldview. A variety of published books and essays in this tradition have appeared since the early 1970s that have functioned as guides to students and faculty striving to do the same.[28] Among other things, these guides typically emphasize Christian presuppositions such as God's divine sovereignty over human affairs, the historical nature of the Christian religion (especially the historical Jesus and other features of special revelation), humans as bearers of God's image (imbued with rationality and free will), the inherent meaning and linear directionality of historical development, Christ's central place in the development of human history, the moral dimensions and responsibilities of human action, the historian's image-bearing capacity (within limits) to know true things about the past, the brokenness of the human condition, and the teleological movement of history toward the final consummation.

Many Christian historians undoubtedly believe the truth of these important theological themes. Far fewer recognize such truths as meaningful or relevant to their scholarship and teaching. The famously unphilosophical ethos so often found among historians often leads Christian writers to integrate faith with history in modest and informal ways. The ideal for many has been to allow the internal convictions of their lives to spill over into the practices of their teaching and research. Donald A. MacPhee observes, "some of the most effective attempts at integration are perhaps not really attempts at all, but are intuitive and unplanned moments of shared insight between instructor and student. If our Christian presuppositions are at peace rather than at war with our conception of our role as scholar-teacher," he concludes, "then applications will come in natural ways—not forced, mechanical, or tacked on for effect, or out of pious compulsion."[29]

The Legacies of Noll and Marsden

A common and largely justified criticism of the faith-history integration project has been its failure to produce an actual research program that demonstrates its presuppositional insights. It is not as though Christian historians haven't written articles or monographs; they have! But when they do, readers are typically hard pressed to find very much in them that is demonstrably Christian. Marxist historiography, by contrast, constitutes a mammoth tradition of Western literature that covers virtually every era, subdiscipline, and continent that has been explored by historical study. Though Christians may have at one time aspired to generate a tradition rivaling Marxian history, they haven't yet shown a lot of evidence that they can.[30]

Two historians are notable exceptions to this rule. The names George Marsden and Mark Noll are synonymous with writing history from "a Christian point of view." Both have been tireless advocates of theories, methods, and compelling reasons for producing Christian-oriented history, and both have achieved international renown for their award-winning monographs, articles, and essays that attempt to display the fruit of doing history Christianly. Whether due to their success in the wider academy or to their peculiar ability to craft compelling and nuanced explanations of their strategies, their approaches to integration have achieved the status of conventional wisdom among historians who identify with this paradigm. If there has been an "evangelical school" of historiography since the 1970s, these two clearly sit at its wellspring.[31]

While the two do not advocate identical ideas about Christian historiography, they have been close friends and allies in this project for decades; both also identify explicitly with the Reformed tradition and are commonly cited in the same breath.[32] Each served for many years on the faculties of two of the nation's flagship Christian colleges. After twenty years at Calvin College, Marsden left for Duke Divinity School in 1986 and then to the University of Notre Dame in 1992. Noll taught history at Wheaton College for almost thirty years before also leaving for Notre Dame to fill the same endowed chair that Marsden vacated upon his retirement in 2006.

Noll's influence on debates over Christian perspectives in history has been considerable, though less substantial or systematic than Marsden's. Whereas Marsden tended to frame the problems of history in philosophical terms, Noll's ruminations on historiography have been more straightforwardly theological. He graduated from Wheaton College in 1968 with a degree in English and earned an M.A. in comparative literature at the University of Iowa before moving toward historical study at Trinity Evangelical Divinity School and Vanderbilt Divinity School. He held memberships in Reformed denominations (the Orthodox Presbyterian Church and the Christian Reformed

Church) his entire adult life. Perhaps it is not significant that nearly all of his historical training came within seminary contexts, but it may help explain his prevailing and consistent interest in theology as the central framework for thinking carefully about the historian's task.[33]

Noll's most important contribution to the conversation about Christian scholarship is undoubtedly his 1994 book, *The Scandal of the Evangelical Mind*. After an already prodigious career in which he had published more than a dozen books and hundreds of articles, Noll presented his case for intellectual life as an ideal to which he believed evangelicals should aspire.[34] In it, he doesn't so much provide a framework for Christian thinking in the disciplines as an explanation for why he believes evangelicals had abandoned the life of the mind and several specific strategies designed to restore a vibrant and faithful tradition of evangelical thought. He described a model of faith-informed scholarship that has had a definite impact on Christian historians, but to understand his specific proposals for faith-informed history, some of his other writing on the subject should be considered.

In a significant 1978 *Fides et Historia* essay, Noll addressed fellow members of the CFH in a way that reveals his confidence that from this group might one day emerge a genuinely Christian historiographic voice with clear implications for the broader profession. Here, he praises some of its members' work in producing scholarship *about* religion. But the production of workaday history was not, in his estimation, the heart of organization's calling. Urging the membership to speak *in* and *to* the profession, while speaking *in* and *to* the church, Noll pressed members to "transcend provincial concerns" and exercise more substantial intellectual muscle on matters of pressing methodological debate. "From us," Noll insisted, "should proceed a clear confession that the existence of a creating and redeeming God must influence historical perceptions." In short, he believed the unique perspective of Christians working in the profession made them ideally suited to "pitch in where the battles are hottest while, however, keeping the home fires burning."[35]

He challenged CFH scholars to combine the highest quality of primary research with an unflinching commitment to viewing the worlds of the past through the prism of Christian theological reflection. This dual priority has been a consistent hallmark of Noll's lifelong program of scholarship. How matters of plausible divine action and human responsibility in the past bore on emergent historical methodologies, Noll cautioned, would undoubtedly raise "philosophical questions with which historians are often very uneasy, but they are the ones we must deal with if we as Christians are to use the new models of historical explanation as servants rather than see them become our lords."[36] With a kind of idealism difficult to find anywhere today, he charged fellow believing historians "not to rest until our historical explanations are brought into the circle of Christian explanations—until, that is, our historical sensitivity to God's work in the world is as vital as our affirmation that he is indeed active among men."[37]

Noll has oriented much of his writing about faith-informed history on the importance of epistemic confidence in what the Christian may say about the past. He argues that his own strong belief in the "truthfulness of historic Christianity . . . has almost completely freed my mind from skepticism about the human ability to understand something about the past." Biblical Christianity asserts the reality that God made a real and knowable world and that humans have been endowed with an ability to know the world, if not always in a complete way.[38]

In a 1990 essay in the *Christian Scholar's Review*, Noll more fully develops his conviction that traditional Christianity provides a sturdy and reliable foundation for the historian's craft; more specifically, traditional Christian foundations make objective knowledge of the past possible.[39] Like Marsden before him, Noll takes up the challenge that epistemological skepticism poses to the foundations of historical knowledge. But for Noll, the epistemological crisis doesn't merely threaten our ability to know the past; it threatens Christian orthodoxy itself. The faith is indisputably historical, and to believe in its truth claims means believing that the events underlying these claims actually happened. He argues that the Christian faith offers "a conserving strategy to meet the epistemological crisis of historical knowledge." And not just any old brand of Christian faith; Noll advocates a faith that "affirms that God is not just the creator and passive sustainer of the world, but also that his energy is the source of the world's energy and his will is the foundation of its existence."[40]

Noll here puts forward what amounts to an argument about the dependability of historical knowledge rooted in the basic "background beliefs" widely held by traditional Christian historians. Namely, he mentions the Christian belief in God's divine creation and sustaining presence, the incarnation and the unfolding of divine redemption, the unity of humankind rooted in our creation in God's image, and the finite and fallen quality of human nature. He assesses each of the primary doctrines, arguing that these fundamental dimensions of a Christian worldview undergird the believing historian to approach the enterprise of learning from the past with relative certainty and confidence. More deeply, Noll makes the grander theological claim that these truths stand at the very foundation of the larger project of human knowledge itself.

But Noll is also quick to concede that the "historical interpretations of nonbelievers are valuable" to any Christian intellectual pursuit. The "cosmological assumptions" of Christian faith undergird the work of all historians not just those who are Christians. God has created the world and all of its potentials so that everything the historian does or observes relies on God's sustenance, whether she acknowledges it or not. "These convictions," Noll asserts, "lead to the intellectually imperialistic conclusions that effective, responsible historical writing exists by the specific grace of the one true God, which is the Trinity named and worshiped by Christians."[41] But this does not mean that Christians are somehow smarter or privileged with deeper insights into the nature of reality. A "self-denying ordinance" of Christian conviction holds that all humans are made in the image of God and that all human labor (including that of nonbelieving historians) should be honored and valued.

In another perceptive and theologically astute essay, Noll explores the unique insights offered to Christian historians by missiologists, theologians who study the global advance of the Christian gospel. Noll believes that these scholars have unique insights to offer Christian historians who, like himself, are attempting to "negotiate between history as theology and history as science." Like Christian historians, missiologists are trained to observe the meaning of Christianity as it is translated from culture to culture while simultaneously reading the historical record of human activity with care and precision. They engage the dicey business of navigating the spiritual realities their subjects experience within the dynamics of thick cultural interaction. "The functional atheism of the academy often makes it difficult for missiologists to keep the realities of faith in focus," writes Noll. "The functional gnosticism of sending churches often makes it difficult to keep realities of lived human experience in view. Yet missiologists, as they attend to the actual dynamics of what they study, keep both atheism and gnosticism at bay."[42]

Again, Noll has consistently insisted that history is a theological endeavor. He concedes that Christian historians have been wise to resist "excessive providentialism," which has weakened and often undermined the project of historical study. But he also believes that the collective push in the other direction has amounted to an overcorrection. He believes that missiology can moderate this overcorrection as missiologists skillfully "show how the beauty, power, and coherence of the Christian faith make it possible to learn from the modern world without falling prey to intellectual confusion or anti-Christian conclusions."[43] And this is an aptitude that Noll believes Christian historians must possess above all others.

While his insights are often striking and his arguments about the place of theology have been uniquely beneficial, Mark Noll has not left Christian historians with a very systematic or well-developed program for integrating faith and history. George Marsden's contribution to this tradition, by contrast, has been a good deal more specific and consequential. Marsden was raised in the Orthodox Presbyterian Church and attended Westminster Theological Seminary before receiving his Ph.D. at Yale University in 1965. But much of his induction into the Kuyperian vision came when he was hired into the Calvin College history department soon after. During what surely must have been Calvin's headiest days, Marsden not only joined an intellectually stimulating department that included Edwin Van Kley, Dale Van Kley, and Robert P. Swierenga, he also befriended several members of Calvin's philosophy department, who would go on to become the most formative Christian thinkers of their generation: Richard Mouw, Alvin Plantinga, and Nicholas Wolterstorff.

While Marsden's ideas about Christian history have evolved through the years, he has always maintained a judicious balance between the demands of traditional Christian conviction and those of traditional scholarship. His unswerving sense of moderation forms both the genius of his program for Christian history and fodder for some of his fiercest critics. Typical of his caution is his 1975 essay, "A Christian Perspective for the Teaching of History," in which he considers how explicit one should be in her Christian perspectives about the past. He observed that while some urged subtlety by keeping their faith orientation implicit, others insisted that it be worked out boldly in a detailed, comprehensive framework. "This essay," Marsden sensibly notes, "will suggest answers that lie between these two extremes."[44] Almost without fail, when Marsden identified points at which one's Christian perspectives might make a distinct and overriding difference in one's scholarship, he would mediate those claims by appealing to the limits of the historian's understanding and her need to mitigate the temptation to indulge in special or partisan pleading. Though bias might be inevitable, Marsden reminded his readers that "an historian should continually compensate for such tendencies with a degree of detachment that will permit him to weigh all available evidence and to present a balanced account of what happened even if it does not readily fit his preconceptions or prejudices."[45]

The tenets of Marsden's more mature formulation of faith-history integration began to take shape in his essay, "Common Sense and the Spiritual Vision of History" (1984). He opens the piece by explaining some of the ways that twentieth-century theories of knowledge had begun making it impossible for observers to lay claim to knowing things *as they are*. Citing the skeptical theories of historians like Carl Becker and Thomas Kuhn, Marsden describes the modern descent into "theory-bound" knowledge that rendered the human capacity to access the *real world* as it truly exists, impossible. We are left with only "ideas of the past" existing in the present, or "paradigms" that prohibit us from making straightforward, objective observations. Marsden admits that this trend in epistemology validates the theory-laden presuppositionalism that characterizes the Kuyperian notion of "worldview thinking," as well as the theological method he learned from Cornelius Van Til while a student at Westminster. But he warns that such views "end up in a morass of subjectivism."[46]

Marsden's moderation is on display as he offers a compromise position that both affirms elements of Kuyperian perspectivism, while situating it within a theory of knowledge consistent with his profession's native instincts of objectivity. He appeals somewhat surprisingly to the eighteenth-century philosopher Thomas Reid, whose epistemology in previous writings Marsden had partially blamed for steering evangelicalism to some untenable conclusions.[47] Reid's common-sense realism, which holds that humans have the ability to see things clearly as they are, Marsden argues, provides a basic and sure-footed foundation for human knowing. "Just as in everyday life common sense leads us to believe that we know something of the real world 'out there,'" observes Marsden, "so it tells us also that we have some direct access to the past and not just to our present ideas about the past."[48]

Marsden contends that when Christian and non-Christian observers fix their gaze on a common object, past or present, they can expect to receive the same common-sense data about that object; in short, they *see the same thing*. With a simple appeal to common grace, Marsden reasons that God endowed all humans with the capacity to know some true things about the real world. But, in seeing the exact same object, one should not presume a universally identical discernment of *patterns* or *meanings* contained in that object. Here, Marsden reasserts a standard reference to Kuyperian perspectivism, appealing to the famous gestalt effect when viewing a certain kind of image; for example, when viewed one way, an observer sees an image of an old woman, and when viewed another way, the observer sees a young woman. In both cases, the essential data under review remains the same and generally accessible to ordinary knowing, but the patterns discerned in the data depend on an added layer of understanding applied to the data. "So it is with distinctly Christian views of history," writes Marsden. "When we add the Christian lens (the lens of Scripture and spiritual insight) to the other lenses through which we view reality," our new lens colors everything we see as it supplies additional insights "that act as controls on our other beliefs; it also provides clues that allow us to see new patterns of relationships among our beliefs."[49]

A few years later, in a "Concluding Unscientific Postscript" to his survey of religion's status in the history of the American university, Marsden attempted to explain some of the ways that his own "fairly traditional Protestant" beliefs had informed the ways he crafted his book. He openly reported that his own Reformed theological heritage "has valued education that relates faith to one's scholarship not just in theology, but also in considering other dimensions of human thought and relationships."[50] Arising from the themes and thesis of his book, which demonstrated the decline and marginalization of religion in academic discourse, Marsden lamented that the current academic climate allowed no such space for scholarly observations rooted in religious conviction. Given the variety of other ideologically derived positions that had been invited into the university, Marsden thought that singling out religion for exclusion was inconsistent and rather capricious. This postscript, which called on the university to reserve a "seat at the table" for religious believers, touched off a heated debate among scholars across the disciplines about the status of religiously informed scholarship.

While Marsden believed his proposal for the inclusion of religiously derived perspectives was modest and sensible, he soon discovered that many found it "outrageous." Many outside the bounds of faith—and a good many within—simply couldn't fathom the notion of grounding intellectual work on foundations usually associated with supernaturalism, divine revelation, and the mysteries of the unseen world. Political scientist John Green described the bafflement expressed by many academics on hearing Marsden's proposal: "If a professor talks about studying something from a Marxist point of view, others might disagree but not dismiss the notion. But if a professor proposed to study something from a Roman Catholic or a Protestant point of view, it would be treated like proposing something from a Martian point of view."[51]

In attempting to explain his views, Marsden penned a slim volume in 1997 entitled *The Outrageous Idea of Christian Scholarship*. In it he more fully unpacked his thinking on the subject and began answering some of his critics. Again, in a tone of almost genteel restraint, he sought to allay the fears over "the return of religion" to the academy expressed by two different groups: (1) those who believed the university should maintain an explicit and formal secularism based on Enlightenment notions of scientific evidentiary verification, and (2) multiculturalists who represented nen, African Americans, gays and lesbians, among other minorities who viewed themselves as historic victims of exclusionary violence from an era when Christianity reigned supreme within the culture.[52]

In reply, Marsden argued that the university should function according to the rules of liberal pragmatism (i.e., a neutral space where a plurality of an almost endless variety of viewpoints can thrive provided that they are mediated by a shared commitment to mutual forbearance and civility) rather than those of scientific naturalism (i.e., a space that only allows a narrowly prescribed set of views defined by Enlightenment rationality) or an establishment brand of multiculturalism (i.e., a space that endorses some politically committed views but excludes those determined to be traditionalist or overly conservative).[53] As long as Christians were willing to serve as a voice among voices within this sphere of liberal pragmatism, there was no legitimate reason for their exclusion.

The key to Marsden's case for Christian scholarship—and for Christian perspectives in history—is the shaping influence of "background commitments" (what Nicholas Wolterstorff calls "control beliefs"). These are underlying personal beliefs "that ultimately rest on scientifically unverifiable theological or moral claims." While much of a Christian's personal faith is rooted in such commitments, they are hardly unique to Christianity or any other religious faith for that matter. Such commitments are universal to the human condition. No one is without prereflective ideas that undergird and inform values and rational thought.[54]

But, as Marsden notes, some background beliefs find a more welcome reception in the academy than others. For example, it's unlikely that someone would be viewed with suspicion if it came to light that, based on Christian conviction, she believed racism and homophobic attitudes to be morally wrong or that U.S. foreign policy in Latin America has been repugnant. Yet these assertions arise from faith commitments no less so than a belief that abortion fits the biblical definition of murder or that God has ordained American support of Israel. The difference between these examples is not that one set is rational and the other religious. All qualify as background beliefs, all are unverifiable and unscientific, and, argues Marsden, none who hold any of them should be excluded from academic discourse for this reason alone.

Marsden objects to those who would dismiss an argument merely because the person making the argument holds religiously derived background beliefs consistent with it. But he *does not* think such beliefs should ever be advanced as *evidence* in support of said argument. As with everyone else, Christians must play by the "rules of the academic game," which means they must marshal publicly accessible evidence and subject this evidence to careful, rigorous, critical, and open scrutiny. This is another way of saying that simply having background commitments does not give the Christian scholar (or anyone else) license to indulge those commitments by playing fast and loose with her sources. And if someone is suspected of arguing a position solely because of a particular background commitment in the absence of solid evidential support, it is perfectly appropriate to expose it as such. Such an argument is purely ideological, not academic, and Marsden believes that fellow scholars are right to dismiss it.

Marsden does not ask that Christians receive special treatment within the academy, nor does he see his position as an opening for Christians to "retake" the university for Christ's kingdom. He believes his arguments require little movement either among believers or among rank-and-file scholars. In drawing from their "control beliefs," he urges Christians to submit to the conventions of their guild, observing and obeying the procedural norms that establish legitimate scholarship. But, in return, he asks the academy to maintain the integrity of these rules, leaving room for personal control beliefs, so that genuine diversity might flourish. In doing so, Marsden has articulated perhaps the most thoroughgoing argument yet for applying genuine and distinct Christian beliefs to scholarly research within the mainstream framework of the modern university. It has become the consensus formulation of "the integration of faith and learning" for Christian scholarship moving into the twenty-first century, and a kind of standard orthodoxy for Christian historians hoping to bring worldview commitments to bear on their research and writing.

Critical Responses to the "Marsden Settlement"

George Marsden's contributions to thinking Christianly about writing history have been so singular, and his proposals—at least among some—so "outrageous," that his program for integration has inevitably generated critical responses from many directions. Traditional academics have worried that Marsden forfeits the important scholarly values of objectivity and universally accessible reason to postmodernism with its endless talk of social location, power, and boundless relativism. On the other hand, postmodern denizens of critical theory and identity-based scholarship fear that Marsden opens the door to a Christian "Reconquista" of the university in which faith perspectives are once again allowed to suppress and marginalize minority voices (women, African Americans, Jews, gays and lesbians, etc.), which only recently gained a footing in the academy. Responses of each of these sorts were developed by both Christian and non-Christian historians.

Bruce Kuklick, a nonbelieving intellectual historian, argues that Marsden's defense of "perspectivalism" degrades the ideal of the university as a broad space for the exchange of ideas among diverse opinions, an ideal that Marsden has otherwise honored in his own career. Kuklick satirically wonders if, in an attempt to implement some of these recommendations, Marsden's employer, the University of Notre Dame, might be inclined to offer "a Roman Catholic chemistry" or if Calvin College might entertain the possibility of teaching "Presbyterian biology." Such thinking, notes Kuklick, will only devolve into academic tribalism that will weaken and ultimately undermine all forms of learning and broker the demise of a universally shared vision of knowledge.[55] Not only is such thinking a blow to the Enlightenment ideal of universally accessible reason, but it doesn't seem consistent with the tenets of Christianity either. Why, Kuklick wonders, would traditional Christians who believe in ultimate truth want to tether themselves to this relativistic account of knowledge? "Their adherence to this ideal," concludes Kuklick, "seems an act of desperation at odds with their fundamental ideas."[56]

Another nonbelieving intellectual historian, David Hollinger, echoes some of Kuklick's concerns while adding a few of his own. He casts doubt on Marsden's basic complaint that religious perspectives have been unjustly excluded from academic discourse. As far as he can tell, there has never been a shortage of Christians working in academic departments in universities across the United States. Believing academics appear to be reasonably well treated, and there does not seem to be a great movement afoot to suppress their voices.[57] But, at a deeper level, Hollinger further believes that Marsden's proposal is not merely asking for a seat at the table. He thinks that Marsden is ultimately calling for a change in "the structure of plausibility taken for granted by the prevailing epistemic communities."[58]

Hollinger believes that Marsden and others conflate an important distinction in research between motivation (the personal origin of a claim) and warrant (the specific argument advanced to justify said claim to a diverse audience). While there might be a great many personal and religious *motivations* for one or another claim, criteria for *warrant* have been established within the university as that which is publically accessible and empirically verifiable. Hollinger submits that Christians like Marsden must now recognize that "the boundaries of the epistemic communities that define discussion in the learned world are no longer coterminous with the Christian community of faith," and, "as a consequence of their de-Christianization, [such communities] no longer count biblical evidence and other religious experience particular to Christianity as relevant to the assessment of a truth-claim or an interpretation."[59] In short, Hollinger believes it matters little if someone claims that their Christian convictions provide the fundamental origins of their research claims. And it matters even less when one considers the fact that most claims supported by Christians are ultimately generic and could be arrived at from many different non-religious motivations. Crediting Christianity with discovering such insights—whether they are insights about history, politics, psychology, or economics—is needless if a great many diverse groups may have arrived at the same conclusions without any appeal to Christian belief or conviction.

Provocatively, Hollinger cites one of the earliest ever anti-tobacco campaigns in the Western world, which was developed by Hitler's National Socialist regime in the 1930s. Yes, the motivation for eradicating tobacco use and stemming the spread of lung cancer was drawn from the well of a broader Nazi ideology that envisioned a particular kind of German society. But no one who believes in the value of contemporary versions of such programs would think it's a good idea to "water the tree" of Nazism to see if it might yield other valuable insights since it brought us this gem of an idea. And no one should

..... any obligation to be the least bit concerned with the original motivation for this enterprise in exploring contemporary warrants for it today. Hollinger likewise believes that, as long as we are agreed about maintaining our current epistemic arrangements, we have no good reason to encourage Christian perspectives within modern scholarship.

Various fellow Christian historians share Hollinger's skepticism about the legitimacy of Marsden's argument, doing so, in some cases, for some pretty explicitly Christian reasons. In a 2001 *Christian Scholars Review* essay, D. G. Hart developed the beginnings of a more complete rebuttal to the Kuyperian ideal of integration, challenging the traditional neo-Calvinist assumption that Christian faith must speak into every sphere of human endeavor.[60] Drawing from the Lutheran tradition's notion of "two kingdoms," Hart urged Christian scholars to accept the procedural norms as they have developed within "the kingdom of man" (i.e., the university) as legitimate expressions of God's sovereignty over creation, and to therefore stop trying to bring "distinctively Christian views" into spheres outside of the church (i.e., "the kingdom of God").[61] Christians should instead strive to do excellent work within those spheres (also including law, politics, and business) and even engage that work with a heady sense of Christian vocation. From the perspective of this "two-kingdom paradigm," scholars working at Christian institutions of higher learning should feel no pressure "to introduce questions of faith in literature or chemistry classes, or to require theological precision from every new hire in sociology."[62]

In the subsequent issue of the same journal, historian Michael Hamilton wondered if all the hand wringing over "integration," in the end, amounted to anything meaningful or substantively different from their non-Christian counterparts. "Despite thirty years of talk about integration of faith and learning, and despite a half-dozen best-selling books that call on Christians to take intellectual life seriously," he lamented, "the idea of Christian scholarship remains elusive for the women and men who teach at and who lead Christian colleges and universities."[63] Taking a more purely pragmatic approach than Hart, Hamilton doubts the value of asking Christian scholars to become theologically sophisticated in negotiating their disciplines' foundational assumptions. While such work might make them second-rate philosophers and theologians, Hamilton believes the energy and resources required to conduct this work robs Christian scholars of valuable time and resources that they could be devoting to making genuine contributions within their disciplines. Rather than spinning their wheels delving into matters of philosophy and theology, argues Hamilton, those whom God has called to steward knowledge of plant biology or medieval France would perhaps serve his kingdom more faithfully by devoting their energies to technical disciplinary research and writing.[64]

If Hart and Hamilton conclude that Marsden's program constitutes a needless, even inappropriate distraction, other Christian historians consider it a recipe for "selling out" to the spirit of the age. It is not Marsden's emphasis on "control beliefs" that this second group finds upsetting. It is his confidence that such beliefs will retain their coherence and power after being domesticated by the demands of the profession. Literary theorist (and atheist) Stanley Fish penned a response to Marsden's proposals in the Christian monthly *First Things* that, oddly enough, anticipated some of the concerns that some Christians would later express. In short, Fish wondered why someone who genuinely believes in the truth claims of Christianity would bother developing an "accommodation to liberalism" by playing the pragmatic game of the academy. In his way of thinking, a religious person confident in God's word wouldn't bother joining the murky mission of the university but would work instead "to shut it down."[65] Though few believing academics would advocate the annihilation of the modern university, at least some of them have feared that Marsden's paradigm invites Christian scholars to strike a bargain with the devil.

Professor of history at Liberty University and theonomist Roger Schultz expresses concerns about what he called "Evangel*histoire*," the impulse of Christians scholars to become embarrassed by and disenchanted with their humble, church-centered origins after pursuing graduate school and settling into a life of scholarship. Schultz' problem with Marsden and others is that they offer a barely detectable window dressing of "faith" but are more fundamentally eager to see Christians develop credibility within the cosmopolitan world of scholarship and to assent wholeheartedly to the academy's culture and worldview. "Desperately looking for respect from their peers and ever fearful of being mistaken for Bible-thumpers," writes Schultz, "neo-evangelicals [who become scholars] try to distance themselves from their potentially embarrassing associations with their hickish and politically incorrect brethren."[66]

Roman Catholic theologian (and former priest) Michael Baxter believes that Marsden's "both and" strategy naïvely places faith in an academic culture that requires its participants to read the world in fundamentally un-Christian ways. The scientific methodologies that shaped the modern discipline of history, for instance, demand that anyone working in the academy today must "labor under a truncated conception of how human events may be understood and explained . . . that favors a pessimistic and unhopeful view of human nature."[67] Baxter believes that Christians should boldly work toward developing genuine institutional alternatives to the secular academy that might enable them to exercise their confessional beliefs in an unfettered way.

Marsden's harshest critic in this stream has been Christopher Shannon, a Yale-trained intellectual historian and Roman Catholic who left the "mainstream" academy to teach at Christendom College in Virginia, an institution that may reflect some of what Baxter has in mind. Shannon takes aim at what he labels "the Marsden settlement," which, he wryly notes, only strives to "make the world safe for professions of faith in scholarship." He rehearses some of the same concerns voiced by Baxter, alarmed that Marsden leaves the soulless procedural norms of the American Historical Association fully intact, which "exclude the substantive moral and spiritual truths essential to any meaningful notion of Christian history."[68] Moreover, the "price of admission" into this world of scholarship is to become a functionary in the profession's moral obligation to churn out monograph after monograph. And to what end?

History as a set of middle-class professional practices, argues Shannon, not only obligates contemporary historians to embrace "naturalistic causality and the procedural norms of the historical profession," but Christians inducted into these practices must also worship at the altar of "human agency." "The modern secular monograph," argues Shannon, "tells us, with pious, mind-numbing regularity that human beings, as individuals and groups, make history," always on a triumphant route toward maximizing "their individual or collective autonomy from imposed restraints."[69] This master narrative of progressive self-liberation—intrinsic to what Shannon labels "providential professionalism"—is such a nonnegotiable feature of the modern historian's craft that most scholars scarcely recognize its existence. Shannon implores fellow Christians to recognize and carefully ponder these insidious practices and warns against donning Marsden's barely perceptible fig leaf as if it functioned as a genuine frame for something called "Christian scholarship."

Conclusion

Aspirations to make Christian worldview thinking foundational to historical scholarship remains a highly regarded strategy for doing history in a Christian manner. And, as this chapter attests, the project has generated some very sophisticated thinking about faith-oriented historiography both among those who support and criticize it. While George Marsden neither originated the approach nor served as its sole advocate, his contribution to the discussions of Christian historiography is in a category all its own. The volume and ferocity of his critics' responses—scarcely covered in this chapter—provides at least one gauge of his importance to the discourse of Christian thinking about the past. Skillfully straddling the perilous challenges presented by two often combative worlds, and doing so with an admirable degree of grace and diplomacy, Marsden may not have developed the final or ultimate program for how Christian faith should engage historical scholarship, but it seems likely that his contributions will continue to serve as a starting point for at least another generation of Christian historians.

3

HISTORICAL STUDY AS APPLIED
CHRISTIAN ETHICS

Most of the world's oldest traditions of history writing envisioned the past as a kind of moral tutor brimming with both good and bad archetypes of how to govern, make war, conduct business, and lead a life of honor. Ancient Greek, Roman, and Chinese historians wrote about past lives and events with the goal of urging their readers to lead virtuous lives. Pointing to the positive and negative consequences of human behavior as lived out on the actual stage of human experience constituted a means of moral instruction that many considered superior to the mere enumeration of abstract rules to be obeyed.[1] It's what the ancient Roman historian Dionysius of Halicarnassus described as "philosophy teaching by examples," and what Cicero called *historia magistra vitae*, "history as the teacher of life." It would have been unthinkable in ancient times for such historical inquiry to resist the urge to apply somewhat explicit moral criteria to judge actors in the past. These were not disinterested chroniclers of human civilization but, in effect, moral guides who wanted their readers to draw particular insights from the good and evil perpetrated by their ancestors.

Historical writing from antiquity was considered not simply an enterprise that allowed for the exercise of moral analysis <u>but as itself a branch of moral philosophy</u>. The Hebrew and Christian traditions of historiography reflected in the Old and New Testament Scriptures bear some of these same characteristics. For example, the historian of ancient Israel's Northern and Southern kingdoms who composed

1 and 2 Kings assessed the monarchy's evolution according to the loyalty particular kings (and their subjects) displayed toward the covenant with God. Along the way, the author—often quoting God himself—appeals to an even earlier moral exemplar who set the standard for covenant faithfulness for all who would follow: "As for you, if you walk before me faithfully with integrity of heart and uprightness, as David your father did, and do all I command and observe my decrees and laws, I will establish your royal throne over Israel forever, as I promised David your father when I said, 'You shall never fail to have a successor on the throne of Israel'" (1 Kgs 9:4-5 NIV). Of course, with few exceptions, the kings of Israel did not act as David acted, and the dissolution of each kingdom is accounted for accordingly.

The New Testament writer of the Epistle to the Hebrews also looks back on the history of ancient Israel, this time enumerating a sizeable catalog of *positive* exemplars whose lives were marked by faith in God. From Adam, Abel, and Noah to Abraham, Jacob, and Moses (among many others), these "heroes" of faith are commended for the sterling lives they lived, trusting in God, often in the face of personal loss, hardship, and violent death: "All these people were still living by faith when they died. They did not receive the things promised; they only saw them and welcomed them from a distance. . . . They were put to death by stoning; they were sawed in two; they were killed by the sword. They went about in sheepskins and goatskins, destitute, persecuted and mistreated" (Heb 11:13, 37 NIV). The implication for the persecuted early Christians reading this letter must have been clear: you are suffering for your faith like the great heroes of old, and, like them, you will be rewarded in due course. This is not a time to give up, but a time to persevere. "Therefore, since we are surrounded by such a great cloud of witnesses, let us throw off everything that hinders and the sin that so easily entangles, and let us run with perseverance the race marked out for us" (Heb 12:1).

Chronicles that observe rewards for virtue and calamities for wickedness have typified Christian historiography from the early medieval period through the nineteenth century. From Einhard's *Life of Charlemagne* (c. 817-833)—the prototype for all future hagiographic Christian biographies, which, borrowing heavily from ancient Roman accounts of the lives of the emperors, obsequiously praises the Frankish king as the embodiment of all Christian virtue—to the late nineteenth-century historian, Lord Acton, who insisted as late as 1884 that "the inflexible integrity of [God's] moral code is, to me, the secret of the authority, the dignity, the utility of history."[2] Despite ever growing objections to morality-based history writing, it should come as no surprise that many contemporary Christian historians continue to see the past through the lens of value-laden commitments informed by Christian faith.

The Christian doctrine of sin holds that humankind has been thoroughly stained by the totalizing effects of "the fall," which has warped the human will and moral compass. Sin has been aptly described as the most empirically verifiable of all Christian doctrines, and, in a vocation that was designed to evaluate the violence, corruption, treachery, and mayhem of the human experience, the Christian historian's application of specifically Christian moral judgments on the past seems a most logical way of "being Christian" when studying the past. But Christians who have attempted to carry forth this old tradition of writing about the past have done so against the grain of some of modern professional history's defining norms.

The Rankean Revolution

Among the many changes that came to historical studies during the nineteenth century, none were as consequential as Leopold von Ranke's (1795-1886) seminar method, in which he institutionalized his emerging ideal of studying the past *wie es eigentlich gewesen*, or "as it actually happened." Although there is considerable debate about what the great German scholar intended by the phrase, it came ultimately to symbolize professional history's goal to make the task of reconstructing the past—using rigorous methods and primary documents—a bona fide *science* on par with other disciplines in the German (and later British and American) university curriculum.[3] No longer would historians aspire to stand in judgment of the past, but would aim instead only to provide a faithful and truthful recovery of past actualities. No more, no less.

The rise of what Ernst Breisach has called "a critical historical science" aimed, among other things, to protect historical study from the historian's personal biases against past individuals, nations, and ideologies, and against temptations to press research projects into the service of one or another campaign of propaganda.[4] In a word, the ideal value to which all professional historians increasingly aspired was a disciplinary practice founded upon *objectivity*. Whether the historians of this or later generations succeeded in achieving this lofty goal is a different (and much debated) question. But the standards that would help erect the modern discipline of history throughout the rest of the nineteenth century, and into much of the twentieth, were defined largely by efforts to write about the past without personal or ideological agendas. And without moral preconceptions.

In one of the most famous and enduring takedowns ever published by a historian, Herbert Butterfield's *The Whig Interpretation of History* (1931) vehemently defended the ideal of objectivity by taking aim at an important (and then still-living) tradition of British historiography. He affixed the label "Whig history" to the persistent tendency among many historians to impose on the past narratives of progress and the irrepressible "spirit of liberty," and "to impute lessons to history which history has never taught and historical research never discovered."[5] A partisan only for truth, the young Butterfield attacked the all-too-common practice of looking at the past with too much concern for today, and an even greater desire to stand in lofty judgment of the past from this all-knowing present. Describing Lord Acton as the greatest exponent of "whig theory," Butterfield held that, "for of this desire to pass moral judgments on various things in the past, it is really something in the present that [Acton] is most anxious about." In the end, Butterfield believed that such whiggish tendencies ultimately undermined all efforts at genuine historical understanding. "In its practical consequences [the whig theory] means the exaltation of the opinions of the historian," Butterfield chastened. "It reaches its highest point in the conception of history as the arbiter, history as the seat of judgment, particularly on moral issues."[6]

As self-consciously Christian historians—Butterfield among them—began to make their mark on the profession during the second half of the twentieth century, they gradually made peace with the ideal of objectivity. And the competing ideal of history as moral philosophy—at least among professional historians—began to wither as a viable interpretive option. In an essay published in 1964, E. Harris Harbison explored the variety of tensions he felt between his identities as historian and Christian. He asserted that, while his Christian beliefs might never be understood or accepted by his secular colleagues, they were ultimately consistent with and reconcilable to the standards of modern historiography. Christian and materialist alike can happily unite around a variety of basic professional standards: the universality of history, the demand to treat the past justly (and mercifully), a commitment to bald realism on matters of the human condition, and a refusal "to deify any hero or cause in history." Although he acknowledged that Christians might sometimes differ from their secular colleagues on an assortment of "underlying motives," Harbison insisted that there "is no inherent and necessary contradiction between being a Christian believer and being a professional historian."[7] But even as Christians like Harbison were resting in Rankean confidence, there were intellectual and cultural tremors rumbling underfoot that would ironically cause many in the profession to revisit the ancient ideals of history as moral philosophy.

The Crisis of Objectivity and the Return of Value-Laden History

During the 1920s and 1930s, Progressive historians like Charles Beard and Carl Becker famously cast doubts on the "noble dream" of objectivity. Not only did they question its foundational assumptions—noting the historian's inability to access the actual past (but only to sources from the past), the woefully incomplete nature of the historical record, and implicit problems of bias in the selection of topics and sources—but they also began to produce scholarship with a political edge. Having given up on the possibility of real objectivity, Beard and Becker (along with a host of others) produced articles and monographs driven by some of their own political concerns and interests. In the service of building a just and democratic society, Beard (especially) conceived of the past in ways that supported his vision for a planned, collectivist social order. Through the influential writings of these relativist progressives, cracks in the foundation of objectivity began to appear.

Although, as Breisach observes, "Progressive history's relativist phase was brief and did not lead to a thorough epistemological debate in American historiography," the seeds of politically assertive scholarship and skepticism over objectivity sown during these years would bloom and thrive in the turbulent political soil of the late 1960s and 1970s.[8] The cumulative impact of the Civil Rights Movement, student unrest on university campuses, and the rising tide of resistance to America's war in Vietnam generated intense volatility and changing norms for the profession. "New Left" historians, anticipated and inspired by Progressives like Beard, were comprised (mostly) of young radical assistant professors who had grown impatient of then-dominant historical narratives, whose consensus themes they believed papered over an undertow of conflict, oppression, racism, sexism, labor exploitation, and state-sponsored violence abroad. The historical profession—under the guise of "objectivity"—had been deemed complicit in the sins of a repressive social and political order. And, they argued, new politically subversive histories designed to expose these crimes were now needed.[9] Entirely new research agendas—ones emphasizing women's history, black history, Chicano history, labor history, and peace studies—gave expression to a new source of grassroots political power (identity politics) through a new medium: advocacy history. This new amalgam of scholarship and political activism aspired both to redress past wrongs and to give voice to historically marginalized and silenced peoples. The resulting pursuit of a "useable past" came to exemplify the profession as it developed during the following generation.

Young radicals like Staughton Lynd and Martin Duberman led the charge to transform the historical profession and to change its conversation. But if there was a single generational exemplar of this kind of activist scholarship, it was surely Howard Zinn (1922–2010). The Boston University professor made no attempt to maintain what he took to be an artificial wall between historical study, on one side, and his personal experiences and political convictions, on the other. All such divisions were false, useless, and typically served to mask the interests of the wealthy and the powerful. In the dialectic between the powerful elites and the oppressed masses—a dialect that, in his judgment, drove the unfolding narrative of American history—there was no doubt on which side he stood.[10]

> Before I became a professional historian, I had grown up in the dirt and dankness of New York tenements, had been knocked unconscious by a policeman while holding a banner in a demonstration, had worked for three years in a shipyard, and had participated in the violence of war. Those experiences, among others, made me lose all desire for "objectivity," whether in my life, or writing history.[11]

Given his leftist politics and the urgency of the political moment, Zinn argued for a "value-laden historiography" that would, among other things, "expose the limitations of governmental reform, the connections of government to wealth and privilege, the tendencies of governments toward war and xenophobia, the play of money and power behind the presumed neutrality of law." In the classic formulation that epitomized this movement, Zinn observed the hallowed practice of "speaking truth to power." Using the words of African American sociologist E. Franklin Frazier, Zinn summarized his vision for history: "All your life, white folks have bamboozled you, preachers have bamboozled you, teachers have bamboozled you; I am here to debamboozle you."[12]

Value-Laden Christian Historiography— On the Left

This scholarship-born-of-moral-outrage appealed to many within a rising generation of young, left-leaning Christian historians, striving to find their place within the post-Vietnam social discourse and now emboldened by the likes of Zinn and others to apply the raw moral insights of Christianity to their craft. In his study of the relationship of contemporary Christians to cultural change, sociologist James Davison Hunter maintains that the Christian Right and Left have each been mobilized by their own distinctive readings of myth and history. Those on the Left, he argues, "have always been animated by the myth of equality and community and therefore see history as an ongoing struggle to realize these ideals."[13] It stands to reason that many of its historians would be drawn to this Zinn-like posture. As

New Left historians had turned a critical eye toward the powerful interests of the "standing order" in government and corporate capitalism, Christian historians like Richard Pierard sought to expose the collusion of fellow Christians with a number of repressive, anti-democratic ideologies in vogue at that time. In a 1972 essay that posited the captivity of evangelical Christianity by right-wing political ideologies—which imagined that the "nation's social turmoil" was "due to the actions of [communist] conspirators, not inequities in the social structure itself"—Pierard enumerated a variety of evangelical traits that he believed led so many of them to forge an unholy alliance with the radical Right.[14] He chastised fellow evangelicals for their individualism, fixation on personal piety, self-righteous moralism, anti-intellectualism, and close-minded separatism.

Pierard's critique of right-wing movements went beyond mere value-laden analysis. Similar to his counterparts in the New Left, he urged action on the part of fellow believers. Such political ideologies had infiltrated Christian churches and other evangelical ministries, he insisted, and was undermining the long witness of biblical Christianity. "The devout Christian must have no part of the radical right," insisted Pierard. And, in a shocking recommendation that raises questions about Pierard's own insistence on ideological purity and conformity, the Indiana State University professor urged Christians to "discontinue giving money to rightists, refuse to support their meetings and publications, and expel them from their churches. . . . Evangelicals must act *now* to purge their ranks of this barrier to the spread of the gospel. Tomorrow may be too late!"[15]

Historian Donald Dayton likewise struggled to reconcile the rigidly conservative politics of American evangelicalism during the 1960s with the tidal wave of social and political change that was simultaneously sweeping across the national landscape. In a series of vignettes first published in the underground newspaper of the "Evangelical Left" published by Jim Wallis, *The Post-American* (now *Sojourners*), Dayton explored the history of nineteenth-century evangelicalism in an effort to demonstrate its surprisingly radical temperament, and to help contemporary evangelicals see that so much of what they considered dangerously destructive to the social order by the late 1960s (civil rights, feminism, social welfare), ironically, had very deep roots

within the evangelical tradition. Later published together as *Discovering* |
an Evangelical Heritage (1976), Dayton looks at the radical abolitionist
founder of Wheaton College, Jonathan Blanchard, along with several
other evangelical anti-slavery activists like Charles Finney, Theodore
Weld, the "Lane Rebels," and the Tappan brothers. Other chapters
consider the evangelical origins of feminism and the similarly framed
roots of social welfare.[16] Throughout these essays, two questions seem
never far from the surface: What happened to the evangelical heritage? And how do contemporary evangelicals continue to justify
resistance and outright opposition to civil rights policies, movements
for gender equality, and programs for social welfare? These spiritual
ancestors, in the pages of Dayton's book, stand in disappointed judgment of what had become of their once-proud heritage.

In yet another case of frustration with evangelical conservatism,
historian Douglas W. Frank penned a book-length survey of early
twentieth-century evangelicalism that, in addition to recounting
actual history, combines left-leaning moral outrage with personal
misgivings about his own fundamentalist upbringing. In *Less Than
Conquerors: How Evangelicals Entered the Twentieth Century* (1986), Frank
begins by voicing much of the same indignation expressed by Pierard
and Dayton at the failure of fellow evangelicals to develop a social conscience attuned to what he took to be the abiding moral issues of the
day—poverty, racism, sexism, the proliferation of nuclear weapons,
and the repressive uses of American power throughout the world—
and the corollary alliance that evangelicals had formed with the Religious Right. Alongside contemporary writers on the Evangelical left
such as Jim Wallis and Ron Sider, Frank believed that the resources
of Scripture and the moral witness of evangelical faith were naturally
(and even historically) aligned with reform movements that advo-
cated spiritual humility, social justice, and egalitarianism. *Less Than
Conquerors* sought to understand how evangelicalism in the twentieth
century went so far off the tracks, selling its birthright of progressive
reform for a mess of right-wing pottage.[17]

Throughout the book, Frank makes no effort to conceal his personal or political views, and seemingly has as little use for "objective"
history as Zinn. His survey explores a series of individuals, ideas,
and movements that led late nineteenth- and early twentieth-century

evangelicals to abandon what he takes to be the essential truth of the gospel; he explores the otherworldly dispensational premillenialism of R. A. Torrey; the triumphalist perfectionism of Phoebe Palmer; the middle-class Victorian moralism of Robert Speer; the gnosticism of Hannah Whitall Smith's "Victorious Life" program; and the militant, moralistic hyper-nationalism of Billy Sunday's revivalism. But it contains a good deal more. Scattered throughout the narrative, Frank indulges in a multitude of personal asides: he engages theological debates with the book's subjects, showing the errors of their ways; he offers personal recollections—testimonials, even—of his Fundamentalist childhood when he still believed in the smug certitudes of evangelicalism; and he provides page after page of heavy-handed biblical exegesis (mostly from the minor prophets), which are intended to convince readers of his "true," radicalized vision for the Christian life.

In a biographical sketch of Frank that appears in Randall Balmer's travelogue of evangelical America, *Mine Eyes Have Seen the Glory* (1989), the author notes Frank's irritation with the evangelical "temptation to moralize." Whether it's right-evangelicals or left-evangelicals, the impulse is the same and equally problematic. Quoting Frank:

> It's not that we shouldn't say things are wrong, but moralism has to do with lines, with pointing fingers. It doesn't make an analysis of evil that's 360 degrees, that says "we're all culpable, we're all encompassed within the same human determinisms." And therefore, that type of moralism doesn't very often acknowledge its own complicity. Moralism assumes autonomous human beings who are free to make autonomous decisions about right and wrong, and even when it notices that people don't often do that, that people generally choose the wrong over the right, it still assumes that those decisions can be made. Therefore, there's a burdensome feel to moralistic analysis. It's the law. It's finger-pointing.[18]

Given this sharp critique of moralizing, it is ironic that it is just such moralizing that stood out most to historian David Edwin Harrell Jr. in his review of *Less Than Conquerors*. "Douglas Frank's book is an exercise in moral instruction," observes Harrell. "Roughly half history, half sermon." Noting that one of Frank's central complaints about his evangelical forbears was their spiritual arrogance, Harrell wryly observes the author's surprise "that some of his evangelical readers thought he had been a bit harsh." Harrell himself notes that he would "be surprised if [Frank] is not labeled a spiritual elitist of the rankest sort himself."[19]

Some like Frank have found their voice of moral concern in history writing by reacting against an overly constrictive, conservative childhood. Others discovered after-the-fact that their moral concern in their historical studies owed its existence to latent, even lapsed religious convictions from their youth. Historian Joseph A. McCartin has written with great sensitivity about the ways that his upbringing among working-class Catholics and his young adult immersion in Catholic social teaching formed his consciousness of class, race, and gender inequities, and, at times unconscious to him, led to a career as a labor historian. In fact, he notes that some of the finest scholarship in American labor history has been written by historians who were shaped by the same kinds of experiences among "cradle Catholics," especially in ethnic urban parishes. Even as McCartin very explicitly discusses his long-standing personal tensions with the official teachings of the church and the repressive quality of the clerical hierarchy, he happily links the moral urgency of his scholarly program to the compelling power of his "Catholic imagination."[20]

Not all Christian attempts at moral analysis through history writing are as self-referential as Frank's and McCartin's, but many have been equally sermonic. Historian Richard T. Hughes in two similarly framed books, *Myths Americans Live By* (2004) and *Christian America and the Kingdom of God* (2009), considers elements of American history with a special concern for how mistaken visions of the nation "have sometimes obscured and subverted the promise of the American Creed, especially for its minority populations."[21] Hughes organizes the structure of *Myths Americans Live By* according to the major periods of American history, identifying distinctive myths of America definitive of each era ("The Myth of the Chosen Nation: The Colonial Era," "The Myth of Nature's Nation: The Revolutionary Period," etc.). Although each myth was in some fashion defined within one era or another, the legacy of each has had a way of traversing all periods of American history. The book, in Hughes' own words, has "a certain melancholy character," largely due to its relentless exposition of how American power has been used to enslave, demonize, exploit, suppress, exclude, invade, and fleece the weakest peoples within its own borders and around the world. Hughes seeks to expose these national offenses because of "my own Christian convictions, for it seems beyond dispute that concern for the poor and disenfranchised stands at the very heart of the Christian message."[22] Hughes goes on to explore, if only briefly, virtually every national sin in every era of the nation's history: from chattel slavery to the expulsion of Native American peoples from their ancestral lands; from American intervention in Cuba and the Philippines to Jim Crow; and from corporate capitalist exploitation of wage laborers to America's war in Vietnam. As with any good sermon, Hughes concludes with an application, hoping readers will learn to "see the world through someone else's eyes, perhaps even through the eyes of their enemies."[23]

In the latter book, Hughes takes a closer look at one of the "myths" covered in the former: the myth of Christian America.[24] Here, the author spends less time covering broad swaths of American history. Instead, similar to Frank, Hughes weaves biblical reflections together with incidents in the American past that illustrate the nation's failure to attain the kingdom ideals outlined in Scripture: justice, nonviolence, and equality. In short, he argues, the United States is not the same as the kingdom of God.'" It would seem an article of common sense that setting the kingdom of God as the criteria to which a nation must conform in order for it to be considered "Christian" (which is what Hughes does) is something like stacking the deck against any claims that might be made on its behalf. But, in Hughes' telling, it would appear that if America could somehow have mustered the moral courage to live according to its own touted ideals, the United States might have been a candidate as "the kingdom of God" after all. But, thanks mainly to the Fundamentalists and other American militarists and capitalists, it hasn't (at least not yet). So it isn't (at least not yet).

Historians James C. Juhnke and Carol M. Hunter may be counted among those who share Hughes' verdict that the United States has failed to approximate the values of the kingdom of God.

In 2001, they published a "relentlessly revisionist" appraisal of American history written from their shared perspective as Christians and pacifists. In *The Missing Peace: The Search for Nonviolent Alternatives in American History* (2001), the authors set out to emancipate "U. S. history from the tyranny of our violent imaginations," believing that a major cause of our national proclivity toward violence has been "the learned history that is shaping us." In other words, they argue, the narrative of national history most Americans take for granted assumes that the national character was forged, preserved, and protected by war. "The U.S. is a great and free country, we are to conclude, because Americans have been effectively violent."[25]

The authors' aim here is not to provide a summative history of American peace movements but rather to renarrate U.S. history "from the perspective of peace values." In this "alternate reading of history," the authors set out to celebrate "those people and those structures and systems which offer nonviolent models in the struggle for freedom and a more peaceful and just society."[26] These moral exemplars supply signposts that the authors believe will help spur students of the past to consider the possibility of nonviolent solutions to pressing national problems. Since the "myth of redemptive violence" permeates American culture and informs the national consciousness, the authors argue, Americans have been prone to perpetuate yet more violence. But the authors invite us to reimagine our history with the values of peace pervading, believing that a history of this sort will enable us to envision a different kind of social order.

Value-Laden Christian Historiography—
On the Right

This look at value-laden Christian historiography has been limited so far to writers producing "mainstream" historical scholarship, or who have at least worked within the bounds of professional history. The moral assessments by each of them followed traditionally left/liberal critiques of the past: appraisals of racism, the exploitation of the poor, sexism, capitalism, empire building, and war. If the Christian Left united around "the myth of equality and community," James Davison Hunter finds that the Christian Right has been galvanized by "a mythic ideal of the right ordering of society, and thus see modern history as a decline from order to disorder."[27] Part of this perceived decline has been conservatives' waning control of higher education, along with other centers of cultural power, and the recent tradition of value-laden Christian historiography reflects this fact. Not only has most right-leaning Christian writing in this vein emerged from outside the academy (often by populist amateurs), it has also been written deliberately against the prevailing culture of professional historiography, real and imagined.[28]

Historians in this group make no secret of their contempt for what they see as the aggressively secular agenda of professional history writing, which distorts and corrupts "traditional" accounts of the past for its own purposes. To many on the Right, academic claims of "objectivity" are dishonest gestures that mask liberal political interests. They contend that universities churn out mostly "revisionist history," defined as the practice of intentionally ignoring, omitting, or misrepresenting details in the past in an effort to bend the past toward their own liberal agendas.[29] Roger Schultz, former chair of Liberty University's history department, agrees with this assessment, but he is not surprised. He surmises that all people—historians included—are guided by and judge the past according to preloaded, deeply embedded philosophical commitments that determine what they see and how they see it. He contends that the modern academy works within a framework captive to a humanistic liberal orthodoxy, and therefore supports and produces scholarship that is twisted and morally bankrupt. What makes the responsible Christian historian different, Schultz insists, is that "he readily admits that he views history from the lens of faith. He can be clear about his presuppositions, the commitments of his worldview, and the scriptural source of his standards of justice and truth."[30]

In this spirit, Christian writers like Schultz cast moral judgments on the past without apology. He reports telling his students that history "is just a way of separating the good guys from the bad guys." The Bible's willingness to speak forthrightly about the good and evil of the men and women in its pages forms, for Schultz, a template that should guide all Christian scholars. He argues, "Our historical judgments are true and fair insofar as they follow God's Word. God is the perfect judge, able to assess the depths of the human heart.

Though we are unable to judge perfectly or exhaustively, we can make judgments with confidence as we depend upon the standards or measuring stick given in God's Word." Schultz goes on to list a number of biblical criteria that he believes Christians should use to judge the people of the past. Did they live in faith or in rebellion? Did they hold views that were consistent with Christian orthodoxy? Did they exhibit personal and public virtue? Did they follow a false religion? Did they contribute to moral or cultural decline? Were their beliefs in league with secular humanism? Were they supporters of overweening forms of state power?[31]

For most Christian writers in this camp, the idea of using history to teach lessons, judge, or edify is such a self-evident feature of what historians *should do* that they rarely discuss or even mention it. History for them remains what it was for Lord Acton: a division of moral philosophy. People—especially young people—should study the past as a way of identifying proper (usually) Christian heroes worthy of emulation and as an important occasion to observe the hideous consequences of sin, the worship of false gods, and the captivity to various worldviews that undermine the truths of the Bible.[32] History in this fashion plays a vital role in the education of children's moral imaginations, making it a vital concern in Christian schooling and homeschooling discussions and a principal reason conservatives feel so invested in finding historical narratives that reflect their Christian values.[33] It also explains why history has so easily found its way to the center of the modern culture wars.

Conservative interest in history is not only about the moral edification of children. Like their liberal counterparts, their concern extends to larger social and political issues. A lot of the Christian historical writing from the Right focuses on the present spiritual and moral health of the American nation, and history has long been a favored method of celebrating the (usually Christian) virtues that they believe made America great, as well as reprimanding the nation's descent into moral and spiritual wickedness. Most defenses of America as "a Christian nation" relate to history in this way.[34] There is an underlying, though usually explicit, message that rides through most of these histories: America is broken, but if we Christians act together, quickly, and on principle, we can "return," "heal," or "take back" America, "restoring" it to its former glory. History provides an important and useful framework to carry this message.

Easily the most popular and controversial Christian writer in this tradition is the political activist David Barton, founder and president of a ministry known as WallBuilders.[35] Since the 1980s, Barton has used history to advance the idea that Christian principles are the bedrock foundation of American greatness. He has been most eager to demonstrate that the American founders were comprised almost entirely of orthodox Christians who set out to build a nation teeming with Christian ideals. He has likewise been relentless in his claims that the so-called separation of church and state, purportedly guaranteed by the First Amendment, has been sorely misinterpreted and never intended by the founders to segregate religious principles from public life. Although he repeatedly insists that he is merely reporting the plain facts of American history in an objective manner, constantly highlighting his "exhaustive" use of primary sources, the moral imperatives of the present social and political order in his commentary are never far from view. His writings are at least as much a public jeremiad decrying the moral profligacy of contemporary culture as attempts at historical writing.[36]

Barton has produced and distributed a vast number of books, videos, CDs, and curricular materials for Christian schools and homeschoolers, all extolling his peculiar version of American history. These resources appeal to many evangelical families who share his anxieties about the state of the nation and instinctively mistrust "secular" accounts of the past. Despite razor-thin academic credentials (a B.A. in religious education from Oral Roberts University) and books that are mostly self-published by his organization, he has become a major "Christian intellectual," media figure, and consultant for the Republican National Committee, with an enormously outsized influence on the cultural ideals of conservative Christian families. In addition to being a regular on conservative cable television and radio, Barton has served as a witness before the Supreme Court, has had a hand in developing history curricula for several state boards of education, and has been invited by at least one member of the U.S. Senate to give "spiritual heritage" tours at the U.S. Capitol.[37] Reflecting the confidence that the conservative political and media establishment has had in Barton, while speaking at the American Family Association's "Rediscover God in America" conference in 2011, former presidential candidate Mike Huckabee stated that he wished "that there would be something like a simultaneous telecast and all Americans would be forced, forced—at gun point no less—to listen to every David Barton message. And I think our country would be better for it."[38]

Barton has been the target of intense criticism by journalists and scholars from virtually every direction due, in part, to his growing status as a vocal and highly partisan force in American politics. But critics have been driven no less by Barton's mishandling of sources, his fabrication of "Founding Father" quotations, and an almost comic tendency to make completely unsubstantiated historical claims. Barton has always brushed off such criticisms as coming from liberal academic and media "elites" who want to suppress the truth. But the public denunciation of Barton reached a crescendo in 2012 with the publication of his book *The Jefferson Lies: Exposing the Myths You've Always Believed about Thomas Jefferson*. Here Barton attempts to make the case that Thomas Jefferson was, among other things, an orthodox Christian believer. A host of Christian scholars, among them even a few sympathetic to his political goals, looked closely at the book and found it to be riddled with errors and falsehoods. After a torrent of public criticism, Barton's publisher, Thomas Nelson, pulled the book from its catalog. But, tellingly, the controversy caused neither Barton nor his supporters to flinch. Undaunted, he continues eagerly to reach an eager audience as he employs the power of history to advance the righteous mission to which he believes he has been called, confirming, as historian Molly Worthen aptly put it, "that truth is no obstacle to a story that people want to believe."[39]

Not all value-laden Christian history writing on the Right has been so irresponsible, even when equally motivated by politics. The conservative Christian journalist, Marvin Olasky has penned numerous works of history that strive to offer a "useable past" for partisans on the Right. He operates from the premise that the United States thrives most when it conforms to the moral principles of the Bible, which, for him, include small government, free enterprise, personal responsibility, compassion for the downtrodden, and sexual purity. Like so many others in this camp, he believes that illustrating the dangers of departing from these principles by showing their consequences in history is the greatest good that written history can achieve. In his most widely read book, *The Tragedy of American Compassion* (1992), he surveys what he sees as the disastrous effects of America's foolish and wasteful welfare state on the lives of the nation's poor since the 1960s. He looks into the nation's longer history, beginning in the colonial era, highlighting different, morally responsible responses to America's poor that actually worked. As he writes in the book's introduction, "The key to the future, as always, is understanding the past," a sentiment that he hoped would lead readers to support more "biblical" models (private charity and church-sponsored help) that ostensibly worked so well in earlier times.[40]

In *Fighting for Liberty and Virtue: Political and Cultural Wars in Eighteenth-Century America* (1995), Olasky explains the American Revolution as an ultimately cultural conflict between virtuous, biblically informed American patriots and sexually deviant British monarchists.[41] And in another foray into the nation's sexual history, *The American Leadership Tradition: Moral Vision from Washington to Clinton* (1999), he explores what he sees as a direct link between personal beliefs and public behaviors. Written amid the Clinton-Lewinsky scandal of the late 1990s, Olasky argues that examining past religious beliefs and sexual morality is "crucial to understanding [the public] motivations and actions of American leaders."[42] He offers thirteen minibiographies of leading American political figures—most of them presidents—and concludes that those who were faithful to their wives and maintained a vibrant personal faith in Christ were likewise successful leaders. Those who were sexually promiscuous and/or irreligious were ineffective as leaders. The practical application to the day's headlines was obvious to Olasky's readers.

There probably isn't a single issue that has mobilized the Christian Right more during the past forty years than its opposition to abortion, and Olasky's *Abortion Rites: A Social History of Abortion in America* (1992) attempts to make sense of the problem historically. In what is perhaps his most nuanced attempt at history, he acknowledges the messiness of the past and presents the story of abortion as such. The book is essentially a reconsideration of an earlier treatment of the same topic, *Abortion in America* (1978), in which historian James

Mohr argues that abortion, at least before "quickening," was a widely accepted practice among most Americans throughout the nineteenth and most of the twentieth centuries. The author found no record of significant organized campaigns against it until after the 1973 Roe decision.[43] In short, Mohr concludes that there has been a long continuity of tolerating abortion in the nation's history. Traversing this same terrain, Olasky discovered a different, far more complicated story: an American past filled with deep moral concern, personal courage in the face of opposition, moderate methods employed to stem the practice, and a great deal of genuine compassion and deep faith within a stout Christian resistance to abortion. In short, Olasky presented a highly *useable history* that he hoped would be employed by the pro-life movement in its efforts. As with all of his historical writings, he concludes this book with an invitation to act: he hoped his readers would allow this history to guide their effort in fighting on behalf of the unborn.[44]

One of the central criticisms many on the Right have leveled against "mainstream history," especially as taught in American colleges and universities, is its seeming obsession with America's flaws: corruption, sexism, racism, exploitation, and an insatiable hunger for empire abroad. Critics on the Right argue that such woefully distorted narratives have had a corrupting influence, especially on American young people, who are discouraged from believing in the promise of the nation's greatness in light of this shameful record. Ever since the appearance of Howard Zinn's big, bold, left-leaning survey of American shame, *A People's History of the United States* (1990), answering Zinn with their own value-laden history became an important priority for at least some historians on the Right.[45]

Few accepted this challenge more earnestly than Larry Schweikart and Michael Allen in *A Patriot's History of the United States: From Columbus's Great Discovery to the War on Terror* (2004). In more than nine hundred pages, the authors set out to renarrate the American story in a manner that aligned with a confidence and optimism reminiscent of Ronald Reagan. Hardly a narrative of "decline from order to disorder," the authors in the book's introduction proclaim "that an honest evaluation of the history of the United States must begin and end with the recognition that, compared to any other nation, America's past is a bright and shining light." The book is guided by an unswerving conviction that, properly told, the history of the United States can do little but inspire "a deepened patriotism, a sense of awe at the obstacles overcome, the passion invested, the blood and tears spilled, and the nation that was built."[46] Though neither author identifies himself as a Christian anywhere in the book, many conservative Christians sensed that the book's heart-felt patriotism reflected their own Christian values, and assumed that it must have been written from a Christian perspective. And, in fact, Schweikart, who is a professing Christian, eagerly took to the airwaves of Christian talk radio to confirm what they suspected and to explain the many ways that this patriotic reading of America's past aligns perfectly with the Bible.[47]

Both Christian Left and Right have indulged the temptation to use history to engage in a brand of moralizing in which contemporary political and social convictions are often crudely propped up through appeals to the past. Sometimes this has led to history writing that helpfully expose great tragedies and crimes in the past, but, more often, it has resulted in moralistic rants that accomplish little more than putting the imperiousness of their authors on display.[48] In the meantime, challenges to "objectivity" on other fronts have continued to mount with the ascendency of postmodern theory, expressing misgivings about the certainties of science, the stability of language, the legitimacy of metanarratives, and the disinterested quality of "truth" and "knowledge" claims. These challenges, in part, helped to chisel away at the seemingly impenetrable firewall that had long partitioned the pursuit of "facts" (traditionally procured through dispassionate truth-seeking) from the application of "values" (traditionally seen as emerging from personal faith or private, subjective experience), leading many to revisit the moral purposes of historical study.

History as Moral Inquiry

In 1998 historians Richard Wightman Fox and Robert Westbrook edited a collection of essays by scholars from across the disciplines that considered what to many seemed an unlikely coupling: moral inquiry and American scholarship. The editors observed that, while most scholars remain committed to the idea of "the university as a haven for disinterested truth-seeking and of the scholar as a pursuer of facts, not a professor of values," the postmodern challenge has blurred these lines. The perspectival (and therefore value-laden) character of all knowledge means that truth-seeking can't be impartial. Unwilling to abandon a needed distinction between "fact" and "value," the writers in this collection have yielded to the interdependence between the careful inquiry of real world facts and judgments of value that are an inexorable and necessary part of any attempt at understanding. "Fruitful inquiry," submit the editors, "is attuned to the moral dimension in all inquiry, and astute moral judgment is alert to the estimate of causes and consequences and to the appreciation of the fabric of lived experience that only inquiry can provide. Inquiry cannot free itself from values, and moral judgment without inquiry is impoverishment."[49]

As noted by the editors, this settlement owes a great debt to early twentieth-century pragmatists, including William James, John Dewey, and Charles Peirce. While Christian scholars are apt to root their moral commitments in beliefs far more normative than anything tolerated within the pragmatist frame of reference—and many within the pragmatist camp would surely distance themselves from such explicitly Christian thinking—at least a few Christians have begun to write about the past in ways that reflect the nuanced relationship between facts and values that Fox and Westbrook describe as "moral inquiry."

Catholic historian Eugene McCarraher's "The Enchantments of Mammon: Notes toward a Theological History of Capitalism," provides one such example. Wearing his left-leaning Dorothy Day brand of Catholic social thought on his sleeve, he sets out to make sense of the manifold moral problems raised in the history of modern capitalism using the grammar of theology. He admires Marxist and feminist historians who comfortably place the study of modern capitalism within their respective moral frameworks. In the same way, he writes, "Christian intellectuals must use theology, not as some invertebrate 'spirit' that 'informs' their work, but as the discursive architecture in which they formulate problems and incorporate insights from other traditions."[50] This essay, which acts as a précis to a forthcoming book-length treatment of the topic, strives to bring clarity to the lived realities of modern capitalism using the rich resources of Christian theological thinking.

A research program housed at the University of Virginia's Department of Religion known as "The Lived Theology Project" may be a species of what McCarraher has envisioned for the Christian intellectual endeavor. The program's director, Charles Marsh, a self-described evangelical Christian, has written historical treatments of two different dimensions of the American Civil Rights Movement. Each treatment attempts to integrate sustained theological and moral reflection with key dimensions in the narrative history of the period. His book *God's Long Summer: Stories of Faith and Civil Rights* (1997) is in one respect a study of the ways that religion shaped the Civil Rights Movement. But it goes much farther, lifting up "the accusing evidence of history" in ways that can be used to promote a theologically distinct vision of racial harmony. He tells the story of five individuals who each represent distinct religious responses—or as he puts it, differing "embodied theologies"—to the struggle as it was experienced in Mississippi during the summer of 1964. He argues that it is possible, "if only with the most modest results, to sift among these narratives to discriminate among the differing, often conflicting images of God." Although he is realistic about the extent to which telling these stories will succeed in laying a new foundation for racial reconciliation, he strongly believes that they can at least "give us clarity for the difficult work ahead."[51]

In *The Beloved Community: How Faith Shapes Social Justice, From the Civil Rights Movement to Today* (2005), Marsh makes a case for the religious essence of the Civil Rights Movement along with the many subsequent programs for community development and racial reconciliation it spawned. Despite the fact that the original movement brought together a multitude of people from different faiths (and no faith), the author is at pains to demonstrate that it was *not*, at base, a secular phenomenon that merely made use of religious language and institutional organization to advance its ultimately secular goals. Marsh argues that it was (and remains) a search for what Martin Luther King Jr. called the beloved community, "the realization of divine love in lived social relation." This specifically Christian theological ideal, Marsh contends, continues to fuel the innumerable projects and programs in urban and rural areas around the United States. Insisting that the book is not a brief on behalf of the utility of religion, Marsh describes the book as, instead, "a portrait of the Christian faith as a set of social disciplines shaped by gratitude, forgiveness, and reconciliation."[52]

Marsh's comparatively subtle attempt at moral inquiry through historical writing in *God's Long Summer* stands in marked contrast to the candid instrumentalism of *The Beloved Community*. The latter work retains the former's careful scholarship with its scrupulous attention to sources and its well-crafted narrative styling. But in *Beloved*, Marsh regularly pauses amid the history he has reconstructed to address the reader directly, reminding her of the lessons she should be learning and principles she should be gleaning from these stories. This often takes the form of broad philosophical and theological questions that his narrative is meant to answer. "What happens to faith," Marsh ponders, "when worldly achievement grows distant; when the partnership of hope and progress dissolves into the brutal ambiguities of history?"[53] "What then sustains a vital affirmation of the human, the protest against avarice and greed, and a lived commitment to social progress and redemptive community?"[54]

While the preceding histories provide plausible examples of how one might conduct moral inquiry while exploring historical topics, none explicitly describe their results as a "moral history." Not so with Harry S. Stout's ambitiously conceived *Upon the Altar of the Nation: A Moral History of the Civil War* (2006).[55] He begins by attempting to explain what might be meant by "moral history"—especially in a book that bears the imprint of Yale University Press! He describes it as "professional history writing that raises moral issues of right and wrong as seen from the vantage points of both the participants and the historian, who, after painstaking study, applies normative judgments." Here Stout claims that he isn't doing anything extraordinary, to the extent that "ordinary language is implicitly ethical," so "all history writing implies moral discernment."[56] But, in the end, he acknowledges that not all history intends to deliver what his moral history aspires to—a verdict: right or wrong.

Stout explains that his goal is not to readjudicate the past or its actors. "The dead no longer care, and they cannot be sentenced." Rather, such moral inquiry is intended for the living in the "hope that lessons for life today may ensue." Drawing from the historian

James Axtell (who, in his scholarship on Native Americans, has never been shy about meting out moral judgments), the task of moral history is to (quoting Axtell) "set the record straight for future appeals to precedent." Stout draws the readers' attention to features of the Civil War that he believes are morally problematic, and, after creating space for readers to draw conclusions of their own, the author does likewise. The framework Stout employs in this endeavor is "the long-established principles of just war."[57] Although he doesn't say so in this text, the author elsewhere makes no secret of his own Christian beliefs. And while he has also, elsewhere, downplayed the particular significance of his faith for how he does history, in this case, his willingness to cast judgment on the actions of the past is framed by the sturdy ethical just-war tradition, long rooted in the discourse of Christian theology.

The Insights of History as Applied Ethics

The introduction alerted readers to the fact that some of the historians grouped together within each "version of Christian history" would differ from one another—sometimes radically—in their respective understandings and applications of their shared historiographic strategy; very often these historians arrive at opposite conclusions. Nowhere in the book is this principle more palpably demonstrated than in the case of history-as-applied-Christian-ethics. Quite a few historians listed in this chapter would be unhappy to see their names grouped together with quite a few of the others (and vice versa, I'm sure). The varied differences among them are obvious: simply believing that there is a place within historical study to make moral judgments and applications does not create unanimity on the question of how such moral analysis should be practiced, nor on the philosophical foundations of such moral criticism (even among Christians), nor, of course, on which features of the past one or another Christian historian will recognize as morally problematic.

The unity in this chapter—as in all the others—is rather one of method, broadly conceived. All here share the belief that morality need not—indeed, should not—be sequestered from the traditionally "hardheaded" task of reconstructing the past. And there are a good many reasons to believe they are right about this. Christians, among all people, should not shrink from the idea that there is a fundamentally moral quality to all of human existence, nor should they pretend that the issues raised when engaging the human condition are anything other than deeply moral issues. To this end, Douglas Sweeney commends Richard Goode's suggestion that Christians take up a distinct form of "radical scholarship," using the "methods of practicing history that promote peace and justice, especially among the oppressed." Writes Sweeney, "These [methods] will never be perfected if we restrict ourselves as Christian to the oft-cited 'canons of the profession.' "[58]

Such canons may no longer mean all that much anyway, argues William Katerberg. He believes that the profession's persistent hopes of holding together claims to "objectivity" may at last have become exhausted. He believes that the main insights of postmodern theory have been largely absorbed by most working historians, and this has been to the good. So, writes Katerberg, historians—especially Christian historians—should consider moving discussions of the historian's craft away from questions of epistemology (what can be known about the past?) to those of vocation (what is history's purpose?). And since "words, truth, facts, and life cannot be disentangled," he argues, Christian "historians should redefine their vocation in terms of history being useful for life."[59]

In *The Degradation of American History*, David Harlan urges his fellow historians to return the craft to its older foundations as a handmaiden of moral philosophy, whose practitioners asked their readers to look at the past with the plaintive assertion, "This is what we value and want, and don't yet have. This is how we mean to live and do not yet live."[60] Michael Kugler agrees. He allows that "Analytical research methods for reaching a defensible, moderate objectivity are necessary to help us figure out what happened in the 'way back then' and to help us give the past a proper context—in other words, to establish the past's meaning." But this commitment alone does not disqualify history from being integrated within what he calls the "moral philosophical arts." Without denigrating the authentic reality of the past, Kugler shows that it was at one time common to equate the work of history writing to that of fiction (citing a variety of historians during the eighteenth-century Enlightenment), whereby such historians sought to use the past to create "reality effects." Like writers of fiction, these historians "crafted 'affecting' portraits of the dead because," says Kugler, "they sought to enlarge the sympathies, to train the sentiments, of their readers—a critical element in moral instruction." Kugler holds that these remain worthy goals for historical instruction, and believes in recovering this kind of vision of historical writing today.[61]

Thomas Albert Howard urges Christian historians to reflect seriously on the relative possibility of remaining morally neutral in the midst of dealing with very human issues of very human history. "By virtue of the very nature of things," writes Howard, "we, *even historians*, are actors in this universe and . . . are always already participants in 'life'—a wonderful, tragic, complex, hopeful moral life."[62] The moral quandaries, reflections, and resolutions humans confront in the messy realities of life are inescapable.

So a modicum of consensus may be building around the project of returning history to its birthplace in moral philosophy, especially among Christians who draw from such a deep well of moral reflection. But a great many old questions about the validity of this arrangement linger, and a few new ones are being posed.

The Limits of History as Applied Ethics

Perhaps the sharpest twentieth-century critic of moral judgments in history was the Christian historian Herbert Butterfield. In a classic essay published nearly twenty years after his iconoclastic *Whig Interpretation of History* (1931), Butterfield pleaded with historians to limit themselves to the simple and austere task of "technical history," advising them to resist the alluring temptation to act as history's moral arbiter. Historians must perform "an act of self-emptying," wrote Butterfield, "in order to seek the kind of truths which do not go further than the tangible evidence warrants, the kind of truths which the evidence forces us to believe whether we like them or not."[63] He doesn't shrink from the notion that human history is a profoundly moral business. In fact, the case he makes against moral judgments ultimately claims that technical history, properly executed, holds the potential of achieving a moral good far greater than anything that might be accomplished by a few "spasmodic incursions into the field of ethics."[64] But Butterfield claims that such moral discourse is, in the end, outside the bounds of the historian's vocation. Moreover, when historians indulge their urge to judge the past—with the well-intentioned hope of increasing their work's gravity—they corrupt the limited but important contribution that technical history can offer: description and explanation pursuant to historical understanding. The aspiration of becoming a transhistorical moral referee has the ironic effect of absorbing the historian's personal moral views—which Butterfield suspects are only veiled political views—into the very structure of the historical narrative. Hence, the keen insights that might have come from solid description and explanation are obscured, rendering the historical narrative itself little more than a polemical weapon that further divides partisans in the present.

Butterfield even speculates a bit on some of the psychology at play in this temptation to exercise moral judgment, and concludes that nothing good can come from it. He believes "moral indignation corrupts the agent who possesses it and is not calculated to reform the man who is the object of it." Laying all his cards on the table, Butterfield baldly claims that "the demand for it . . . is really a demand for an illegitimate form of power. The attachment to it is based on its efficacy as a tactical weapon" noted for its "ability to rouse irrational fervour and extraordinary malevolence against some enemy."[65]

Despite what its practitioners claim, Butterfield believed that moral evaluation adds nothing of substance to historical understanding. It is not as though readers need the historian's expert guidance to recognize the monstrosity of human evil when they see it. The capacity for naming such evil is not the peculiar skill the historian brings to her subject.

> The truth is . . . we need no help from the historian to bring us to the recognition of the criminality of religious persecution or wholesale massacre or the modern concentration camp or the repression of dissident opinions. And those who do not recognise that the killing and torturing of human beings is barbarity will hardly be brought to that realisation by any labels and nicknames that historians may attach to these things.[66]

Historians may aid in moral understanding, certainly, but they do so by "merely describing, say, the massacre or the persecution, laying it out in concrete detail, and giving the specification of what it means in actuality."[67] Those who are not moved by such descriptions surely will not be persuaded by the pontifications of the pious historian.

The Scottish evangelical church historian Iain Murray, a writer never shy about making pious pronouncements upon the past, has for many years warned against what he sees as the perils of "mere" technical history. Murray believes that the critical method in historiography has functioned as little more than a pitiable fig leaf among Christian scholars who have abandoned the prophetic mission of exercising biblical judgments upon the past in their writings. In *Revival and Revivalism: The Making and Marring of American Evangelicalism, 1750–1858*, Murray expresses dismay at the failure of historians to render theological verdicts in explaining how the American church lost its way during the nineteenth century. He uses the study to draw an unambiguous distinction between "revival," a reawakening of genuine piety brought about by the movement of God's spirit resulting from sound biblical teaching, and "revivalism," a manufactured human enterprise designed to manipulate the masses, whipping them up into emotional hysterics. In telling the story of American evangelicalism, Murray doesn't simply narrate. He advocates. Those who share his strong Calvinist sympathies—such as Samuel Davies and George Whitefield—are lionized as heroes we today must emulate. Those who do not—such as Charles Finney and D. L. Moody—led American Christianity into a regrettable morass of theological lethargy and compromise, and their examples should be avoided at any cost.[68]

Many like Butterfield have observed that this tendency to moralize has the ironic effect of thinning rather than expanding historical understanding. Responding to Murray's latest diatribe against professional historians' timidity in "right or wrong" judgments of the past, historian Carl Trueman notes that, instead of gaining a richer and deeper appreciation of the past, Murray's strategy nets results that are simplistic and, in the end, pointless. He cites a hypothetical response to the Holocaust that employs Murray's approach: "Germans hated Jews, and that was a very wrong thing." Trueman observes that such a verdict tells us nothing about why the Holocaust happened, or how to avoid another such evil. The historian must instead be focused on an assortment of questions that hope to understand *why* such an event happened, which can only be achieved by putting one's hand to the difficult task of Butterfield's "technical history." "To do this," Trueman writes, "is not to remain personally neutral on the moral status of the Holocaust; it is simply to acknowledge the need to explain complex human behaviour in a suitably complex manner." This important practice "does not exclude the truth question; it simply reassigns it."[69]

James LaGrand believes that historians like Murray maintain a relationship with the pastbest described as instrumentalist. "By advocating that we view things ontologically rather than historically," he writes, "instrumentalism tends to rely on static ready-made models rather than evidence and historical detective work." Such strategies are therefore ill-equipped to "deal with the 'messiness' of history, its unexpected twists and turns, the surprise of finding evil people doing good things and virtuous, moral people revealing a fatal flaw in some of their actions."[70] He wonders if Christians are especially prone to such instrumentalism because they fear that history, on its own, is too "worldly" to serve the prophetic interests of *radical* Christian living. Perhaps Christians are more interested in stories that serve up crystal-clear marching orders (whether from the Left or the Right) rather than tales of complexity with uncertain lessons.

In defense of history *as history*, LaGrand turns to the resources of Christian humanism. In light of the truth that God made humans in his image and then took the form of a man, himself, we must conclude that no human endeavor may ever be reducible to a mere worldly enterprise. Humans have a rich and complex relationship with the world, and should not resist the urge to exercise stewardship over it, or to celebrate its beauty and goodness. "Thus," LaGrand maintains, "carefully crafted history (or literature or music or art) is a faithful Christian response to the world around us. Inquiry and understanding are valuable tasks for Christian historians just as they are for others." The fundamentally humanistic work of observing and appreciating the ways people of all times (including we ourselves) have been woven into the fabric of time counts as a good and earnest calling that requires no additional justification or utility.[71]

Gordon Wood has argued that writers whose primary aim is "to change the present" rather than "to elucidate the past" should stop calling themselves historians. In a review of a book by John Patrick Diggins on Abraham Lincoln, which explores a wide variety of seemingly present-minded concerns, Wood makes the provocative claim that Diggins is "not a historian at all," but rather a cultural critic. Wood later said that an editor had changed his original formulation, "not primarily a historian," for dramatic effect. Still, he stood by his review's underlying sentiment: in his opinion, "not everyone who writes about the past is a historian. Sociologists, anthropologists, political scientists, and economists frequently work in the past without really thinking historically."[72] Though I vigorously disagree with Wood's overly restrictive (and frankly self-serving) limitations on who may and may not call themselves historians, I believe his concerns about historical thinking are valid and need to be considered carefully.

Conclusion

The Christian tradition is unimaginable without the inclusion of its thick and sturdy moral framework or its prophetic witness to the world (and to itself). It's not surprising that Christians writing about the unfolding human drama have drawn deeply from Christianity's considerable moral resources to think through, evaluate, and even judge ideas, actions, and institutions from the past. Understanding history as a form of moral inquiry and an expression of Christian moral philosophy is a long-standing feature of Christian historiography, and a practice older than Christianity itself. To be sure, the application of Christianity's moral math in writing about the past has been as varied and diverse as the membership of the Christian church. And not all contemporary writers drawing from this tradition have done so in the same way; there is, to be sure, a fairly wide gulf separating careful and nuanced moral inquiry from brute moralizing and judgment. Regardless where one stands on the inclusion of moral categories in historical study, perhaps all can agree that there have been responsible and less than responsible ways of applying them.

It may be that moral discernment is ultimately so enmeshed in the humanity of historians and within the human dramas they study that engaging in some kind of ethical assessment when writing about the past is simply unavoidable. And perhaps Christians have a responsibility to do so more consciously and conscientiously. But historians also bear a moral responsibility to reconstruct the past with as much dispassionate, clear-minded understanding as possible. The tension between understanding the *dead past* on its own terms and using it to provide moral instruction to the *living present* is one that believing historians may never resolve. But they must remain vigilant in understanding the challenges and potential pitfalls found in moving too far in either direction.

4

HISTORICAL STUDY AS CHRISTIAN
APOLOGETIC

Believing historians largely affirm that the central claims of the Christian faith are true, even if they can't always agree on which ones should be called "central." But one particular strain of Christian historiography has aspired to *demonstrate* the truth claims of the faith in its presentation of the past. For some, this impulse involves attempts at establishing the historicity of the faith itself. For others, history functions as a sphere that reliably illustrates the cultural and intellectual benefits that Christian beliefs, values, actions, and institutions have supplied to past human societies. Or, accordingly, when Christian ideals have been absent, obscured, or suppressed, history inevitably reveals a resulting pattern of chaos and despair. The truth of Christianity is established among such historians by showing how well Christianity *works*. Such thinking and writing conceives of *history* as a form of *Christian apologetics*.

The branch of Christian thought known as apologetics endeavors to defend the faith by demonstrating that particular Christian claims are true. From showing the philosophical coherence of God's existence (e.g., the cosmological and ontological arguments) to supplying (for instance) geological evidence in support of a literal version of the creation story in Genesis 1 and 2, Christian apologetics attempts to provide rational foundations for Christian belief. And history has long been employed in the service of this endeavor.

Defending the Historicity of the Faith

Evidentialist apologetics uses the traditional study of primary sources to validate the historical claims of the Bible, especially those events that are foundational to belief, including the Genesis account of creation, the incarnation, the life of Jesus, the crucifixion, the resurrection, the beginnings of the Christian church, and the historicity of the biblical authors themselves. For Christians who subscribe to the doctrine of biblical inerrancy, it has become necessary to verify and defend the historicity of all events recorded in the Bible, or at least those intended to be read as history.

Since at least most Christians believe the Bible contains true accounts of people who actually lived and events that actually happened, historical study has long played an important role in defending the faith. "Christianity is basically a vigorous appeal to history," writes Georges Florovsky, "a witness of faith to certain particular events in the past, to certain particular data of history. . . . Emphasis is put on the ultimate cruciality of certain historic events, namely, of the Incarnation, of the Coming of the Messiah, and of his Cross and Resurrection."[1] Especially since Enlightenment-era attacks on miracles and the authority of the Bible put church leaders on the defensive, Christians have been compelled to justify religious beliefs on empirical and rational grounds. For instance, the great nineteenth-century "quest for the historical Jesus" generated a flowering of biblical scholarship intent on trying to distinguish the first-century Jewish carpenter "Jesus" from the "Christ" of traditional church dogma. In the face of a massive tidal wave of books and articles that have attempted to "demythologize" the historical Jesus, by scholars ranging from Albert Schweitzer and Rudolf Bultmann to Morton Smith and John Dominic Crossan, believers in traditional Christian doctrine have attempted to reintegrate the "Jesus of history" with the "Christ of faith."[2]

Perhaps the greatest area of concern for historical apologetics has been verifying the historicity of the resurrection. For, as the Apostle Paul wrote in his first letter to the Corinthians, "If Christ has not been raised, your faith is futile; you are still in your sins. . . . If only for this life we have hope in Christ, we are of all people most to be pitied" (1 Cor 15:17, 19 NIV). Noted ancient historian and Christian Edwin Yamauchi devoted much of his scholarly career to exploring the texts of early Christianity, and believed one of his principal tasks as a historian of faith was to demonstrate the truth of the faith. In a two-part 1974 essay published in *Christianity Today,* Yamauchi lays out the debate surrounding the historical resurrection.[3]

Yamauchi explains and dispenses with each of two predominant nineteenth- and twentieth-century theories of the resurrection: that it functions as a myth akin and even related to Egyptian mystery religions and other ancient Near Eastern stories, and that the eyewitnesses who reported it as fact were actually undergoing hallucinations. Yamauchi observes that even among those who believe Jesus to have been a historical figure, many dismiss all supernatural elements of the Gospel accounts as impossible to believe. For neoorthodox theologians such as Emil Brunner and Karl Barth, the resurrection is an "event," but one that cannot be understood or verified as any other historical event. The resurrection has happened in some kind of existential way "for us" as believers.

Yamauchi pokes holes in each of these theories, demonstrating by means of meticulous, traditional historical research that Jesus lived as a Jewish man in first-century Palestine, died the death of a common criminal at the hands of the Roman authorities, and rose from the dead after three days, just as he predicted he would. Although Yamauchi contends that the problem of the resurrection is a tangible historical reality that can be understood using the methods of traditional research, "it differs from other historical problems in that it poses a challenge to every individual." It stands both within and beyond history. Yamauchi concludes, "For the Resurrection of Christ to be more than a beautiful Easter story, each person needs to believe in his heart that God has raised Christ from the dead and to confess with his mouth Jesus as Lord."

Another noted scholar from the 1970s who defined historical study as a species of evidentialist apologetics is John Warwick Montgomery. While more a formal apologist than a historian, Montgomery explicitly defined the central work of Christian historiography in terms of defending the historicity of Christian foundations.[4] The stakes for Montgomery are stated somewhat wryly by Carl Braaten:

If God's revelation to mankind comes *as* history, and if the historical method is our only reliable way of dealing with the past, it would seem to follow that Christian faith is made totally dependent on the results of historical research. If faith claims to be based on truth and reality, not on opinion and fantasy, historical science seems to offer the only objective canons of discernment. The basis and content of faith then seem to be in the hands of the historian, and faith must, apparently go begging for its certainty.[5]

While Montgomery would surely have disputed the suggestion that any "begging" was necessary, he did see the historian's role as decisive in shoring up the foundations of faith. As Ronald Nash put it, Montgomery "believes that since historical objectivity is possible and since the Bible measures up to the canons of scientific history, it follows that there is a conclusive historical proof for the Christian faith."[6]

In making a case for the faith, Montgomery held that nothing could be more important than showing the historical validity of the biblical account of reality, and, of course, establishing the historicity of Jesus Christ. In *Where Is History Going?* (1969), Montgomery challenges what he takes to be the dominant philosophies of history—those of Kant, Hegel, Marx, Spengler, and Toynbee—because each, in their attempt to craft a picture of "total history," fail to grapple with God's knowledge and superintendence of the whole of human history. And none give credence to the central event of this history: "that God entered the human sphere and revealed to men the origin and goal of the historical drama, the criteria for significance and the value in the process, the true nature of the human participants in the drama, and the ethical values appropriate to the process."[7]

Montgomery contends that there can be no "Christian conception of history" without first demonstrating the historicity of Jesus Christ, the linchpin of history itself. In *History and Christianity* (1972), Montgomery takes on philosopher Avrum Stoll, who stands in for Montgomery as a representative of all those who, while believing Jesus to have been an actual historical figure, thought the man from Nazareth was shrouded in so many layers of legend and myth that accessing him through historical study is inconceivable. Montgomery goes on to deal with the historical record, but his analysis is more concerned with problems of logic, methodology, and misinterpretation that he believes leads skeptics like Stoll from accepting the historicity of Jesus as presented in the Bible. After overcoming each of these problems, Montgomery concludes, "I have tried to show that the weight of historical probability lies on the side of the validity of Jesus' claims to be God incarnate, the Savior of man, the coming Judge of the world. If probability does in fact support these claims . . . then we must act in behalf of them." Like Yamauchi, he ends with an appeal to honest readers to submit to the God of the universe. "If God is 'closing in on you,' why not let the gap be closed entirely? As Pascal so well put it, you have nothing to lose and everything to gain."[8]

Both Yamauchi and Montgomery approach history in a way that leads inevitably to an invitation to respond personally to the claims of Scripture by accepting Jesus Christ as Savior and Lord. Such historical study as apologetics is direct and simple. Although historical scholarship designed to validate Christianity's historicity is the most explicit brand of history-as-apologetics, another kind of history writing is somewhat less direct but no less determined in its attempts to defend the faith in the wake of its many cultured despisers.

Demonstrating Christianity's Historical Successes

Many writers have turned to history not only to show that Christianity is true but also to demonstrate its success in forging the enduring pillars of Western civilization. As a set of ideas, a collection of moral assertions, and even a prescription for social organization, these writers argue that Christianity provides the ideal framework within which God intended human beings to live, and, since the age when Jesus walked the earth, Christian faith has been the primary engine of cultural progress and moral order for human civilization. Validating the successes of societies that have been shaped by Christianity—and the failures of those that haven't—has thus been the chief task of historical writing within this tradition.

There is tremendous anxiety today among many Western Christians over the perceived pace of secularization cutting through what they understandably view as a civilization built on historically Christian institutions, ideas, and values. Rather than defending the Christian features that underlie Western culture, many Christians have been apt to apologize for and criticize the undemocratic, repressive, and even abusive legacies of the faith. Conservative writer Dinesh D'Souza notes that many "liberal Christians" have become the world's missionaries to the church rather than Christianity's top defenders to the world. He decries this concession to secularism as an appalling and inexcusable intellectual retreat, and urges Christians instead to push back against the secular assault on Christianity's place in history.

D'Souza encourages Christian believers to "show that Christianity is the very root and foundation of Western civilization," and "to argue that Christianity is responsible for many of the values and institutions that secular people cherish most."[9] He insists that the strong-armed press against the faith by secular elites is based on a warped understanding of history that has whitewashed the powerful influence that Christian ideas and people have had on human culture. "Christianity is responsible for the way our society is organized and for the way we currently live," notes D'Souza. "So extensive is the Christian contribution to our laws, our economics, our politics, our arts, our calendar, our holidays, and our moral priorities," continues D'Souza, "that historian J. M. Roberts writes in *The Triumph of the West*, 'We could none of us today be what we are if a handful of Jews nearly two thousand years ago had not believed that they had known a great teacher, seen him crucified, dead, and buried, and then rise again.' "[10]

Historical writing in this tradition is polemical in nature. Histories of the sort D'Souza promotes advance particular kinds of arguments about the character of Christianity, namely that it is capable of building free, prosperous, inventive, well-ordered, and compassionate societies, and has proved its capacity for doing so through two thousand years of development. Writers in this stream of thinking tend to assume that, where the West has been great, it owes its greatness to the genius of Christianity. And where the West has been vicious or close-minded, it has been due to its failure to maintain the tenets of the faith. A great deal is at stake for many of these writers. D'Souza warns, "Secularists want to empty the public square of religion and religious-based morality so they can monopolize the shared space of society with their own views. In the process they have made religious believers into second-class citizens."[11] Christians, he concludes, must rise up to rightfully claim the Christian origins of society. And establishing their claims by looking to the past is an important dimension of this struggle.

Challenging the assumption that Christianity has been an obvious blessing to humanity is commonly traced to the Enlightenment's more general attack on the teachings and abusive authority of the church. Perhaps most famously, Edward Gibbon's magisterial six-volume *The History of the Decline and Fall of the Roman Empire* (1776–89) argued that Christian ideas of pacifism and the afterlife, along with celibacy, all of which grew in popularity during the Christianization of Rome during the fourth century, weakened the empire's internal strength and drive, leading to its eventual demise. He further argued that Christianity plunged post-Roman Europe into what widely became known as "dark ages" of superstition and irrational church authority, from which it didn't begin to recover until Gibbon's own enlightened age of science and reason.[12]

Since Gibbon, it has become all too common to challenge the validity of Christian faith by looking to its deleterious effects in history. Rather than leveling a philosophical argument about its incoherence or even a historical argument about its specious origins, the truth of Christianity has more commonly been challenged on the basis of its ignominious history of social harm. Such arguments point to Western civilization's long history peppered with Christian-inspired religious warfare, corrupt and abusive church hierarchies, complicit endorsements of totalitarian regimes, obfuscation of scientific (and other academic) inquiry, and sponsorship of socially regressive practices from patriarchy and chattel slavery to anti-Semitism and homophobia. How can a religion that has brought so much harm to so many people be deemed worthy of belief?

Debate over Christianity's social benefits and liabilities has been a primary site of cultural warfare during the past generation. When contemporary skeptics and humanists enumerate reasons for rejecting the faith, one is as likely to hear a recitation of past Christian hypocrisies and episodes of church-sponsored violence as a list of intellectual challenges to Christian beliefs. While he also entirely rejects Christianity's metaphysical claims, frenetic writer and impassioned atheist Christopher Hitchens found the sordid history of Christian-led violence to be a central reason for his aggressive attacks on religion generally, and Christianity in particular. In *God Is Not Great: How Religion Poisons Everything* (2007), Hitchens lumps all religions into a single mass and cites example after example of religious peoples doing horrific things on the basis of their beliefs and moral codes.[13]

Practicing Christians typically view the faith as encompassing the essence of goodness and a dependable safeguard *against* social, psychological, and physical harm. Contending with reports that portray Christianity as the source of the world's greatest troubles—slavery, sexism, militarism, and economic exploitation—can be understandably vexing to many believers. Contemporary Christian writers have responded to this strategic historiography in various ways. Some concede that past Christian generations, intoxicated by worldly power, have often failed to live by the true teachings of Christ. In fact, it has become popular for many Christian writers to argue that the church took a calamitous turn in the years following Roman Emperor Constantine's conversion to Christianity in the fourth century. Ironically contradicting Gibbon, this argument says that Constantinian Christians traded their ethic of pacifism for one of power, and fundamentally reoriented the relationship of faith to the predominant institutions of this world. What followed was an increasing propensity of Christians to wed religion to military and political power, a move that explains much of the church's unfortunate legacy of social malfeasance.

Christian ethicists John Howard Yoder and Stanley Hauerwas have been very influential proponents of this "Constantinian thesis." Yoder claims that the vast majority of Christian history has been tainted by an implicit justification of violence and power due to the absorption of political power into the ministrations of the church. He writes that "pre-Constantinian Christians had been pacifists, rejecting the violence of army and empire not only because they had no share of power, but because they considered it morally wrong," whereas "post-Constantinian Christians considered imperial violence to be not only morally tolerable but a positive good and a Christian duty."[14] As Christianity again today recedes to the margins of the dominant culture, Hauerwas has passionately urged Christians to embrace their status as "resident aliens" as a return to the more faithful pre-Constantinian arrangement of powerlessness and Christ-like love.[15]

A variety of more recent books informed by this thesis include Gregory A. Boyd's *Myth of a Christian Nation: How the Quest for Political Power Is Destroying the Church* (2007), Brian McLaren's *A New Kind of Christianity: Ten Questions that Are Transforming the Faith* (2011), and Lee C. Camp's *Mere Discipleship: Radical Christianity in a Rebellious Age* (2008). These authors look to Christianity's checkered past with a sense of bewildered embarrassment, while doing little or nothing to defend past Christians against negative historical portrayals. However, they remain buoyant about the essence of Christianity itself. The problem in history, they insist, has been *Christendom* not *Christianity*, and they argue that Christendom's violent past serves as a useful caution against pursuits of political and social power by contemporary believers.[16]

But Marvin Olasky, editor of the conservative Christian *World Magazine*, describes such contemporary concessions to this deeply critical historiography as expressions of evangelical "self-hatred." Just as many believe that the only possible explanation for contemporary Jewish criticism of Israeli foreign policy (among other things "Jewish") is an unconscious, but deeply nurtured "self-hatred," so Olasky concludes that criticisms of past Christian actions in the post-Constantinian era emerge from the same kind of personal pathology. "For some self-hating evangelicals," writes Olasky, "the story of the past 2,000 years is: 'Christ came, Christians have pillaged, we're sorry.'"[17] Many conservatives like Olasky equate historical accounts that critique Christianity with attacks on the faith itself. According to Olasky, failing to counter such attacks betrays a lack of "strong church worship and preaching." He believes that Christians have an obligation to write and read historical accounts of Christianity that show it to be the positive, transformative force for social good that he instinctively knows it to be. For Olasky and other culturally conservative evangelicals, it is necessary for Christianity to have been an honorable, virtuous, even transformative influence on humankind. Its victory over past evils is a presumptive article of faith that *must be* embraced and accepted without serious debate, and then demonstrated in history.

Conservatives like Olasky have led the way in writing histories that endeavor to link some of humankind's most celebrated moral, technological, artistic, and intellectual achievements to their inevitable origins within Christianity. Some of this writing is intended as self-conscious rebuttals to attacks on the faith, answering what is often described as secularist, left-leaning, revisionist history that twists the facts in order to destroy the credibility of Christianity. The baldest example of this kind of writing is D. James Kennedy and Jerry Newcombe's counter-factually titled, *What If Jesus Had Never Been Born?* It imagines how the world might have turned out without the establishment of the Christian church and all that it spawned, and lays out an enormous number of civilizational pillars that they believe owe their existence to Jesus, the Bible, and the church.

"Despite its humble origins," write Kennedy and Newcombe, "the Church has made more changes on earth for the good than any other movement or force in history."[18] The list of contributions they attribute to Christianity includes but is not limited to hospitals, universities, literacy, free-market capitalism, representative government, civil liberties, modern science, the elevation of women, the protection of human life, and the eradication of slavery. The authors do spend one chapter exploring the "sins of the Church," including the Crusades, the Inquisition, wars of religion, and anti-Semitism, though in each case, they notably go out of their way to pin each of them on Roman Catholicism (drawing on the useful distinction between Christianity and Christendom not that different from Yoder and Hauerwas). Still, they make it clear that, in studying the impact of Christianity in history, "the good far, far outweighs the bad."[19]

In his book, *What Has Christianity Ever Done for Us? How It Shaped the Modern World* (2005), Jonathan Hill strikes a much less defensive tone. He claims that he is "certainly [not trying] to argue that Christianity is true . . . and I don't have an agenda of my own that I am trying to push," wanting nothing more than to take an "objective look at some of the positive contributions that Christianity has made to the world over the past two thousand years."[20] He asserts a basic contention contained in one form or another in all such books: that the culture of Western civilization, even as it has formally rejected the norms and beliefs of Christianity, owes more than it imagines to historical foundations rooted in the faith.

Hill draws selectively from Western history a series of familiar and somewhat less obvious legacies that came into existence only by way of the Christian tradition, from the way the liturgical calendar continues to structure the rhythms of our years to the ways Christian ideals came to undergird themes of Western art, music, and literature, even to this day. The most predominant feature in Hill's survey is the priority Christians gave to literacy and education from the earliest period of the Middle Ages through the Reformation, and the ways they fueled powerful movements of philosophy and scientific inquiry, as well as the institution of the world's greatest universities.

The author concludes his book by looking to the Christian origins of two aspects of the contemporary political order that seem today to war against one another: the birth of both the modern self and the modern state. Citing crucial Christian works such as Augustine's *Confessions* and Descartes' *Meditations*, the West elevated the value and sanctity of the individual as a fundamental unit of social organization, endowed with the power of empirical observation and rational deduction and likewise imbued with irreducible rights worthy of protection. But the individual cannot exist in isolation from larger social organisms. Christians never viewed themselves as autonomous creatures but as members of a larger body with a communal identity and communal responsibilities. Hill writes that Christians have long believed that "it is only in peaceful community that people can become truly human."[21] Though Christians value the individual, the Christian tradition has also placed enormous value on the protective and defensive state and the need to engage in social action that promotes the common good. This dual legacy has been a formative element of the contemporary West.

In *How Christianity Changed the World* (2001), Alvin J. Schmidt offers a more substantial, though ultimately interchangeable, survey of Christianity's grand contributions to cultural betterment. His list has a familiar ring. Christianity was both the author and preserver of the sanctity of human life, sexual morality, the dignity of women, charity and compassion, and Western education. It laid the foundations for economic freedom, scientific study, political liberty, and much of what we understand as the great art of Western civilization. And it stamped out slavery and other forms of tyranny.

In the foreword to Schmidt's survey, historian Paul Maier bemoans the impact of secularization and multiculturalism in contemporary society, which he believes have caused "the massive impact that Christianity has had on civilization" to be "overlooked, obscured, or even denied." He commends Schmidt's work as "long overdue, not only in the interests of defending the faith, but more urgently to set the record straight."[22] He categorizes Schmidt's analysis as a fresh and powerful work of apologetics in its effort to demonstrate Christianity's "record of being *the* most powerful agent in transforming society for the better across two thousand years since Jesus lived on the earth."[23]

In terms of "setting the record straight" about the benefits of Christianity to human civilization, no author has written more voluminously or zealously than Rodney Stark. A sociologist by training, Stark made a decisive turn toward writing history in the early 1990s, and has made a veritable cottage industry of turning conventional historiographic wisdom about religion's cultural implications on its head.[24] In more recent years, he has taken explicit aim at the so-called New Atheists like Hitchens and their dismissal of religion as inherently destructive. From the cultural savvy of early Christians through the first four centuries after Christ to the buoyant piety of Americans during the early republic, Stark has been an indefatigable defender of religion's cultural cachet. As the *New York Times* observed, Stark "is sick and tired of reading that religion impeded scientific progress and stunted human freedom. To those who say that capitalism and democracy developed only after secular minded thinkers turned the light of reason on the obscurantism of the Dark Ages, he has a one-word answer: nonsense."[25]

Stark's most widely discussed book, at least in recent years, is probably *The Victory of Reason: How Christianity Led to Freedom, Capitalism, and Western Success* (2005). Although similar to Schmidt, Hill, and Kennedy/Newcombe in several notable ways, Stark's treatment differs in one important respect: as the title indicates, he attributes Christianity's successes less to its doctrines than to its assimilation of reason. Stark doesn't credit Christianity with establishing reason (that goes to the Greeks) but rather praises the Christian tradition for integrating reason into the ways it has functioned in the world. As he writes, "Christianity alone [among all the world's religions] embraced reason and logic as the primary guide to religious truth."[26] While other religions remained mired in mystery and instinct, only

Christianity developed a capacity to orient itself to the future by embracing an account of progress that enabled it to adapt successfully to an ever-changing world.

In Stark's account of Western civilization, we are again treated to a sizeable list of social, political, and cultural goods that have been ushered into the world on the coattails of Christian institutions and ideas. What he calls "the blessings of rational theology" helped to grease the wheels of liberal democracy, capitalism, and other impulses that he considers socially beneficial. To put the matter plainly, Starks asserts, "Christianity created Western Civilization. Had the followers of Jesus remained an obscure Jewish sect, most of you would not have learned to read and the rest of you would be reading from hand-copied scrolls." Stark takes for granted that the fruits of modernization have been desirable, without serious negative consequences. Christianity created modernization, and modernization has been beneficial to everyone. "Without a theology committed to reason, progress and moral equality, today the entire world would be about where non-European societies were in, say, 1800: a world with many astrologers and alchemists but no scientists. A world of despots, lacking universities, banks, factories, eyeglasses, chimneys, and pianos."[27]

Stark's priority for *reason's influence on Christianity* over the role of *Christianity itself* might be explained partly by his own nebulous personal faith. About a year before the publication of *The Victory of Reason*, he admitted in an interview that, although he was raised in the church, "I don't know what I believe."[28] By 2007 Stark was willing to describe himself as "an independent Christian," but more of a cultural Christian without ties to any church. He likened his personal sense of being Christian to his personal attraction to the power and the rational elegance of Western civilization, not unlike the theme of his book. So Stark offers a curious case: a firm-minded apologist for the faith who, in the end, hasn't been convinced of its ultimate claims in his own life.

The history of science is especially well traveled territory for historians hoping to demonstrate the Christian origins of prosperity and goodness in the modern world. Arguably the greatest indictment contemporary Christians often receive involves their lack of scientific rigor and their unwillingness to accept the consensus of scientists when it comes to issues ranging from human origins to climate change. Powerful antidotes to such criticisms have therefore been aggressive illustrations of how much modern science relies on underlying Christian presuppositions and the yeoman work of past Christian scientists.

While historian of science James Hannam concedes that life within medieval Europe was disease-ridden, corrupt, repressive, and typically short, he urges skeptics to rethink assumptions about the period as "dark ages." In a deeply researched and nuanced study, Hannam demonstrates that virtually all of the important foundations that built what is commonly called "the Scientific Revolution" were laid by Christians within the Middle Ages.[29] In *God's Philosophers: How the Medieval World Laid the Foundations of Modern Science* (2009), Hannam provides a long list of scientific insights and breakthroughs that would have been unthinkable were it not for the specifically Christian ideas of thinkers toiling away in premodern Europe.

Aside from sweeping surveys of civilization that give Christianity a heroic, starring role, dozens of other microstudies have also been produced during the past thirty years that strive to explain the emergence of particular spheres of social progress by looking to the legacy of Christian faith. In the area of politics, for instance, "liberty" is regularly described as the unique purchase of the Christian tradition. This is especially the case in attempts to understand the origins of the American system.

Many writers have suggested that the modern idea of liberty in contemporary America has been shorn of its deep and richly Christian roots. Douglas F. Kelly finds these roots by looking to the theology of John Calvin and his progenitors in the sixteenth, seventeenth, and eighteenth centuries. In *The Emergence of Liberty in the Modern World* (1992), Kelly cites Calvin's Geneva, Hugenot France, Scotland during the age of John Knox, and Puritan England as the most vital wellsprings of thought and practice that produced the key documents of America's founding. This thick heritage of theology that informed America's understanding of liberty was imbued with nuances and assumptions about God's sovereignty, sin, and redemption that were lost over time. "By the latter part of the eighteenth century," writes Kelly, "there was a growing tendency for many of the major practical implications of Calvinism for civil government to enter the political

'market place' disconnected from the theology that shaped them."[30]
He notes that, while American liberty today is unthinkable without Reformed theology, this process of secularization weakened the
power and vitality of liberty as it was carried forward in the American system.

Benjamin Hart's *Faith and Freedom: The Christian Roots of American
Liberty* (1988) also explores the underlying structures of the American government and economic system. He asserts, "The history of
America's laws, its constitutional system, the reason for the American
revolution, or the basis of its guiding political philosophy cannot be
discussed without reference to its biblical roots."[31] The faith and moral
ideals espoused by Christianity, according to Hart, are everywhere
evident in functions of the American system of government, from
George Washington to (then president) Ronald Reagan. He points to
a wide variety of religious-themed customs, such as beginning each
session of the Supreme Court by invoking God's protection and oversight, and posting "In God We Trust" on the national currency, to
demonstrate the basic religious tenor of the nation. "These laws and
customs all have their origins in America's Christian past," observes
Hart, "and provide a clue as to the assumptions guiding the creation
of America's form of government, assumptions the founding fathers
had about man's nature, his place in eternity, and the character of the
God to whom he is accountable. It is these ultimate concerns that
determine the shape of our society."[32]

In a similar vein, Gary T. Amos' *Defending the Declaration* (1996)
confronts and criticizes what he takes to be an overwhelming consensus that the Declaration of Independence was a "bastard offspring of
anti-Christian deism or Enlightenment rationalism. The ideas in the
Declaration," Amos retorts, "are Christian despite the fact that some
of the men who wrote them down were not."[33] Like so many other
writers, Amos believes that most prevailing accounts of America's past
have been clouded by myths designed to whitewash the true Christian origins of the nation's founding documents and the character of
America itself.

A very different, hard-to-categorize kind of apologetic is found
in Steven J. Keillor's *This Rebellious House: American History and the
Truth of Christianity* (1996), which is an attempt at renarrating the

sweep of American history in defense of the faith. Keillor's book challenges the premise behind many attempts at historical apologetics that seek to defend Christianity's truth by demonstrating the successes and sterling faithfulness of its people, ideas, and institutions. He observes that Christianity's status as ultimate truth has increasingly been determined and challenged within the arena of history (how it has fared over time) rather than philosophy (its internal rational coherence), and while he doesn't believe Christians ought to be in the business of producing historical narratives we "can tell ourselves to prop up our faith," neither does he deny history's standing as a legitimate venue for defending the faith.

Keillor boldly proclaims, "Jesus Christ is Lord," as a "public fact" of history—an undeniable truth—and that "Christ will return" as an equally undeniable public fact. Within the frame of this irrefutably true Christian metanarrative, Keillor takes license to sift through the record and interpretations of history drawing from revisionists and traditional historians alike, to tell a "truer" story of America's past, warts and all. He understands and does not flinch from the fact that there are many lamentable features of the human past. So exposing the past foibles and flaws of the faithful (slavery, exploitation of native peoples, and patriarchal mistreatment of women) and happily rejecting the "Christian America" thesis presents no credible challenge to the faith's truth claims. In fact, he argues, showing the rebellions of (quoting Ezek 24:3 NIV) "this rebellious house" (i.e., the United States of America) "tends to confirm" Christianity's truth claims.[34]

If the logic of historical apologetics typically (Keillor notwithstanding) suggests that Christianity must be shown to have prevailed as a force for human good everywhere that it was rightly observed, then it follows that narratives of cultural decline and disorder are best explained by the absence, suppression, or abandonment of true Christian conviction. The latter argument drives C. Gregg Singer's *A Theological Interpretation of American History* (1964). Singer begins with the assumption that history must be interpreted through the lens of the Bible's message of redemption, assessing the philosophical and theological systems that undergird human society at each point in its development. As an explicitly devoted Calvinist, Singer holds that the closer past societies conformed their thinking and practices to the world and life view of Calvinist orthodoxy the more successful they were in ordering their lives.

The genius of American society, argues Singer, has been its foundation in "the Puritan way of life." Even as its purity diminished over time through heretical and humanist philosophies, some kernels of its essence were sustained for more than three centuries. But the story Singer reports in his "theological interpretation" of history is decidedly one of decline. While the Puritans boldly enthroned God as sovereign over the political affairs of society, subsequent generations became intoxicated with democratic beliefs that sought "to enthrone man as sovereign in his own right."[35] Rather than seeing individual liberty and economic individualism as the great bequest of Christianity in the West, Singer sees these emerging impulses as radical departures from biblical orthodoxy. Puritanism's "dethronement from a position of supremacy has cast its shadow over every succeeding epoch and generation," writes Singer. And "its effects are seen not only in the life of the churches but in American political, social and economic development as well."[36]

Singer details the American departure from Calvinist orthodoxy from its dabbling in deism during the colonial era, to its embrace of Transcendentalism during the antebellum period, to its assent to social Darwinism and the Social Gospel by the early twentieth century. In each case, Singer sees a growing acceptance of a "man-centered" understanding of the world coming to trump God's sovereignty. Singer describes nearly every negative social and political development in American history as a direct consequence of this theological declension. He states, "Calvinism in particular and the older evangelical theology in general, have lost their hold on the American mind to such an extent that they are no longer the dominant forces in the formulation of our political and economic thought."[37] By the 1920s and 1930s, even the last vestiges of theistic leavening were drained from American social thought; Singer sees the descent into various forms of socialism, statism, and internationalism as the natural destination of a people who have abandoned "the Scriptures as the norm of all truth and accepted the dictum that man is the measure."[38] He concludes his "theological interpretation" by imploring the U.S. government to condense its power, overseeing only "those spheres which are clearly conferred upon it by the Scriptures and [to] surrender . . . those extra-biblical powers which liberal political philosophy and practice have given to it during the last one-hundred years or so."[39]

Francis Schaeffer's *How Should We Then Live: The Rise and Decline of Western Thought and Culture* (1976) offers a far more ambitious and influential look at historical decline. Schaeffer (1912–1984) is widely recognized as a pivotal figure in the resurgence of American evangelical engagement with culture and ideas during the 1960s and 1970s. The Presbyterian pastor, writer, and speaker began to reconsider his own Fundamentalist separatism during the 1950s, beginning a lifelong ministry of cultural inquiry and involvement. Although not, strictly speaking, an academic himself, Schaeffer made the arts, philosophy, and history spheres of serious concern, believing that Christians could never speak to the modern human condition with the gospel if they weren't listening to the questions modern (especially young) people were asking. He believed that the political and cultural tumult of the late 1960s signaled a cataclysmic point of crisis and despair for Western civilization, and that young people "searching for answers" had become more ready to hear the message of Christian hope than at any point in history. While he quite frequently struck the pose of a reflective intellectual, Schaeffer was—from beginning to end—an apologist for Christianity.[40]

Whether welcoming conflicted young people to live alongside his family at L'Abri, his Swiss mountain retreat, or delivering talks throughout the United States on college campuses, Schaeffer dedicated himself to reading, assessing, and diagnosing the human condition, and to inviting seekers to consider the claims of the Bible. While most of his books (almost all taken from transcripts of his lectures) focused on philosophy and the fine arts, *How Should We Then Live?* was his only real foray into history. He conceived the project as a multipart documentary film produced with his son Franky, with the book as a companion piece. The film series and the book begin with the same basic premise: contemporary society has lapsed into a state of moral and cultural degradation. He observes the youth rebellion of the 1960s with its countercultural attitudes toward authority, sexual experimentation, use of hallucinogenic drugs, and embrace of leftist political ideologies, and he explores the question of how Western culture came into its current state of near anarchy. He does not blame the 1960s youth for this radical turn and, in fact, sympathizes with their restlessness and frustration. This story of cultural decline is instead rooted in a yearning for human autonomy and a thirst for what he calls "personal peace"—a desire to "live one's life with minimal possibilities of being personally disturbed"—that is rooted deeply within the history of Western civilization itself.[41]

Rather than finding in Western Civilization a flowering of Christian ideals, Schaeffer identifies a host of impulses that would increasingly come to marginalize and suppress Christian values. He places strong emphasis on the ways that worldview thinking governs the beliefs and practices within every age of history. In some instances, non-Christians have adopted Christian ideas to good effect, while in other cases Christians have taken on corrupt, non-Christian presuppositions with predictably negative implications. So the rise of Western culture, even as it was marked by the presence of Christian institutions, regularly became debased, mixing humanistic assumptions of human autonomy with traditional Christian theology.

Schaeffer biographer Barry Hankins calls the book a jeremiad, "that is, a sermon in the tradition of Jeremiah, who often preached about decline." He summarizes *How Should We Then Live?* this way: "Early Christianity was pure and biblical; medieval Roman Catholic Christianity became increasingly corrupt; the Renaissance introduced humanism; then the Reformation recaptured true Christianity and held humanism at bay until the twentieth century."[42] Hankins also notes Schaeffer's focus on the Enlightenment, which deepened the Renaissance commitment to secular humanism. In trying to preserve its Christian origins, Schaeffer argued that the American system of government was a legacy of the relatively untainted Protestant Reformation. To contrast the American system with the twentieth-century European descent into dictatorship and communism, he traced these latter developments to the Enlightenment-based French Revolution.

Just as Schaeffer believed American democracy was an inheritance of Christianity, he made similar arguments about modern science. He explained that Christianity supported the idea of an objective, knowable reality that was understood as God's creation. The created order was worth studying and, moreover, scientific study counted as an ropriate response to the dominion God called humans to exercise over it. "Since the world was created by a reasonable God," Schaeffer argued, scientists "were not surprised to find a correlation between themselves as observers and the things observed. . . . Without this foundation, Western modern science would not have been born."[43] So, although Schaeffer ultimately generates a narrative of decline, he is careful to isolate features of Western culture that he deems positive, and he studiously preserves their distinctively Christian roots.

This survey of literature provides a mere sampling of a much larger body of writing that endeavors to persuade the skeptical—and encourage the faithful—by helping them see the power of Christianity to transform the world with its unique and divine fruits, and to offer cautionary tales of what it means to live in a world without such leavening. For many of these authors, history could serve no nobler task than to illustrate such soaring truths. As noble as this task is, and as well-intentioned as its authors have been, the use of history as an apologetic for the Christian faith is plagued with problems that must be addressed.

Problems with History as Christian Apologetic

The essential problem with history's use as a Christian apologetic is that it invites—and sometimes requires—historians to cajole and stretch historical evidences to fit neatly within the frame of their presuppositions and expected results. Such endeavors often begin with a set of vague premises. Consider Robert L. Waggoner's essay "Why Genuine Christianity Makes the World Better." The author offers a list of such starting assertions: (1) Christianity considers every individual person of great worth; (2) Christianity produces a sense of universal kinship and equality, which, among other things, abolishes slavery and elevates womanhood; (3) Christianity's message of love overcomes sin, produces salvation, and transforms humanity; (4) Christian love produces self-sacrifice for both humanitarian efforts and evangelism; and (5) Christian love produces a higher moral standard of life for individuals and civilizations.[44]

These are not bad principles. In fact, most Christians would probably find it easy to embrace all of them. The problem is that Waggoner states these principles as if they are iron laws of necessity, and thereby feels emboldened to begin cobbling together evidence from the past that demonstrates their experiential validity. The problem is that if someone is intent on finding evidence that will support any particular set of broadly generic truisms, such evidence will be found. The past is overflowing with personalities, events, and anecdotes ripe for the picking that can be used to support just about any claim imaginable. But such habits will only wreak havoc on what might otherwise be honest attempts at truthfully reconstructing the past.

Introductory history students learn to describe these tactics as "source mining," which, according to J. H. Hexter, "is the examination of a corpus of writing solely with a view to discovering what it says on a particular matter narrowly defined—going through the indexes and leafing through the pages of the appropriate works . . . to find what they had to say about the cultivation of asparagus or spiritual pride."[45] It's easier to mine sources in search of evidence that support our preconceived convictions about the past than it is to engage in a painstakingly thorough evaluation of primary texts to develop a rich, complex, and oftentimes surprising picture of the past. The evidence rarely cooperates with our presuppositional expectations, and we must learn to make peace with this fact.

Mark Noll suggests that the production of such literature stems from the conviction "that historical writing exists in order to illustrate the truth of propositions known to be true before study of the past begins."[46] Armed only with the conviction that my beliefs are true, I will use them as a guide, locate just the right sources, and bend them to my purposes. "It is probably the most widely practiced form of Christian history," observes Noll, "for it specializes in exploiting historical data to show why my group is right and the opponents of my group are wrong."[47] Noll calls it "tribal history." Another, less polite term for this kind of writing is propaganda.

We must also contend with the fact that historical writing in this tradition equates Christianity uncritically with cultural progress and worldly success. Many of the books listed here take for granted that the civilizational pillars that Christianity is said to have built are not only desirable but, by implication, authentically Christian. When Christianity is credited with democracy, liberty, capitalism, and technological development, readers are urged to celebrate these advances as inherently good and manifestly Christian. Del Tackett, director of Focus on the Family's *Truth Project*, gives voice to this vision of worldly success: "The truth claims of God are consistent and logical," writes Tackett. "They make sense; they work. And even in a fallen world, when we follow them, they lead to peace and prosperity and happiness."[48]

The notion that Christianity is perceived to have been a pathway to personal prosperity and happiness—much less a cornerstone of civilizational progress—should strike anyone as odd when considered in light of its origins and earliest expectations. The perspectives from which the New Testament Scriptures were written were not ones of worldly power or cultural success. The writers of the Bible were almost without exception marginal and vulnerable in relation to real social and political leverage. Why should one assume that civilizational "success" is the "way things are supposed to be" from a biblical point of view? In what sense are the kinds of scientific, political, and technological growth written about in these books reflective of genuinely Christian notions of "success"? It isn't altogether clear that "peace and prosperity and happiness" are the trajectory of the Christian life, or that the authentic development of societies under Christian sponsorship should be free, peaceable, and technologically savvy.

Compare Tackett's anticipated fruits of Christian faithfulness with those described in Hebrews 11. Although some of the faithful described here achieved great victories and enjoyed recognizable success, a greater emphasis is placed on those who "were tortured . . . faced jeers and flogging . . . even chains and imprisonment. They were put to death by stoning, they were sawed in two; they were killed by the sword. They went about in sheepskins and goatskins, destitute, persecuted, and mistreated. . . . They wandered in deserts and mountains, living in caves and holes in the ground. They were commended for their faith, yet none of them received what had been promised" (NIV). The account of Christian living presented here doesn't lead one to expect a trajectory of grand social formations or prodigious cultural triumphs as the natural consequences of faithfulness. Why should such cultural progress be a reliable measure of Christian faithfulness today?

Simply put, writing in this vein too often fails to account for the genuine complexities of the human experience. It tends to posit an idealized world of coherence and clarity, where Christian principles are neatly translated into corresponding Christian actions. But humans have instead been left with a topsy-turvy world in which up is sometimes down, black is sometimes white; a world in which Christians often behave in deplorable ways, while pagans are apt to bear the fruit of the Spirit; where pious men willfully ignore a beaten man left for dead beside the road, while a wretched Samaritan provides a grand example of self-sacrificial love.

None should be surprised to find a sizeable gap between the way the world *ought to be* and the way it actually *has been*, between the world our Christian convictions *long for* and the world *we actually inhabit*. And yet Christians often feel defensive when critics remind us of the abuses of the Crusades, the thoroughly "Christian" arguments on behalf of chattel slavery, and the "biblical" mission to invade and exploit raw materials from Africa's interior. Christians grow nervous when hearing reports of wisdom, kindness, and genuine human flourishing found among people who appear to have completely abandoned God's law. Lived reality has always been a good deal messier than the theological axioms Christians hold, and historians must somehow contend with this messiness.

Though not immune from his own brand of (anti-Christian) apologetics, the great eighteenth-century English historian Edward Gibbon provides some insight here. He helpfully reflected on this conundrum, comparing the tasks of the theologian and the historian—two vocations that this apologetic tradition too often conflates: "The theologian may indulge the pleasing task of describing Religion as she descended from Heaven, arrayed in her native purity. A more melancholy duty is imposed on the historian. He must discover the inevitable mixture of error and corruption, which she contracted in a long residence upon earth, among a weak and degenerate race of beings."[49] In other words, it's one thing to affirm a theological truth and to hold it as a personal presupposition. But it's quite another to use such theological truths to cobble together a story of the past in order to make those theological truths more compelling.

Gibbon's perceptiveness likewise bears on the criticisms of faith by anti-Christian writers like Hitchens. While rightly pointing out many embarrassing episodes in the history of Christianity, Hitchens' reproaches no more thwart the truth of Christianity than pointing to its "successes" can vindicate it. Christianity is not authenticated by the faithfulness of its followers, who remain largely feckless and mired in sin. No, the only one who can certify Christianity is Jesus himself, who is the same yesterday, today, and forever, ever faithful to his Father in heaven. "He causes his sun to rise on the evil and the good, and sends rain on the righteous and the unrighteous" (Matt 5:45 NIV).

Conclusion

The problems raised by the use of history in service to apologetics reach to the heart of questions many Christians ask when thinking about tensions between faithfulness to Christ and responsibility to the past. How can someone maintain her commitment to Christian belief and practice without resorting to a kind of "special pleading" on behalf of Christianity in our study of human history? How can Christians be honest and forthcoming about the messiness of the past—which repeatedly challenges our expectations—without calling the essential and eternal truths of the faith into question?

In answering these, Christians must abandon their allegiance to something that might be called "Christian exceptionalism," or the perceived need to assert the unique and uniquely superior contributions to human culture by explicitly Christian people, working in explicitly Christian institutions, using uniquely Christian ideas. This well-meaning project to manage Christianity's reputation, while understandable, ironically hurts the cause of Christ in at least two important ways. First, it implicitly admits that the development of human culture is a legitimate sphere for the vindication of Christianity, as if arguments for its truth somehow rely on demonstrating its unsullied success. Those who put their hope *here* are bound to lose their faith. And second, it turns Christian scholars into utilitarians who have stopped seeking *the truth* about the human experience and have become interested only in knowing how they might best *use* some comfortable version of it to reinforce their already settled opinions. Doing so reduces Christian scholarship to a species of propaganda that needlessly discredits Christian learning and weakens a broader Christian witness both inside and outside the church.

In the end, I suspect that at least some of the authors reviewed in this chapter—and more than a few of their readers—are motivated by a certain kind of fear. Not necessarily fear of secularism itself but fear that a credible case for the faith cannot be made in a world that has been known to experience relative stability, peace, and prosperity without deference to Christianity, and a world that has, at times, suffered greatly at the hands of those who have called themselves Christians. Believers would do well to resist such fears for they are rooted in a lie. Christianity does not require a record of worldly success or cultural sponsorship in order to vindicate itself to the world. Christians may therefore boldly encourage one another to examine human culture without fear, eyes wide open, come what may.

5

HISTORICAL STUDY AS SEARCH FOR GOD

Narrating God's role in the human past is probably the most commonsense contemporary understanding of "Christian history." Advocates of providentialism or "HIS story" assume that when Christians look to the past, their unique contributions must consist of questions about God: Where is he? What is he doing? And can we better understand his character and his eternal plans by looking to the past? It should come as no surprise that providentialism is the *least commonly employed* version of Christian historiography among believing historians who are professionally trained (more on this later). But providentialism's lack of academic respectability has discouraged very few popular Christian ministries, worldview training courses, history textbook publishers, or ordinary Christians from making the "search for God" the centerpiece of historical study. This providential sense of history is the default setting for Christian thinking about the past among ordinary believers.

This vision for history follows a simple logic. God rules over every square inch of creation, and governs it according to his perfect, holy will. So the honest believer, when looking at the past, should expect to find it brimming with evidence of God's purposes and plans. In fact, it seems hard for many to imagine that anything short of this formulation could be described as a "Christian understanding of history." But a closer look at the doctrine of providence and its varied applications reveals a more complicated picture.

The Christian Doctrine of Providence

The doctrine of providence is a basic, even central pillar of historic orthodox Christian belief. It contends that, as creator and sustainer of the universe, God maintains an ongoing, active, controlling, personal involvement in the affairs of his creation. He made all things, owns all things, knows all things, and guides all things according to his desires. The doctrine bears on his omnipotence: God is all-powerful; his omnipresence: God is everywhere at once; his justice: God governs all affairs with equity and good order; and his love: God lovingly cares for that which he made. It specifically rules out-of-bounds the Enlightenment, deist concept of God as a detached creator who established governing laws before the foundation of the earth and, after setting the world in motion, views it from a safe distance. Although God is bound by neither time nor space, he enters the human drama to sustain, to judge, and to save. Here we see God as our heavenly Father who actively attends to his children and all else he has made.

The Old and New Testament Scriptures are filled with passages that emphasize and elucidate God's providential relationship with the world he made.

> I am God, and there is no other; I am God, and there is none like me. I make known the end from the beginning, from ancient times, what is still to come. I say: "My purpose will stand and I will do all that I please." (Isa 46:9-10 NIV)

> The Most High is sovereign over all kingdoms on earth and gives them to anyone he wishes and sets over them the lowliest of people. (Dan 4:17)

> You alone are the Lord. You made the heavens, even the highest heavens, and all their starry host, the earth and all that is on it, the seas and all that is in them. You give life to everything, and the multitudes of heaven worship you. (Neh 9:6)

> The God who made the world and everything in it is the Lord of heaven and earth and does not live in temples built by human hands. And he is not served by human hands, as if he needed anything.

Rather, he himself gives everyone life and breath and everything else. (Acts 17:24-25)

For from him and through him and for him are all things. (Rom 11:36)

In him we were also chosen, having been predestined according to the plan of him who works out everything in conformity with the purpose of his will. (Eph 1:11)

His sovereign care is not limited to humankind. The seas and the streams, the grasslands and the hills are all overseen and lovingly tended by God, a most wise and merciful gardener (Ps 65). Jesus likewise reminds his disciples, "Look at the birds of the air; they do not sow or reap or store away in barns, and yet your heavenly Father feeds them" (Matt 6:26 NIV). God also intervenes in the everyday affairs of individuals, families, and nations to accomplish his purposes. When Noah, his family, and all the animals entered the ark, it is God who shuts the door (Gen 7:16). It is God who both established Nebuchadnezzar on his throne (Dan 5:18) and similarly forced him down to the status of a "wild donkey" who "ate grass like the ox" (Dan 5:21).

The Bible portrays God as one who providentially enters the human story both to bless and to judge. He fed manna and quail to the children of Israel while they wandered in the wilderness (Exod 16:4, 13); on numerous occasions he gave infertile women children (Judg 13:3; 1 Sam 1:19-20; Luke 1:13); and he rescued Daniel from certain death while locked in a den of lions (Dan 6:16-28). But he likewise turned Lot's wife into a pillar of salt for returning to take a quick glance at Sodom and Gomorrah's destruction (Gen 19:26), hardened Pharaoh's heart rendering him intransigent (Exod 9:12), and struck Ananias and Sapphira dead for dealing dishonestly with their offering to the church (Acts 5:1-11).

God's most dramatic and consequential providential entrance into human history is the incarnation. In his determination to turn back the curse of sin and defilement, "the Word became flesh and made his dwelling among us. We have seen his glory, the glory of the one and only Son, who came from the Father, full of grace and truth" (John 1:14 NIV).

Within the Christian tradition, theologians and church leaders have commonly distinguished between "ordinary" or "general" providence (God's sovereign oversight working through natural laws, secondary causes, and even human agency) and "extraordinary" or "special" providence(s) (signifying God's direct and decisive interventions in the creation, often suspending the laws of nature). This distinction acknowledges everything that happens in the universe as a function of God's commands and will, even those things that appear to be unfolding according to the normal, orderly operations of nature. These classifications have provided a way to assert the supreme principle of God's sovereign control in all things, while preserving the idea that God sometimes acts in very direct and exceptional ways.[1] However, many applications of the doctrine of providence make no such distinction; the doctrine asserts that every detail observed in the human and natural worlds provides hints and clues of God's intentions and desires. Every thunderstorm, every political election, and every trip to the grocery store expresses some feature of God's eternal purposes.

Providentialist History

Since the Christian Scriptures reveal a God who, by virtue of his character, regularly enters the sphere of human affairs, it is not surprising that a significant theme in Christian historiography has been God's continued maintenance of and superintendence over the created order: the doctrine of God's providence applied to the reading of past and contemporary events.

In the wake of the Barbarian invasion and plunder of Rome in AD 410, for instance, Augustine of Hippo (354–430) interpreted the event as an act of divine judgment. In his theological masterwork, *The City of God*, Augustine asserted that "God can never be believed to have left the kingdoms of men, their dominations and servitudes, outside the laws of His providence," and that, if contemporary observers had "any right perceptions" of the catastrophic events in Rome, they would "attribute the severities and hardships inflicted by their enemies to that divine providence which is wont to reform the depraved manners of men by chastisement."[2]

At its most basic level, providentialism is an attempt to apply the insights of the doctrine of providence to the study of "ordinary events" beyond those recorded in the canon of Scripture. Reverend John Cumming opened his 1852 tract, *God in History*, by helpfully summarizing this most common of sentiments in Christian historical thinking: "The Christian delights to trace everywhere the footprints of his God—to hear in every sound the voice of his Father, and to gather new proofs of his love, his power, his acting in and through and by all things for his glory."[3] In a manner that essentially mimics the tenor of biblical historiography, Cumming believed that contemporary historians had the duty and the privilege to interpret human events from the perspective of God's sovereign intentions within creation. At least until the modern era, Christians writing about the past would have taken for granted the appropriateness, even the necessity, of taking up this task in just this way.

The basic frame of divine action in the world is not without meaning or direction. In other words, God would never indiscriminately enter the human story without teleological purposes or long-term goals. Most providentialist historians have recognized that God's overarching purposes in the world followed a narrative established in the Bible known as "salvation history" (or *heilsgeschichte*). The deep story of the world is the sacred narrative of redemption, in which history unfolds from creation (God's original purpose of harmony and fellowship with humankind in Eden), to fall (human rebellion that resulted in being cast from Eden and living in the midst of a world colored by the curse of sin), to redemption (Christ's atonement that established the foundation for the conquest of sin, death, and Satan), and finally to consummation (the completion of Christ's redemptive work at the end of the ages and the establishment of a new heaven and a new earth).

So the story of God's salvation is not entirely contained within the biblical timeframe. Contemporary events unfold as part of God's purposeful intervention in which he is moving to accomplish redemption on a grand, glorious, and cosmic scale. Human history—from the close of the biblical canon until Christ's return—fills out the balance of salvation history. The challenge of providentialism has been to understand how the common, ordinary events of traditional history relate to the sacred story of redemption. While some have argued that the site of this redemptive activity is Christ's church and that providential historians should therefore limit their attention to describing and interpreting God's guidance of the Christian church, many others see this drama impinging upon every sphere of human existence. "He is in the counting-house, the shop, the exchange, the market," writes John Cumming, "on the deck, the battle-field—in the parliament, the palace, the judgment hall."[4]

Although much of the providentialist tradition of history writing emerged as a reasonable application of the doctrine of providence and as, quite often, an attempt to continue to narrate salvation history beyond the biblical era, providentialism has never been motivated by a simple desire to present the past *as it happened*. Again, like much of the history written in the Bible, providentialist historians consider the impact their writings will have in the lives of their readers. At the beginning of Luke's Gospel (traditionally thought to introduce a larger work encompassing both Luke and Acts), the author addresses himself to "Theophilus" (lover of God), explaining that since he has "carefully investigated everything from the beginning, I too decided to write an orderly account for you . . . so that you may know the certainty of the things you have been taught" (Luke 1:3-4 NIV). Similarly, the Apostle John writes his Gospel so "that you may believe . . . and that by believing you may have life in his name" (John 20:31).

The Gospel chroniclers wrote history designed to elicit a particular sort of response and to shape their readers' lives in distinctive ways. In these examples, the biblical authors produced their accounts with an expressed hope of encouraging belief, certainty in that belief, and a vibrant life in Christ. Many contemporary providentialist historians are doing the same thing. David A. Fisher, professor of history at Bob Jones University, summarizes the benefits of teaching providential history. Building "a foundation of biblical truth so students can view history from a biblical perspective" enables them "to see the hand of God readily at work in history." They can then "make practical application of history—its lessons, its warnings" to their own personal lives. He concludes, "Teaching the providence of God in history becomes a valuable vehicle to communicate to our students not only that God's providential hand is over history, but also that His concern and care are over their lives."[5]

The practice of teaching piety with history is a common theme throughout the Old and New Testaments. As the psalmist proclaims, "One generation commends your works to another; they tell of your mighty acts. They speak of the glorious splendor of your majesty— and I will meditate on your wonderful works. They will tell of the power of your awesome works—and I will proclaim your great deeds" (Ps 145:4-6 NIV). The Apostle Paul uses the past in a similar way in his first letter to the Corinthians. Here he recounts God's faithfulness to Israel, along with Israel's accompanying unfaithfulness, and concludes, "These things happened to them as examples and were written down as warnings for us, on whom the culmination of the ages has come. So if you think you are standing firm, be careful that you don't fall!" (1 Cor 10:11-12). Using this biblical model, Edward Panosian, another Bob Jones University professor, sees a great opportunity to disciple students in the classroom through teaching them providential history. "If young people are to be taught to trust their present and their future to the wisdom, power, and goodness of the God of heaven," Panosian writes, "they must be taught to see the evidence of His gracious hand in times past. If they are to mature in understanding and are to learn to remain balanced in the face of the vicissitudes of their own generation, they must know something of whence they have come."[6]

Providential history's greatest contribution to student learning has been its power to reinforce the truths of the faith and to instruct the moral imagination. By observing that God acted in the past, both in the Bible and in "ordinary history," young Christian readers will be more inclined to believe that he is at work in their lives and circumstances. Whether a student is learning about the French exploration of the St. Lawrence River or the Compromise of 1850, Garrett Heyns and Garritt E. Roelofs reminded their readers in their 1928 manual for teachers, *Christian Interpretation of American History*, they should "want to teach [their students] to see the hand of God in all things, to appreciate all things are under Divine guidance, so that he may learn to entrust himself to his Father who is in Heaven."[7]

Especially since the nineteenth century, Christian historians have agonized over what they perceived as aggressive secularization that threatened to eclipse trust in God's provision in favor of blind fate, naturalistic causality, and rootless, random human action. Heyns and Roelofs write, "The foundation . . . of the Christian conception of history lies in the belief in the unity of God who has created and governs all things." The Christian history teacher can therefore never be satisfied with mere facts but must always dig down to determine their underlying source and purpose. "But back of all events," argue Heyns and Roelofs, "the Christian sees not blind force or chance but the Providence of God. To him God is the center of all things, and all events occur under His control and to His glory."[8]

It is evident among nearly all arguments for providentialist history that "secular" historical scholarship has had a destructive impact on the faithful. Telling stories of the past that do not place God explicitly and squarely at their center is to deny his existence and to settle for life in a world of random chance. Pastor (and sometimes historian) Steve Wilkins chastises Christians who use secular textbooks to learn about the past. Such books "are filled with terrible distortions and inexcusable omissions." According to Wilkins, history books that lack explicit references to God's provision are not merely deficient; they are willfully anti-Christian and actively aim to undermine the convictions of the faithful. He believes that Christians have willingly allowed themselves to learn history from "theological Canaanites" who would have us believe that "God is practically irrelevant to solving any problem outside our souls."[9]

Of course there are many alternatives available to those unhappy with secular textbooks. Perhaps the best-known and most widely read such version of American history is Peter Marshall and David Manuel's *The Light and the Glory: Did God Have a Plan for America?* (1977). Marshall and Manuel admit that neither of them are trained historians, but due to "the extreme gravity of America's present spiritual and moral condition," and their belief that a book of this kind would help "Americans rediscover our spiritual moorings," they were "led" to write it. While the authors insist that the book is "not intended to be a history textbook, but rather a search for the hand of

God in different periods of our nation's beginnings," it has been used by countless thousands for just this purpose.[10] Marshall and Manuel's account of American history extends from Columbus' voyage through the end of George Washington's second term as president, musing at every turn how each detail displayed evidence of God's "specific and unique plan for America." God established a covenant with America, which the authors view as God's special project, and as long as "her people" remained committed to the Lord's ways, God would bless this land. Whether talking about the abuses of the Spanish Conquistadors ("At first glance, it would appear that God's plan for America was doomed almost before it could be set in motion"),[11] or the events leading to the Pilgrims' *Mayflower* voyage ("It became increasingly clear that God wanted them to go to America"),[12] or evangelist George Whitefield's tussles with local churches in England ("God's solution: preach in the open"), the authors knit every detail of their story into a seamless divine saga.[13]

Books like *The Light and the Glory* have played a significant role since the 1970s in energizing not only Christian education and home-schooling movements but also an intense grassroots interest in finding God's hand in the past. Several years ago, a group of homeschooling advocates invited Christian young people from around the country to Omaha, Nebraska, to spend several days presenting their God-centered research essays, dramatic reenactments, and other history projects. "The Providential History Festival" has since become an annual event. One of its organizers, Phillip G. Kayser, wrote a small booklet, *Seeing History with New Eyes: A Guide to Presenting Providential History* (2008), in which he offers a framework and general tips for doing good providential history. He begins by explaining that historical study is inevitably warped and futile unless it is fully grounded in God's sustaining and Christ's redemptive work. In other words, all knowledge claims are entirely presuppositional, and unless one begins with the proper—orthodox Christian—presuppositions, then there can be no true or valuable knowledge. "The starting point for Christianity must not be assertions of *man*," notes Kayser, "but must be the assertions of *God*."[14] So secular history is not simply wrong about the facts it emphasizes and the interpretations it offers. It isn't even merely engaged in an ideologically divergent agenda. Its failure to acknowledge God's presence in history renders everything it proposes totally and fatally flawed.

Providential history and secular history are, in Kayser's view, irreconcilable. Since one starts with "God" and the other with "man," they proceed in two completely different directions, and the providentialist may feel free to disregard all "insights" of the non-providentialist. As opposed to traditional history, in which dispassionate observation is considered a welcome virtue, Kayser invites young providentialists to pledge themselves fully to biblical precommitments that will determine what they see and how they read the past. Obviously one of those precommitments is the active presence of God, but to this Kayser adds others: the belief that "history is the record of the success and victory of the sovereign purpose of God," that free-market economic principles are both true and always yield prosperity, that "polytheism is not compatible with science," and that "Christian nations have historically been the least racist, the least class conscious and the most prosperous."[15]

With increasing frequency, providentialists like Kayser see their efforts as part of broad-based counterinsurgency. They are convinced that Christians in the United States are under siege by secular elites aiming to destroy Christianity and to tear apart the nation's moral fabric. One way to push back against this assault is to provide a God-honoring alternative to the soul-withering, aggressively anti-Christian history produced within the secular academy.

Mark Beliles and Stephen McDowell direct the Providence Foundation, a national parachurch organization that aims to "turn America back to its foundational principles." The Foundation's "National Transformation Network" sees the Bible's command to "overcome evil with good" as a basis for its strategy to return God to the center of moral, educational, financial, and political spheres of American life. A central plank in this program is their effort to refurbish American history, cleansing it of what the Foundation takes to be the lies and distortions of secular history that have led so many to believe that God neither founded America as a biblical nation nor led to its original (and future?) greatness.

The Foundation makes various resources available for its supporters. *America: A Christian Nation* provides "abundant evidence from

primary sources that America was founded upon Biblical principles."
The American Dream looks at "seven foundational ideas that produced
the American dream, all of which are Biblical in their origin and were
planted by the early settlers." It also shows how "God's hand was evident in preserving the [Jamestown] colony and in the lives of many
of its founders." Beliles and McDowell's own book, *America's Providential History*, isn't so much an attempt at writing providential history
as an ambitious program for wholesale cultural change. The authors
describe their goal as equipping "Christians to be able to introduce
Biblical principles into the public affairs of America and every nation
in the world, and in so doing bring Godly change throughout the
world. We will be learning how to establish a Biblical power and
form of government in America, and we will see how our present
governmental structures must be changed."[16] They describe a host of
besetting cultural problems, from abortion and rampant sexual pro-
miscuity to poverty and the national debt, and boldly argue that all of
these problems will be eliminated if the United States can return to
its historic Christian principles and its reliance on God.

America's Providential History argues that the principles of individual liberty, limited government, free-market capitalism, homeschooling, and American territorial expansion are both rooted in
the nation's Christian past and the obvious result of God's shaping
hand. "To see Godly change occur in America we must renew our
minds to view the world from God's perspective as revealed in the
Bible—we must infuse the Faith of our Fathers into the life of our
country. In other words," continue the authors, "we as Christians
must learn what it means to disciple a nation. The study of America's
history provides the best example of this, because colonial Christians
discipled their nation."[17]

Wilkins shares the urgency of these authors, and likewise places
an almost exultant optimism about the implications of studying history in this way. "This is our glorious task in this generation. We
must not shirk it. For the glory and honor of God and the future of
our culture," concludes Wilkins. "Let us give ourselves to knowing
and telling the great things He has done. To do otherwise is to surrender future generations to the slavery that always follows unholy
forgetfulness."[18]

One of the most ambitious recent purveyors of a providential view of history is the Minnesota-based historian, Steven J. Keillor. An earlier book took up questions about Christianity's truth claims by staging an unconventional survey of American history.[19] While he appealed to divine guidance in history in this first effort, Keillor's unusual survey functions more as a work of apologetics than as genuine providential history. A second book addresses the question of God's activity in human affairs—and the mortal historian's capacity to make sense of it—head on. In *God's Judgments: Interpreting History and the Christian Faith* (2007), Keillor asserts that one cannot have a "Christian perspective *on*" history—explicitly rejecting all worldview-oriented approaches to historical study—because Christianity *is* an interpretation of history. And, as such, the faithful Christian historian has no choice but to read history according to its frame, which can have no "alternate readings" or perspectives. The Old and New Testaments present God as an active, interventionist personality who is working to bring his eternal purposes for this world to fruition. Throughout the biblical narrative, God acts (often in the form of judgment) in what Keillor contends is a long, unfolding process of refining or "sifting out" the divine plan for humankind.[20]

If, as Keillor insists, *Christianity is an interpretation of history*, we have no choice but to consider the possibility that events we observe in the past (and the present) might in fact be part of this providential "sifting out" process. Provocatively, he begins his study by asking readers to contemplate even the horrific September 11, 2001 terrorist attacks on the United States as an expression of divine judgment. He is fully aware of the temptation to manipulate this language toward political ends, and he hopes to assure readers that God's judgments tilt both toward the Left and the Right. But simply because talk of God's judgments has been abused, Keillor sees no good reason to avoid asking hard questions.

The most interesting feature of this study is that Keillor moves beyond theological reflection and philosophical speculation about divine providence in history, and spends considerable time looking at actual events. After a substantial overview that explores the theology of divine judgment and Christian historiography, he spends the balance of his study analyzing specific test cases in American history. Namely, he considers the burning of Washington, D.C. in 1814 and the American Civil War. He concludes that each, on the basis of various divergent factors, can reasonably be described as God's judgments on the United States and its leaders. Though unpopular, and surely fraught with difficult choices, <u>Keillor urges Christian historians to take seriously "divine judgment" as an essential category in historical study.</u>[21]

The Insights of Providentialism

Although, as will become evident, I find little to recommend in providentialism as a historical method, there are definitely some positive things to say about it more generally. There can be no doubt that the providential sense of history properly elevates the importance of the doctrine of providence, as it also urges us to think of ways to be more mindful of its consequences for our studies. The living God *yeah* stands as an active, sustaining, guiding presence in the world, and, in a basic way, with certain important qualifications, this theological fact should rest firmly at the foundation of any Christian idea of the past.

Providentialists appropriately fear that life in the modern, secular, mechanized West has too easily tempted us to live as if God *doesn't* exist. Some call this tendency in modern Christianity *practical deism*—an abstract assent to God's providence without it having any discernible impact on our priorities, our choices, or our decisions.[22] Our technologically sophisticated, highly specialized, fast-paced lives move along in a fashion that gives us the illusion of mastery and control. We flip a switch and light appears. We enter a grocery store and, lo and behold, the shelves are stocked with food. We set our trash by the curb and it goes "away." In an age of heroic science, we come ever closer to believing that nearly everything our ancestors might have attributed to God or unseen supernatural forces may now be explained and managed through science and technology. Doctors heal the sick. Mechanics fix cars. "This world" is not "with devils filled," as Martin Luther's was. As long as it is filled with Wi-Fi and plenty of cheap gourmet coffee, we have little recourse to *actual* belief in God's overarching governance in our lives.

The scholarly term for this propensity within historical studies (as well as the natural sciences) is *methodological atheism*. Although believing historians may confidently assert that God "holds it all together" and may live otherwise active, faith-filled Christian lives, there is often little or nothing in the way they see or reconstruct the past that shows any deference to the active governance of God. While not *actual* atheists, many of us, with respect to *method*, practice our craft in an as-if-God-doesn't-exist kind of way.

Though not a providentialist—at least not in the way described here—the great twentieth-century British historian Herbert Butterfield helpfully conveyed the implications of divine providence for life and vocation. Among the many features of modern life that have weakened the resolve of religious faith, Butterfield believed that nothing has done more harm than

> the notion of an absentee God who might be supposed to have created the universe in the first place, but who is then assumed to have left it to run as a piece of clockwork, so he is outside our lives, outside history itself, unable to affect the course of things and hidden away from us by an impenetrable screen. . . . If God cannot play a part in life, that is to say, in history, then neither can human beings have very much concern about him or very real relationships with him.[23]

Though there may be distinct reasons to reject the providentialist program, as a whole, Butterfield understood the importance of maintaining a consciousness of providence in all areas of life.

Providentialism also holds the potential of providing genuine spiritual encouragement to those who are instructed by it. Since the principal goals of providentialism typically focus on the spiritual and moral benefits to its recipients, it is worth noting the relative value of this enterprise. While I can offer little agreement with the providentialist paradigm, it is uncharitable to suggest that those who practice it do so in bad faith. Most who espouse a providentialist reading of history are moved by genuine belief, and many who read histories guided by its insights undoubtedly come away with a deepened confidence in God's care for their lives and conditions. When David Fisher says that teaching providentialist history "allows the students to see that the Lord of the Bible is the Lord of history and wants to be the Lord of their lives," he is probably right.[24] As a fellow

Christian I support these goals and wish him every success, even if I remain ultimately troubled with the representations of the past such an approach yields.

These faith-building benefits of learning providentialist history are probably most compelling among grammar school children, at an age in which history instruction is commonly little more than "teaching lessons" drawn from the past. Making a case for this approach to history instruction at this level makes some sense. But can the good yielded by girding up a child's (or an adult's) faith in this fashion sufficiently override what appear to be its deep flaws as an understanding of history? I think the answer is no. There are better, more sustainable ways to establish one another in the faith that do not require a providentialist interpretation of history.

A final benefit of providentialist history is that it helpfully reminds us that faith can play a shaping role in how Christians read the past, and that it will—or at least should—eventually put them at odds with available secular historical accounts. Providentialists are not wrong in their assertions that history writing can never be "neutral" in perspective and orientation. All situate their propositions about the past upon deeper beliefs about the nature of humankind and reality itself. Christopher Shannon observes that modern historical "monographs are not proofs of fact; they are reflections of value," and, as such, he argues, most of them "take autonomy for granted as something like an inalienable right."[25] And to the extent that human autonomy is not a Christian virtue, there are ample and adequate reasons to mistrust the visions of the past that modern scholarship often advances. Providentialism attunes Christian sensibilities to the potential dangers of simply assenting to modern historiography.

Providentialism has some clear and unassailable spiritual benefits for Christians in reminding them that God remains present and active in human history, in encouraging and spiritually bolstering the faithful, and in leading them to question the implicit value of secular history. But these, by themselves, do not validate its methods or warrant its use. Providentialism's tenuous theological reasoning, in the end, produces results that are difficult to defend.

The Limits of Providentialism

In 2001, *Christianity Today* ran a cover story that asked, "Whatever Happened to Christian History?" Within the first paragraph of Tim Stafford's essay, it became evident that, when referring to "Christian history," the author was thinking of only one sense of the term: the historical treatment of God's movement in the past. Although all of the believing professional historians Stafford interviewed upheld the doctrine of providence and viewed it as a general framework of human history, he managed to locate just one who seemed open to writing about the past with an explicitly providentialist bent. Stafford lamented, "Historians seem determined to tell the story of the world without recourse to 'the God hypothesis.' "[26]

This episode highlights an inner-cultural tension that should be addressed before moving to critical reflections on reading God's hand in history. Why is it that providentialism, so nearly ubiquitous among a certain subset of Christian laity, is almost nonexistent among professionally trained Christian historians who otherwise hold pretty much the same basic beliefs? A common answer offered by many providentialists is that professional historians have made an idol of academic respectability and status among their secular peers. They have been educated beyond their native beliefs and have too willingly adapted their understanding of the world to suit the secularist agendas they learned in graduate school. In a kind of devil's bargain, they have learned to be embarrassed by the "plain folk back home" who used to teach them about God's providential guidance in Vacation Bible School. Higher education has spoiled what was once a simple, childlike faith.

It is difficult for me to evaluate these claims, in part because they are directed at people exactly like me. Almost any response I might offer to such an accuser is likely to be construed as rationalization and self-justification. Moreover, such claims admittedly contain a good deal of truth. There is no use denying that my graduate training has had an impact on how I experience the world; or that the practices of the secular academy have clarified and refined how I read, interpret, and write about the past; or, that my desire for professional success and recognition often produces an inevitable and often unhealthy desire to be taken seriously among my secular counterparts. Guilty as charged! But this is all little more than subterfuge. While it may explain some of the personal and psychological factors that tend to create an unfortunate divide between believing academics and the broader Christian laity, these claims entirely sidestep the question of whether there might be some genuinely thoughtful *Christian reasons* for challenging the search for God in history. To dismiss an academically informed critique of providentialism for these reasons is to assume that academic training can only ever move a believer *away* from faithfulness and never *toward it*. At the risk of being accused of selling out the faith of my childhood, let me offer a critical analysis of providentialism.

The problems of providentialism as a method for doing history are too many to enumerate here. A brief consideration of its chief and most consequential liabilities will need to suffice. The central problem of providentialism's claims is its contention that human readers possess the capacity to see and understand the purposes of God by studying specific events. Given the profound limits of human knowing and the incomprehensible character of divine action, the providentialist program seems neither practically possible nor theologically permissible.

Let us begin by exploring the nature of historical knowing and its relationship to traditional Christian belief about the knowledge of God. No discussion of historical method can avoid the challenges of epistemology (i.e., the extent and limits of historical knowledge). The past hundred years have witnessed a long and contentious debate among historians over the question of objectivity.[27] Without getting too deeply into this debate, suffice it to say there are today pretty sound and widely accepted reasons to treat the claims of historical knowledge somewhat modestly. Without descending into a kind of postmodern despair (i.e., nothing firm or final can ever be known about the past because the record is too fragmentary, the historical knower is too fully ensconced in her social and political situation, and the plausible interpretations too endless), typical practicing historians understand that the complicated business of reconstructing the past can never provide a complete or incontestable picture of the past. While it is possible to say a good many true and relatively definite things about the past, historical knowledge is best thought of as limited, provisional, and subject to ongoing revision.

There are good theological reasons to support these academically derived conclusions. Human beings are finite, embedded within particular times and particular places, and profoundly limited in our capacity to know all we might like to know. This is simply how God made us. Even with these limits, we should marvel at the extensive knowledge that humans have attained about the world and how it works. It's hard not to admire such human achievement when looking at the inner workings of a microcomputer or studying the fully mapped human genome. Even so, what we know—even what we are capable of ever knowing—remains a small droplet in a vast ocean.

In addition to human finitude, historical knowledge is further constrained by the curse of sin, a factor that hasn't simply corrupted our *moral sense* (our propensity to commit sins). The comprehensive effects of the fall have also warped our *cognitive faculties*. These "noetic effects of the fall" place additional restrictions on our already limited, finite knowing selves. One writer has described the resulting condition of our historical (and more generally human) knowledge as "the congenital blurriness of our vision."[28] The partial knowledge I can obtain about the Armenian genocide of 1915, for instance, through what remains (and can be accessed and translated) of the fragmentary documentary record is apt to have been originally reported in error, may be observed faultily by me within an archive, and later misinterpreted in the production of a scholarly article on the subject. Our cognitive and empirical lives are shot through with the foibles of sin. This may be what the Apostle Paul had in mind when he spoke of seeing "through a glass darkly."

But the main object of historical knowledge for the providentialist is not *the ordinary human past* (e.g., the Armenian genocide), but *God's hand moving within the ordinary human past*. The epistemological problems that bewilder basic historical knowledge seem small when compared with those that attend the knowledge of God's actions amid the Armenian genocide. Providentialists will say that they derive insights about God's will by drawing out a variety of "biblical principles" that reveal his desires, his promises, and the ways he has acted in comparable situations within the canon of Scripture. But, unlike economic forces (e.g., tax rates, wages, stock portfolios) or political impulses (e.g., elections, coronations, street protests), the providentialist must contend with the simple fact that God is, as the old hymn put it, "immortal" and "invisible." Believing that God was present and active amid the horrors of the Armenian genocide is quite different from giving an account of his attending purposes and intentions in that tragedy. To understand the difficulties in claiming to *know* God's ways in any given era or event, the ways Scripture represents God's providence need to be looked at more closely.

As much as providentialism gives greater attention to our dependence on God's provision, its application within ordinary history ironically weakens and distorts classic theological beliefs about God. Providentialists generally assume a self-evident correspondence—even a logical necessity—between the doctrine of providence and a providentialist rendering of history. In other words, affirmation of the former should oblige us to practice the latter. But I think this assumption badly misreads and underestimates the practical and theological issues raised between them. In fact, I would argue that the doctrine of providence, when understood more completely, actually *prevents us from embracing providentialism*.[29] While we can be confident that God undergirds the creation with his loving, divine will, the Bible consistently describes the ways he does so as hidden and unknowable. In fact, one of the clearest attributes of God's character is his inscrutability. "For my thoughts are not your thoughts, neither are your ways my ways, declares the Lord. As the heavens are higher than the earth, so are my ways higher than your ways and my thoughts than your thoughts" (Isa 55:8-9 NIV).

God's ways are *only* revealed selectively through the small bits of revelation that he chooses to disclose. "The secret things belong to the Lord our God," writes Moses in Deuteronomy 29:29 (NIV), "but the things revealed belong to us and to our children forever, that we may follow all the words of this law." Through *general revelation* (the creation) we are enlightened on certain features of his character (Ps 19:1-4), and through *special revelation* (in the person of Jesus Christ, his son, and in holy Scripture) we see other, much more vivid features of his character and his long-term agenda with regard to the world's salvation, but only in the broadest of outlines. The vast majority of what there is to know about God and his plans for the world remain hidden from us. Jesus himself did not know everything of the Father's plan for the world (Mark 13:32). As the Apostle Paul states in his letter to the Romans, "Oh, the depth of the riches of the wisdom and knowledge of God! How unsearchable his judgments, and his paths beyond tracing out! Who has known the mind of the Lord?" (Rom 11:33-34a) Who, indeed!

The Old Testament book of Job can be read as an extended commentary on the impenetrable quality of God's actions and the contemptible audacity that attends the human presumption of knowing his ways. For reasons that are never revealed, God permits Satan to wreak havoc on Job, robbing him of every vestige of family, friendship, health, and status that had given his life its savor. The prolonged discourses that follow between Job and his three "comforters," and between Job and God himself, serve to disabuse us of the fatal human misapprehension that God's ways among humankind are anything less than shrouded in mystery, and that God somehow owes us some kind of explanation for what he does and why he does it. Job begins to gain an inkling of God's incomprehensibility in chapter 26. After describing the most general outlines of God's work in holding up the cosmos, he remarks, "These are but the outer fringe of his works; how faint the whisper we hear of him! Who then can understand the thunder of his power?" (Job 26:14 NIV).

There is little in the providentialist paradigm that seems prepared to acknowledge or submit to the considerable limits of historical knowledge imposed on us by virtue of our finitude and our fallenness. There is even less that seems reconciled to the profound mysteriousness of God's purposes. Providentialists often speak of awe and wonder in the face of God's majestic works, but rarely do they exhibit awe in sufficient enough magnitude to resist making outlandish assertions about God's purposes within, say, the American Revolution. The entire approach seems designed to make everbolder claims, not only about exactly what has happened at virtually every stage in human history, but regarding its grand directionality and the divine will standing behind it. But can we hope to know his peculiar ways, century by century? Much less, event by event?

In the end, providentialist accounts like these fail to make a sufficiently bold distinction between the history written in the Bible (special revelation) and nonbiblical, ordinary history (general revelation). The record of divine action found in the Bible is admittedly appealing. What Christian historian wouldn't want the ability to narrate the American Civil War in the manner the book of Judges describes the battles to subdue Canaan? "Then Jephthah went over to fight the Ammonites, and the Lord gave them into his hands" (Judg 11:32 NIV). But our capacity and our warrant for doing so simply does not exist.

C. T. McIntire explains the problem of discontinuity between the biblical era and today. He observes that the biblical era had "emissaries from God" such as Moses, the prophets, and the apostles whose "messages were authoritatively and authentically the words of God." By contrast, we in the postbiblical era have no such emissaries. Also, the events covered in Scripture were unique revelatory acts of God, a status given to no events of this day and age.[30] Without the aid of revelation, we have no eyes to distinguish the "wheat" sown in God's kingdom from the "weeds" that grow in their midst. As Jesus recounts in his parable, the historian of ordinary events must be satisfied to "let both grow together until the harvest" (Matt 13:30 NIV). "I do not dispute that History is a story written by the finger of God," wrote C. S. Lewis. "But have we the text?"[31]

In his book *Christianity and History*, Herbert Butterfield compares human history to "a piece of orchestral music that we are playing over for the first time." It is our presumptuous tendency, observes Butterfield, to want to assume the role of music's composer. "But in reality," he continues, "I personally only see the part of, shall we say, the second clarinet, and of course even within the limits of that I never know what is coming after the page that now lies open before me." In fact, no one playing the music is privy to the whole score, and we can really only claim to know the parts we have experienced thus far. And, even then, "the meaning of a passage may not be clear all at once." He concludes, "no single person in the orchestra can have any idea when or where the piece of music is going to end."[32] A confession of human finitude should never be taken as a faltering confidence that, in many wonderful but wonderfully hidden ways, God is working in the world. We are not God and are not privy to knowing and seeing the things that he knows. Nor should we be.

In the end, providentialism is arguably not a method of doing history at all, but a kind of rhetorical strategy designed to rally the faithful by reconfiguring their sense of the past and assuring them of God's attentiveness to their plight. This "useable past" functions as a compelling aid for advancing various kinds of social, political, and religious goals within Christian communities. As a rhetorical strategy, providentialism has little to do with critical methods for reconstructing the past. Sociologist Christian Smith has argued that one of the keys to explaining the social dynamics of American evangelicalism, for example, is to discern the causal link he sees between its numerical success and its heightened awareness of its own imminent doom. In other words, evangelicalism remains a strong social movement because it constantly perceives itself to be under siege by a host of secularist forces that threaten to undermine its way of life. It is "thriving" because it is ever "embattled." Big government, the public schools, abortion rights activists, Hollywood, sexual immorality, the ACLU, liberal churches, "the homosexual agenda," and feminists all seem to conspire against the integrity of the faith and the American way of life. And the stronger and more dastardly the perceived scheme, the more determined evangelicals become to fortify their ranks and preserve their heritage.[33]

Historian R. Scott Appleby observes this impulse not only among evangelicals but among conservative religious believers of other faiths as well. A major part of this shared religious imagination has been the tendency to read history in terms of divine intervention. He contends that such communities are gripped by an abiding fear that secularism is eroding the foundations both of faithful religious commitment and of civilization itself, and he further argues that such believers regularly employ history as a way to protect themselves against and to encourage the faithful amid this catastrophe. They aim to overcome their feelings of powerlessness amid the decline of public righteousness and the rise of godlessness and moral perversion by placing the human drama in a much larger, divine framework. "The enemy seems to control the centers of power. And yet, to the eyes of the true believer, even now God is bringing this dour history to an unexpected, dramatic, and rewarding culmination."[34]

"History," as the old aphorism goes, "is written by the winners." And Christians inclined to write, teach, and consume providentialist history undoubtedly believe that—despite their current status as a dispirited and besieged underclass in an overwhelmingly secular world—they are on the winning team. Christianity will come out on top. The truth of Scripture will ultimately prevail. God will have the final word. Providentialist history is an important rhetorical strategy that prompts the faithful to remember that this is so, and urges Christians to remain vigilant in the ongoing culture war against the enemies of the faith. Reminding those in the fight that "there was once a time" when God's presence and purposes were properly honored in civilization, and that God will have the final word in judgment, plays an important role in preserving the identity of Christians in a challenging age.

But such a rhetorical strategy should not be mistaken for an honest, critical Christian reading of the past. History has long been employed as one of the bluntest weapons in the culture wars—and it hasn't only been those on the Right who have used it this way—because of its power to justify the assumptions of one party about itself to itself. It's hard to imagine a more potent use of this weapon than to align one's own personal, political, and social interests in the course of history with the eternal purposes of God Almighty. In sum, it is a crude but often effective strategy for worldview maintenance. In carrying it forward, however, narratives of the past too often become little more than occasions for brute sloganeering that neither help their readers understand the complexities of the past nor honor the profound reality of God's presence in the world.

Conclusion

I am sensitive—maybe oversensitive—to the tensions created by discussions of providentialist history among Christian believers. On one hand, I recognize that affirming God's real, personal, and active presence in the world should probably have some pretty distinct implications for how the Christian historian handles descriptions of the world's human unfolding. I understand the ways in which secularizing methodologies of historical reconstruction have made it both practically difficult and professionally perilous to identify divine or any other supernatural forces as genuine explanations of past events. I also appreciate the tremendous faith-building value that can often attend historical instruction that reminds its students that God's presence among us abides—yesterday, today, and forever. However, criticisms of and resistance to providentialist history does not necessarily reflect cultural accommodation or an unfettered desire for professional recognition. There are ample *Christian* reasons for criticizing and resisting providentialist history. The hope of preserving the theological integrity both of God's providence and of human finitude—along with an honest recognition of our capacity to bend history to suit our ideological needs—lead me to conclude that there is little in providentialism worth salvaging.

CONCLUSION

Historical Study as Christian Vocation

The theological vocabulary of "vocation" made a comeback in various Christian circles during the early 2000s. Aspirations to resurrect theological purpose within American higher education led the private philanthropic foundation, the Lilly Endowment to offer substantial grants to "church related" colleges and universities that would aid in helping students and faculty consider their respective purposes in learning and life, and to encourage at least some of them to consider careers dedicated to some kind of formal Christian work.[1] Dozens (if not hundreds) of schools were drawn to Lilly's Project for the Theological Exploration of Vocation, and the term "vocation" began cropping up with frequency in discussions about faith, learning, and life.

For some, introducing the language and ideals of vocation provided a welcome antidote to what had become a tired, almost clichéd discourse on "the integration of faith and learning." This latter model that so many Christian colleges and universities had come to adopt since the 1970s was viewed in some quarters as overly "Reformed" in its formulation and encouraged thinking within various academic disciplines that did not cohere meaningfully with how non-Reformed theological traditions envisioned the task and ends of Christian learning.[2] Vocation, on the other hand, provided a comparatively broad, more diverse template for engaging the life of the mind and the Christian's task in the world, and promised to enliven and deepen conversations about the meaning of faith for each.

It is no surprise that this language quickly made its way into discussions about Christian historiography.[3] While the notion of historical study as Christian vocation was hardly new, its resurgence in popularity served to complicate the interpretation of other "versions" of Christian historiography discussed in this study. On one hand, history-as-Christian-vocation might be seen as its own peculiar strategy for relating the complex facets of personal faith to the equally challenging work of the historian (indeed, even a strategy that rules all of the others out-of-bounds). On the other, it might just as easily stand in as a "catch-all" category that in some manner reflects all of the aspirations and methods of every writer discussed in these pages. Since it can arguably function well in either case, exploring the idea of historical study as a Christian vocation seems a fitting way to sum up and conclude this survey.

Vocation in the Christian Tradition

The term vocation comes from the Latin verb *vocare*, "to call." And the more familiar biblical rendering of vocation is, of course, "calling." Although there are several different ways that calling is used in the Bible, the most relevant here are those by which God calls humanity either into some kind of relationship with himself, or into a prescribed station, work, or manner of living. British theologian J. I. Packer helpfully summarizes the "developed biblical idea of God's calling" as that of "God summoning men by his word, and laying hold of them by his power, to play a part and enjoy the benefits of his gracious redemptive purposes."[4] God's active will in the world, carried forth by divine decree, is regularly conveyed in the Scriptures using this language.

The central picture of God's call in Scripture is his summons to relationship. The Old Testament abounds with stories of God's covenant bond with Israel whereby God *called* Jacob's descendants to be his people and to live in righteousness (Isa 42:6; 43:1; Joel 2:32). The New Testament presents the story of a perfected and comprehensive covenant relationship made available through the life, sacrificial death, and resurrection of Jesus Christ. This is the covenant of grace by which God *calls* all people to new life through faith in Christ. God extends his call beyond Israel to include all humankind: the "external call" to repent of sin and enter communion with God through Jesus is universally offered but only selectively answered (Matt 22:14). More demonstrably in the New Testament, however, God's call signifies "that by which God invites people and *causes* them to be drawn to Him," otherwise known as his "effectual calling."[5] In Christ, God's elect (those who are effectually called) are consequently also called to peace (1 Cor 7:15), holiness (1 Thess 4:7), hope (Eph 4:4), eternal life (1 Tim 6:12), and to God's kingdom (1 Thess 2:12), among other fruits of regeneration. In sum, the relational conception of calling expressed in Scripture "denotes God's verbal summons, spoken by Christ or in his name, to repentance, faith, salvation, and service."[6]

The Bible, thus, uses God's "call" typically to mean God's summons of people, collectively and individually, into a covenant relationship. But effectual Calling (designated with a capital "C") should be distinguished—though not entirely disconnected—from the familiar sense of vocation as generic "work," or, more broadly, that place in the world, accompanied by distinct tasks and responsibilities, to which God places any given person. That is to say, wherever one finds oneself in life—excluding those areas that, by definition, break God's law—reflects the sovereign will of God and constitutes a kind of sacred calling (hereafter designated with a lowercase "c"). Even though a distinction is made here between these two senses of calling, they are ultimately linked in purpose and direction. The Puritan divine William Perkins in his *Treatise of the Vocations or Callings of Men* (1603) wrote, "A particular calling must give place to the general [Calling] of a Christian . . . because we are bound unto God in the first place and unto man, under God."[7]

Historian Paul Marshall argues that this latter sense of calling—the "idea that people are called by God to a specific mundane work or duty as a sphere and means of religious obedience"—constitutes a uniquely Protestant contribution to the idea of vocation.[8] While Roman Catholics had for many centuries associated "callings" with specific stations in life, these were limited to church-related work such as those belonging to nuns, priests, and others "set apart" for "holy" work. Beginning with Martin Luther, Protestants expanded the concept considerably. Early in the Reformation era it was a term by which Christianity was coming to condone and even sanctify all manner of work as "unto the Lord." "Hence," writes Marshall, "views of calling came to form the core of much of the economic and social theory of Protestantism at a time when such theory was culturally and politically important," a development that would both chasten and, unfortunately, justify many harmful practices in the Western history of human labor.[9]

Douglas J. Schuurman suggests several themes that underwrite the notion of vocation in Christian theology, and believes that understanding and adapting these ideals will clarify the goodness of vocation as a theological insight for our times and enable us to recognize some of the barriers that keep us from experiencing our overall lives as responsive to God's Call.[10] A brief look at two of these themes will help to frame the subsequent discussion of Christian historiography.

The first theme considers the ways vocation imbues every facet of human life with religious significance; all aspects of life are holy.[11] *All* human activities have a sacred quality as one recognizes that God has directed humans into those activities, having designed them to serve his divine purposes in shaping the common good. Protestants developed a biblical rationale for this conception of vocation largely from 1 Corinthians 7:20: "Each person should remain in the same *calling* wherein he was *called*" (NIV). The verse appears to make use of both senses of calling as delineated above, urging that one should remain in the same "calling" (God-directed human work in the world) that one was doing when one was "called" (God's summons to covenantal fellowship). Martin Luther developed this interpretation of *calling* by his peculiar translation of *klesis* as *beruf*, or "an external condition" or "station." Luther's translation was no doubt informed by his strong notion of the "priesthood of all believers," as well as his critique of any hierarchical relationship that, until that point, placed clerical "work" on a higher spiritual plane than any other type of mundane "work." Priests and monks were to be considered no more holy than farmers or merchants. In his *Babylonian Captivity*, Luther writes:

> Therefore I advise no one to enter any religious order or the priesthood, indeed, I advise everyone against it—unless he is forearmed with this knowledge and understands that the words of monks and

priests, however holy and arduous they may be, do not differ one whit in the sight of God from the words of the rustic laborer in the field or the woman going about her household tasks, but that all works are measured before God by faith alone.[12]

On the basis of such claims, many generations of Reformed and Lutheran Christians have gradually developed a full-orbed doctrine of vocation that has affirmed worldly work and looked on all stations in life as ordered by the Lord. The work of our hands and the sweat of our brow, as a result, have eternal and divinely appointed worth.

The Puritans arguably did more than any other group to expand the notion of particular callings to include, in Edmund Morgan's words, "all honest human activities. God called men from sin to salvation; called them to be husbands or fathers, masters or servants; called them to be the particular trade by which they served society and made a living."[13] Morgan notes that before any Puritan man or woman assumed "any new enterprise, voyage, or job" they must discern their "call" from God to it. Protestants do not, thereby, designate one kind of activity as "Christian" (i.e., missionaries, pastors, teachers in Christian schools), while other kinds of work (i.e., butcher, baker, candlestick maker) as "secular." All of life is religious, and humans are directed into all (lawful) callings providentially. The conviction that every activity we pursue has religious significance has been difficult to defend and embody in an increasingly secular, scientistic, capitalist, compartmentalized, and religiously privatized age. The rediscovery and development of this insight for our times has the potential to reenergize our work in the world.

The second theme holds that the tasks and duties of any vocation are ordained and directed by God. In other words, just as vocation has religious significance, it also contains a distinct moral mandate.[14] William Perkins asserted that a "vocation or calling, is a certain kind of life, ordained and imposed on man by God, for the common good."[15] But by this claim, notes Marshall, Perkins was not only saying that God had called individuals to unique and fixed estates in life but that God also required certain duties of individuals regardless of their estate (as long as that estate was lawful). In Perkins, then, there "appeared to be a fusion of the . . . idea of calling as estates with the . . . idea of calling as godly duty."[16]

So the Protestant vision of vocation sees no human activities as morally neutral or inconsequential, and Perkins importantly understands the moral responsibility resident in vocation as having clearly social emphases intended to service the "common good." Philosopher Lee Hardy contends that this sense of vocation leads to a vision of human life "lived out in a society of mutual service and support, each member contributing according to his specific talents and receiving according to his need."[17] Love of neighbor, in short, must find a central and immovable place in any Christian exploration of calling and identity.

Theologian Cornelius Plantinga pushes the social emphasis in vocation's moral mandate to its logical conclusion. For Plantinga, the Christian's calling in the world can only be understood in the perspective of her place and tasks in God's kingdom and in diminishing herself to the point of seeing all priorities only in that light. Such a Christian's primary sense of identity is found in seeking *first* the kingdom of God and all his righteousness. "Christians follow their main vocation," writes Plantinga, "by playing a lively part in institutions and endeavors that, consciously or not, seek the interests of the kingdom."[18] This charge urges the *called* to move in directions that are not necessarily attractive by typical worldly standards (prestige, money, security). Plantinga reminds us that following Jesus in our callings requires us to give substantial consideration to its moral implications and our responsibility to care for "the least of these."[19]

The rich theological heritage of vocation provides Christians today with profound resources for navigating the world and confirming the meaning of faithfulness in their daily work. By establishing the value of all human endeavors as God-ordained, and thereby holy, and by reminding the believer that all such activities are also framed by moral imperatives and kingdom responsibilities, an enlivened sense of Christian vocation can help propel believers toward lives of useful, thoughtful, and godly service. That it has served as a wellspring of help for Christian scholarship generally, and Christian historiography in particular, is hardly surprising.

The Ordinary Holiness of Historical Study

The initial appeal of thinking about history as Christian vocation is the way it elevates this otherwise mundane work and infuses it with holy purpose. There is deep, God-ordained legitimacy in the tasks of selecting and reading primary sources, asking thoughtful historical questions, consulting the work of other historians, developing interpretive theories, and reconstructing past events using story and critical analysis. It is important to note that the basis of history's holiness here is neither the quality nor even the existence of the historian's religious faith. It does not depend on the historian, the choice of topics, the strategies of interpretation, or the "worldview" employed in reading the past. To the degree that the work of the historian falls within the domain of what God deems as lawful, it is sacred work. In this way, whether she acknowledges it (or would especially be pleased to know it) or not, the atheist historian writes her history of eighteenth-century farming in Virginia to the glory of God! She participates in an estate ordained by God, and it is God who enables her to do it.

This account of vocation conceives of historical study and the institutions that facilitate it—universities, departments of history, professional organizations, archival repositories, scholarly journals, publishing houses, etc.—as extensions of God's creation. They are good. Even as they have been twisted by the curse of sin (as all persons and social formations have been), they remain among God's excellent gifts and may be joyfully utilized as such. And, as extensions of creation, they are all subject to God's mandate to human dominion and stewardship. So when conferences are convened, lectures delivered, documentaries filmed, museums visited, dissertations defended, books published, and students educated, Christians are invited to join these activities wholeheartedly with a holy sense of worship. All such work is part of and done in response to God's calling.

Given the machinations and handwringing that so often attend questions about "the difference faith makes" in doing history, these insights about vocation can be liberating to Christian historians. God honors the work of their hands, and they are free to direct their principal energies toward simply doing it well. This straightforward, realist account of Christian historiography seems perfectly suited to the typical historian's native sensibilities, which is to just "get on with the work" of doing history. This feeling is expressed somewhat sardonically bythe Catholic historian John McGreevy: "I've never taken a course on method, and tend to view historical method as an extension of common sense; never felt a particular philosophical orientation was a predilection of good historical work; [and] never felt embarrassed by such quaint sounding phrases as 'empirically sound' and 'objective.' "[20] With no philosophical "grounding" or other theological "reflecting" needed, this account of vocation encourages Christian historians to be confident that their work is "Christian" simply in the faithful doing of it.

Vocation also recognizes that the "secular" work produced by historians has enduring value in God's kingdom. And, from this perspective, Christian historians may also see their own work in a new, more encouraging light. But such thinking runs against the grain of many standing norms within Christian scholarship. Christians have often been inclined to defend scholarly work as "Christian" only if it bears some kind of obvious religious theme, challenges "secular" disciplinary norms using Christian "presuppositions," or promises to produce some kind of clear positive benefit to the church or the world that Christians can celebrate. Most ordinary "secular" scholarship rarely does any of these things, at least not in any obvious or explicit way.

In a 2001 *Christian Scholar's Review* essay, Michael S. Hamilton reported on feedback he received from a survey of Christian college and university administrators that gauged present attitudes toward specialized disciplinary scholarship. He became troubled by what he found. Hamilton notes that respondents regularly decried specialized research believing it to be at odds with Christian values due to its perceived secularism; they also assumed that this kind of scholarship could only feed the careerist egoism of individual researchers. A waste of time for Christians! From a framework of Christian vocation, Hamilton couldn't have disagreed more heartily. He defends the research programs of scholars doing work regarded as "esoteric" and "pointless" by the public (and even by their own deans!). He posits that God has called some people to this kind of scholarship, and that, while very specialized research might initially appear impractical and

self-indulgent, such work in time could prove revolutionary. "H₁
tells us that technical disciplinary scholarship redirects human af.....s.
If this is true," wonders Hamilton, "isn't it just as likely that God uses
academic research to accomplish purposes that are just as inscrutable?
And if *this* is true, is it likely that God calls some of those who serve
him to undertake this work?"[21]

In significant ways, by placing every element of the historian's
vocation under the broad banner of God's calling to cultural development, there is good reason to wonder if it makes sense any longer
to speak of something called "Christian scholarship" (or "Christian
historiography"). Indeed, some have suggested that the time has come
to stop using the term. Richard Horner argues, "The term 'Christian' functions far better as a noun with reference to persons, than
as an adjective with reference to practices or the products of those
practices."[22] While it is still appropriate to talk of scholars who are
Christian, calling specific practices "Christian" presumes that there
might be something about them that fundamentally differs from those
produced by nonbelieving scholars engaged in the same work. Building on the Lutheran idea of "two kingdoms," on which much of the
Protestant doctrine of vocation was built, D. G. Hart suggests that
the work Christians and non-Christians share in together within the
"kingdom of man" is equally God-ordained and will differ little from
one another. Just as the prophet Daniel embraced and excelled within
the arena of "Babylonian scholarship," Christians have more reasons
than commonly assumed to play "by the academy's rules and [keep]
their faith private."[23]

If what Hart says is true, then the idea of historical study as Christian vocation invalidates other versions of Christian historiography
discussed elsewhere in this study, and, indeed, nullifies the standing of any approach that would distinguish Christian labors in the
craft from those of their secular counterparts. This account of vocation offers Christians a strategy that is really an anti-strategy. While
it provides a rich theological lens through which to see one's ordinary efforts as holy and meaningfully ordained by the Creator—the
importance of which should not be underestimated—the historian's
work and its worth can here only be measured by the standards of the
God-ordained "powers that be" (e.g., the University of Wisconsin,

the American Historical Association, Yale University Press, etc.).[24] The theological heritage of vocation, however, contains additional resources that cast serious doubts on Hart's proposition.

Vocation's Moral Mandate to Christian Historians

As much as Christian historians might want to simply "get on with the work" of doing history, which the doctrine of vocation seems to countenance, the second theme of calling developed by Schuurman seriously complicates this disposition. While vocation renders all ordinary work "sacred," it also imposes upon it a distinct set of God-ordained moral mandates that obligate Christians to work in the world in ways that conform to his will and extend his good purposes. The work of ordinary history and the present institutions that go about promoting it are indeed part of God's good order and fall within the divine call to develop the creation, but it appears that a distinctively *Christian vocation* within this order comes with a variety of special responsibilities and priorities that are likely to cause the specific efforts and concerns of believing historians to diverge (at times radically) from those of their secular colleagues. In short, if the calling of the Christian historian is indeed to be a *Christian vocation*, then the professional needs, norms, and priorities of academia will prove an absurdly small space in which to encompass the vision of God's kingdom on which its sights must be set. And even within academia, the calling of Christian historians would seem to demand much more than the mere fulfillment of their professional duties.

Douglas A. Sweeney urges Christian historians to think of themselves as no less than "priests" with a calling and a mission to reflect the ministry of Christ in their scholarship. Sweeney has written solicitously about the Christian vocation of believing historians to pour out their lives in humble service to their students and colleagues "as priestly ministers to the guild." In this, he urges them to take up a "special calling to worldly ministry" that strives in every way to model their scholarly lives after the fashion of Jesus. In a discipline that encourages and rewards cutthroat ambition, incessant self-promotion, and ruthless competitiveness, Sweeney writes, "[W]e are called to model a counter-cultural style of scholarship." He urges the use of "radical" historical methods that champion peace and justice and, as scholars, a willingness to stand in the margins with the poor and the oppressed. He likewise encourages the faithful to resist the siren call of professionalism and acclaim, which promises safe passage within the scholarly consensus. Rather, Christian historians should be marked by a mix of humility and boldness that at once offers kindness and solace to the hurting in their midst, and willingly lays claim to features of their faith that makes them genuinely different. In doing so, Sweeney believes, "We can encourage a deeper *faith* in God's vocation on our lives, strengthen one another in our common, priestly service and—precisely in so doing—help each other become much better Christian scholars."[25]

A quest for understanding the Christian vocation of history put historian Beth Barton Schweiger in tension with "the profession" in different ways. Rather than wondering what Christian historians owe their colleagues, she has asked what they might owe to the dead people they are called to study. Her answer is, in a word, love. Wrestling through her Christian responsibility to love the subjects she studies—along with the tangled questions of personal identity and moral complexity it entails—led Schweiger to reflect deeply on her calling as a Christian historian. In doing so, she came to the realization that her *career* as a historian was in an awkward almost irreconcilable conflict with her *vocation* as historian. Delving into the varied theological dimensions of love and the quandaries of historical "knowing," she gradually settled on an insight that would sit at the heart of her vocation: a "pastoral imagination towards" those voices and images of the past she longs to know. Her problem is that the "world of professional history does not reward charity or wisdom."[26] It was her *vocation* as a *Christian* historian that led to the most important discoveries in her encounter with the past, but she is called to work it out within a professional context that is, by turns, unimpressed or hostile to the Christian sensibilities she needs most to do her work.

Some of the same tensions between the vocation of the Christian historian and work in the current profession were confirmed in the experience of historian Robert Tracy McKenzie. He speaks to the issue as a former tenured professor at a major public university who left his post to take a job at a Christian liberal arts college. He makes it clear that he retains no dreamy-eyed idealism when it comes to the grand promise of doing scholarship in the secular academy. His decision to leave his prominent academic post for Christian higher education was directly tied to his belief that his calling as a *Christian* historian could never be realized serving out his career writing monographs and directing graduate students where he had been. Prior to making this move, McKenzie wrote, "I do not want my perspective to 'fit nicely' at the secular university where I teach, although I fear that I say and do too little to prevent that. I teach out of a sense of calling, and I have increasingly come to view my vocation as *redemptive* and *sacred*."[27] He found that the dual accomplishments to which every professional historian aspires—the publication of his first book by a highly esteemed university press and notification of his tenured status—had left him "profoundly disturbed" and that there was little in achieving these pinnacles of success that he could identify as having enduring spiritual or eternal value.[28] He concluded that there must be more important things he could and should be doing with his calling as a historian.

In response to this crisis of conscience, McKenzie began to expand his conception of vocation by moving more thoughtfully into a sadly neglected sphere: the church. Due largely to professional snobbery, he believes Christian historians have ignored and failed to speak to the broad community of ordinary Christians. In so doing, these professional scholars have allowed a battery of poorly conceived, schlocky, and ideologically charged books about history to fill the vacuum within the Christian marketplace.[29] Both in speaking to local congregations and in endeavoring to find a larger audience in publishing works accessible to ordinary Christians, believing historians can (and do) render a valuable service to God's kingdom and will develop a more vital love for the faithful along the way.

The idea that history done well is both good for the world—and that, while it's being done, is good for the historian—is the root of its status as a Christian calling. In this account, quality historical scholarship in order to be "Christian" needs no additional Christian justification. Carefully crafted history—regardless of who writes it, fro mwhat perspective, or toward what ends—is inherently valuable to the kingdom of God, and is itself a viable "version" of Christian historiography. But it may also be argued that "Christian vocation" is better thought of as the vital thread that knits together all of the various "versions" of Christian historiography covered in these pages into a broad tapestry of noble, valuable, yet always flawed work done in God's service. Whether bringing an empathetic ear to the lives of past religious people, striving to exercise background faith commitments in assessing primary sources, applying Christian values to past human events, defending the truth of Christianity by looking at its presence in history, or aspiring to see God's hand in the events of cultural development, the enterprise of historical study has and will remain a vital interest to Christians everywhere and stands as a necessary calling in service to God's kingdom.

The Christian Historian's Vocation

More than a few writers have made the subtle yet profound observation that, for the Christian believer, history can never be reduced to a mere pastime or triviality reserved for a few "buffs." So thoroughly are its central claims rooted in the historical record that, as historian Frederick Maurice Powicke emphatically put it, "the Christian religion is a daily invitation to the study of history."[30] Christianity is not a faith of timeless or extrahistorical abstractions. God has infused the unfolding events of time with meaning and significance, from the defining acts of creation and redemption to the smallest deeds of human kindness and cruelty. In this light, Christians bear a discipleship responsibility to live their lives with a heightened consciousness of historical development. This fact alone probably goes a long way toward explaining the many divergent, multifaceted attempts at history writing by Christians discussed in these pages. Indeed, Christians have a specific, existential stake in the historical claims that are recorded in the Old and New Testaments.[31] But human endeavors recorded by "ordinary" history fall no less under the sphere of God's reign. To live fully and faithfully in the reality of history constitutes a central part of what it means to fulfill our calling as Christian believers. The vocation of history is, in short, every Christian's calling. But it may be equally claimed that the vocation of every Christian historian is a calling wholly defined by the transforming power of faith.

.hur S. Link (1920–1998), among the most distinguished American historians of his generation, was surprisingly candid about the place and consequences of Christian faith for his work. Religious themes played a minor role, at best, in his more than thirty books (he was his generation's foremost scholar of Woodrow Wilson and the Progressive Era), and he wasn't the least bit interested in developing a "Christian interpretation of history." And yet, Link maintained that his faith in Christ entirely defined and shaped his work as a historian. In fact, Link admitted that any ambition he might have had to become a "good and faithful" historian was nothing but "a snare and delusion" apart from the regenerating work of the Holy Spirit in his life.

Appealing to the Pauline dichotomy of law and grace, Link believed that traditional scholarship was captive to the ruthless "law of historical methodology," which, while giving historians some valuable tools and insights, ultimately leaves them in "vast darkness." He conceded that, left to his own devices, "I have found . . . that my ego drives inexorably toward its own control, that is to say, it seeks to impose its own pattern upon events, selects its own evidence and discards evidence when it is not useful." Living under the tyranny of this law, the historian flails about hopelessly in a vast, overwhelming sea of incoherent facts and fragmentary evidence. "At best," he continued, "we will have seen only the small tip of the historical iceberg."[32]

If, as Link argued, the law of traditional scientific history "pronounces a death sentence" on all who trust in it, he was convinced that being set in a right relationship to God was the only path to true liberation. The Holy Spirit's work of regeneration radically transforms the whole person: mind, body, and spirit. And in doing so, the believing historian is made entirely new. She is no longer under law, but grace. But what, in Link's estimation, does regeneration specifically do for the Christian historian as historian? Does it grant her special knowledge of God's hidden purposes in history? Does it endow her with perfect objectivity? Is the woefully incomplete historical record, in the hands of the regenerate historian, somehow made whole? Can the regenerate historian abandon the rules of conventional history to produce something altogether better? Hardly. Link would have answered each of these questions with a resounding, "No!"

The only special power bestowed upon the believing historian, Link argued, is the freedom to practice history unreservedly, fully at rest with God and herself. In a telling paradox, Link reasoned that, freed from its tyranny, believing historians are uniquely free to *obey the law* of historical methodology and to follow its statutes with faithfulness and rigor. Unchained from the burdens of selfishness and pride, and freed to love God and his creation, the way is now open for them to do historical study aright. Having made peace with their finitude, their mortality, and their ongoing frailties, such historians are liberated from "the compulsion to be original, masterful, cosmic," and are more accepting of the hard truth that "imperfection and mortality stamp [their] work with ephemeral character." Though her work may prove no better or freer from error than nonbelieving scholars, Link holds that the believing historian uniquely profits by receiving eyes to see that she is "called to be a mere chronicler of the past."[33]

The church and the world are in desperate need of "mere chroniclers" who are devoted to truth-telling and eager to see the past in ways uncluttered by ego, personal agenda, and ulterior motive. Perhaps Link was right in thinking that Christians are uniquely free, and therefore uniquely suited to this task. But there is ample evidence to suggest that, if we are, we fail far more than we succeed. Still, it seems that Christian believers have especially good reasons to keep trying. The craft of history is a powerful enterprise with a unique capacity to expand the ways we see ourselves and our world. As Christian disciples committed to this good calling, let us continue to draw from the vast treasure house of faith as we strive to meet its many challenges. May God help us to do so with prayerful discernment and a humbleness of heart.

NOTES

Introduction

1 Whenever I use the term "Christian history" throughout this book, unless specified otherwise, I am referring to history done by self-consciously Christian historians (often in self-consciously Christian ways) rather than the history of Christianity.

2 The list of works in this tradition is vast and diverse. For a taste of some of the more notable ones written during the twentieth century, consider the following: Nicholas Berdyaev, *The Meaning of History* (New York: Scribner's, 1936); Hendrikus Berkhof, *Christ and the Meaning of History* (Richmond, Va.: John Knox, 1966); Emil Brunner, *Christianity and Civilization* (New York: Scribner's, 1948); Jean Daniélou, *The Lord of History* (Chicago: Regnery, 1958); Langdon Gilkey, *Reaping the Whirlwind: A Christian Interpretation of History* (New York: Seabury, 1976); Karl Löwith, *Meaning in History: The Theological Implications of the Philosophy of History* (Chicago: University of Chicago Press, 1950); Jürgen Moltmann, *Religion, Revolution, and the Future* (New York: Scribner's, 1966); Reinhold Niebuhr, *Faith and History: A Comparison of Christian and Modern Views of History* (New York: Scribner's, 1949); Wolfhart Pannenberg, *Revelation as History* (New York: Macmillan, 1968); Herman N. Ridderbos, *The Coming of the Kingdom* (Philadelphia: Presbyterian and Reformed, 1962); and Roger Shinn, *Christianity and the Problem of History* (New York: Scribner's, 1953).

3 The art of classification is a necessarily reductive one. As in any such attempt, subtle distinctions within each model have surely been sacrificed occasionally for the sake of simplicity and explanatory power. For this I can only offer my apologies preemptively. The "versions" of Christian historiography covered in these pages are largely constructions of my own making. Although it is often said that historians are expert splitters, there is no way around it: this book is an exercise in lumping. I hope that what these models lack in accounting for fine-grade distinctions will be made up for in their overall capacity to illuminate the contours of a bigger picture.

4 There are surely key historians and works that I have neglected. And despite striving to consider a wide and diverse array of historical writings, I anticipate with relative certainty that some readers will find my examples too white and male, disproportionately Anglo American, and excessively evangelical Protestant. This undoubtedly reflects what I know best, but it also points to what strikes me as the real centers of gravity for discussions about faith and history. One absence that will be quickly noted by some is any discussion of Mormon historiography. Mormon historians have been increasingly present and active in conversations relating faith to history, and I have found many of their insights and contributions unusually helpful. But given the way my commitments as a confessional Protestant lead me to define Christianity, I have decided to leave their notable additions to this discourse outside the bounds of this book. I would draw the reader's attention to the thoughtful collection of essays by Mormonism's most distinguished historian, Richard Bushman. In *Believing History: Latter-Day Saint Essays* (New York: Columbia University Press, 2004), Bushman mixes autobiographical reflection together with faith/history-oriented discussions. Most notable among them are some of his attempts to square his training as a technical historian with his continued belief in the witness of Joseph Smith and the miracles that are the foundation of Mormon belief. For an engaging review of Bushman's essays, which may also help to explain some of my own reasons for leaving Mormons out of this volume, see Elesha Coffman, "The Historian as Latter-Day Saint," *Books & Culture*, November/December 2004, http://www.booksandculture.com/articles/2004/novdec/18.38.html, accessed February 1, 2014. For a further and highly illuminating discussion of these essays and Coffman's review, see a follow-up forum that brought Bruce Kuklick, Richard Bushman, and Mark Noll into conversation about the challenges of asserting religious belief amid the task of doing history. See "Believing History," *Books & Culture*, March/April 2005, http://www.booksandculture.com/articles/2005/marapr/4.06.html, accessed February 1, 2014.

5 Harry Stout acknowledged this sensibility when asked to reflect on his own theological beliefs in relationship to his scholarship. He wrote, "Whether owing to our preoccupation with the dead or our own peculiar temperaments, historians are not inclined toward philosophical questions regarding the meaning of history and its relationship to theology. . . . We are story tellers who spend most of our waking hours imaginatively living in past societies so that we might bring them back to life." See Stout, "Theological Commitment and American Religious History," *Theological Education* 25 (1989): 44.

6 Edward T. Linenthal and Tom Engelhardt, eds., *History Wars: The Enola Gay and Other Battles for the American Past* (New York: Henry Holt, 1996); Peter Novick, *That Noble Dream: The "Objectivity Question" and the American Historical Profession* (New York: Cambridge University Press, 1988); Joyce Appleby, Lynn Hunt, and Margaret Jacob, *Telling the Truth About History* (New York: Norton, 1995).

7 Bernard Bailyn probably spoke for many historians when he admitted that, while he maintained "a good deal of interest in th[e] questions" of objectivity, the nature of a fact, and problems of interpretation, he "never once felt it necessary

to work out precise answers to such questions . . . in order to advance my work in history." He wasn't at all certain that anyone's "work in history has been affected one way or the other by such considerations." See Bailyn, "The Problem of the Working Historian: A Comment," in *Philosophy and History*, ed. Sidney Hook (New York: New York University Press, 1990), 94.

8   Leslie Woodcock Tentler, "One Historian's Sundays," in *Religious Advocacy and American History*, ed. Bruce Kuklick and D. G. Hart (Grand Rapids: Eerdmans, 1997), 212.

9   Although once considered a supporter of evangelically informed historiography, whose main practitioners include George Marsden, Mark Noll, Nathan Hatch, and Joel Carpenter, Hart has retreated decisively from the kinds of "integration" strategies that are its hallmark. See Hart, "Christian Scholars, Secular Universities, and the Problem with the Antithesis," *Christian Scholar's Review* 30 (2001): 383–402. Anxieties that faith-informed concerns are apt to produce poor thinking and scholarship are well expressed in Ronald Numbers' review of a book written by fellow-Adventist historian, George Edgar Shankel, *God and Man in History* (Nashville: Southern Association, 1967). "Essentially, Shankel wants to abandon the training of professional historians in Christian colleges in favor of a program that would produce historically oriented theologians trying to answer 'the great questions of human destiny' by the aid of faith and revelation." See Numbers, "In Defense of Secular History," *Spectrum* (1969): 64–68.

10   The importance of quality work and the use of reliable methods seems also the central concern of Reformation historian, Carl R. Trueman, as expressed in his book, *Histories and Fallacies: Problems Faced in the Writing of History* (Wheaton, Ill.: Crossway, 2010). Aside from the many examples he gives from his studies in historical theology, his peculiar concerns as a specifically *Christian* historian are nowhere discussed. And, apart from a burden that fellow Christians should also make use of these same responsible methods to produce credible work, Trueman never explains the peculiar decision to pitch this book to a *Christian* audience using a popular *Christian* publisher.

11   Jon H. Roberts, "In Defense of Methodological Naturalism," *Fides et Historia* 44, no. 1 (2012): 62–63.

12   C. T. McIntire, "The Ongoing Task of Christian Historiography," in *A Christian View of History?* ed. George Marsden and Frank Roberts (Grand Rapids: Eerdmans, 1975), 53–54.

13   It is also worth noting that both are *also* historians of religion.

14   Paul D. Feinberg, "History: Public or Private? A Defense of John Warwick Montgomery's Philosophy of History," *Christian Scholar's Review* 1 (1971): 325–31; Earl William Kennedy, "John Warwick Montgomery and the Objectivist Apologetics Movement," *Fides et Historia* 5, nos. 1–2 (1973): 117–21.

Chapter 1

1   The best synthesis on this topic, at least as it bears on the American academy, is George M. Marsden, *The Soul of the American University: From Protestant*

Establishment to Established Nonbelief (New York: Oxford University Press, 1992).

2 While Hume opens *The Natural History of Religion*, first published in 1757, proclaiming, "The whole frame of nature bespeaks an Intelligent Author; and no rational inquirer can, after serious reflections, suspend his belief a moment with regard to the primary principle of genuine Theism and Religion," the succeeding pages deliver a whithering blow to the idea that religion has been an intrinsic feature of human nature or that its practices correspond in any meaningful way to transcendent realities. David Hume, *The Natural History of Religion* (Stanford, Calif.: Stanford University Press, 1956), 9–20.

3 Brad S. Gregory, "The Other Confessional History: On Secular Bias in the Study of Religion," *History and Theory* 45 (2006): 132–37. Andrea Sterk and Nina Caputo have edited a promising collection of essays that strive to "be faithful to the demand of critical analysis and sensitive to the beliefs, ideals, and struggles of their religious subjects." The contributors to the volume recognize and have sought to redress the many problems brought on by the tendency of historians to treat religion reductively. See "The Challenge of Religion in History," in *Faithful Narratives: Historians, Religion, and the Challenge of Objectivity*, ed. Andrea Sterk and Nina Caputo (Ithaca, N.Y.: Cornell University Press, 2014), 4.

4 Bruce Kuklick, "On Critical History," in *Religious Advocacy and American History*, ed. Bruce Kuklick and D. G. Hart (Grand Rapids: Eerdmans, 1997), 54.

5 Robert Handy, "Christian Faith and the Historical Method," in *History and Historical Understanding*, ed. C. T. McIntire and Ronald A. Wells (Grand Rapids: Eerdmans, 1984), 84. See also Van A. Harvey, *The Historian and the Believer: The Morality of Historical Knowledge and Christian Belief* (Philadelphia: Westminster, 1966), 3–37.

6 Edward G. Purcell, *The Crisis of Democratic Theory* (Lexington: University of Kentucky Press, 1973), 21.

7 See William R. Hutchison, *The Modernist Impulse of American Protestantism* (Cambridge, Mass.: Harvard University Press, 1976).

8 Quoted in Handy, "Christian Faith and the Historical Method," 85.

9 Though overshadowed in later years by his classic study, *Christ and Culture* (1951), Niebuhr's *Social Sources* was in many ways his more original and influential contribution to religious scholarship.

10 H. Richard Niebuhr, *The Social Sources of Denominationalism* (New York: Henry Holt, 1929), 17. In a 1934 letter to his brother, Reinhold, Richard Niebuhr confessed that "the trans-historical, absolute point of reference, the *x* beyond all *x*', has no particular significance. This religion of the absolute remains to my mind an aspiration, not a faith, a trust, a hope, a surrender." Quoted in Richard Wightman Fox, "The Niebuhrs and the Liberal Protestant Heritage," in *Religion and Twentieth-Century American Intellectual Life*, ed. Michael Lacey (New York: Cambridge University Press, 1989), 109.

11 See William McGuire King, "An Enthusiasm for Humanity: The Social Emphasis in Religion and Its Accommodation in Protestant Theology," in *Religion and Twentieth-Century American Intellectual Life*, ed. Michael Lacey (New

York: Cambridge University Press, 1989); see also Harry Elmer Barnes, *The Twilight of Christianity* (New York: Vanguard, 1929).

12 Robert Skotheim, *American Intellectual Histories and Historians* (Princeton, N.J.: Princeton University Press, 1966), 77.

13 Quoted in Skotheim, *American Intellectual Histories*, 84.

14 Shirley Jackson Case, *The Christian Philosophy of History* (Chicago: University of Chicago Press, 1943), 149.

15 David Bebbington, "Response: The History of Ideas and the Study of Religion," in *Seeing Things Their Way: Intellectual History and the Return of Religion*, ed. Alister Chapman, John Coffey, and Brad S. Gregory (Notre Dame, Ind.: University of Notre Dame Press, 2009), 240–57.

16 Emile Durkheim, *The Division of Labor in Society* (New York: Free Press, 1964), 169.

17 Wilfred McClay, "Teaching Religion in American Schools and Colleges: Some Thoughts for the 21st Century," in *Historically Speaking* 3, no. 2 (2001): 13–17.

18 Quoted in Marsden, *Soul of the American University*, 408.

19 Carl E. Olson, "Rediscovering Christopher Dawson: An Interview with Bradley Birzer," *Ignatius Insight*, February 4, 2008, http://www.ignatiusinsight .com/features2008/bbirzer_interview_feb08.asp, accessed January 10, 2014. For more on Dawson, see Bradley J. Birzer, *Sanctifying the World: The Augustinian Life and Mind of Christopher Dawson* (Front Royal, Va.: Christendom Press, 2007); and Stratford Caldecott and John Morrill, eds., *Eternity in Time: Christopher Dawson and the Catholic Idea of History* (Edinburgh: T&T Clark, 1997).

20 Christopher Dawson, *Religion and Culture* (New York: Wade and Sheen, 1948), 49.

21 Christopher Dawson, "Prevision in Religion," in *The Dynamics of World History*, ed. John Mulloy (Wilmington, Del.: ISI Books, 2002), 97. See also Dawson, *The Movement of World Revolution* (Washington, D.C.: Catholic University Press, 2013); and *The Gods of Revolution* (New York: New York University Press, 1972).

22 C. T. McIntire, "Kenneth Scott Latourette," in *God, History, and Historians: Modern Christian Views of History* (New York: Oxford University Press, 1977), 46. For a quite substantial survey of Latourette's life and scholarship, including an in-depth assessment of his views on history, see Richard Pointer, "Kenneth Scott Latourette," in *Historians of the Christian Tradition: Their Methodology and Influence on Western Thought*, ed. Michael Bauman and Martin I. Klauber (Nashville: Broadman & Holman, 1995), 411–30.

23 Kenneth Scott Latourette, "The Christian Understanding of History," *American Historical Review* 54 (1949): 271.

24 Kenneth Scott Latourette, "The Christian Understanding of History," 276.

25 William F. Buckley Jr., in his famous diatribe against the anti-religious atmosphere of his undergraduate alma mater, *God and Man at Yale*, identified Latourette's classes as a very rare exception to the rule of godlessness within the school's curriculum. See Marsden, *Soul of the American University*, 12.

26 M. Howard Rienstra, "Christianity and History: A Bibliographical Essay," in *A Christian View of History?* ed. George Marsden and Frank Roberts (Grand Rapids: Eerdmans, 1975), 184.

27 E. Harris Harbison, "The 'Meaning of History' and the Writing of History," in *Christianity and History* (Princeton, N.J.: Princeton University Press, 1964), 47.

28 Harbison, "Meaning of History," 50–51.

29 Henry F. May, "The Recovery of American Religious History," *American Historical Review* 70 (1964): 79–92.

30 See Anne C. Loveland, "Later Stages of the Recovery of American Religious History," in *New Directions in American Religious History*, ed. Harry S. Stout and D. G. Hart (New York: Oxford University Press, 1996), 487–502.

31 John Coffey and Alister Chapman, "Intellectual History and the Return of Religion," in *Seeing Things Their Way: Intellectual History and the Return of Religion*, ed. Alister Chapman, John Coffey, and Brad S. Gregory (Notre Dame, Ind.: University of Notre Dame Press, 2009), 6.

32 Irwin Unger, "The 'New Left' and American History: Some Recent Trends in United States Historiography," *American Historical Review* 72, no. 4 (1967): 1238–39. Unger's assessment of the New Left is mildly sympathetic in places, but largely critical.

33 Jeffrey Russell, "Religious Commitment and Historical Writing," *Christian Scholar* 45 (1962): 18–19. See also Burr C. Brundage, "The Crisis of Modern Historiography," *The Christian Scholar* 37 (1954): 385–95. Brundage gave voice to the despair and anxiety shared by many Christians in the historical profession during the generation that preceded the founding of the Conference on Faith and History (CFH). Brundage believed that impulses within the profession were aggressively excluding the very categories of faith and devotion that had once given Western historical study its life force. Sensibilities like those of Brundage animated many in the founding generation of the CFH.

34 Russell, "Religious Commitment and Historical Writing," 19–21.

35 D. G. Hart, "History in Search of Meaning: The Conference on Faith and History," in *History and the Christian Historian*, ed. Ronald Wells (Grand Rapids: Eerdmans, 1998), 72–73.

36 The varied interests of the CFH over the years help to account for its origins and frequent mentions throughout this book. It is the only professional organization in existence designed around the personal religious beliefs of its membership. In his 2000 CFH presidential address, William Vance Trollinger lamented that the organization had not done enough to forge an identity tied to its unique mission. While exploring the ways personal faith informs historical study was its originating genius, it had become primarily a venue for the presentation and publication of scholarship *about* religion. He noted that, of 150 articles published in the organization's journal *Fides et Historia* up to that time, 78 percent (or 114) of them were standard research essays on religious history. See Trollinger, "Faith, History, and the Conference on Faith and History," *Fides et Historia* 32, no. 1 (2001): 6. Compare CFH to the American Catholic Historical Society, which, while comprised mostly of observant Catholics, is

more officially an organization for those who study Catholic history, and is open to scholars without respect to their personal religious affiliation.

37 While there isn't much evidence of political alignment between the CFH and the New Left, California State University historian Ronald Rietveld drew inspiration from some of these young radicals and implored fellow members of the organization to take up the call to use their scholarship in the service of socially responsible action. "The Christian historian is in a better position than other persons, even other Christians, to help meet social needs. God can give him or her compassion and understanding for the unlovely, a constraining love that results in outer acts of love with the perspective of historical insight. Although they may not know clearly God's precise purposes in events, the 'activist' Christian historians can be assured that they cannot escape history and that God is personally at work now." Rietveld, "The Christian Historian as Activist," *Fides et Historia* 9 (1977): 9.

38 Christian Smith's *American Evangelicalism: Embattled and Thriving* (Chicago: University of Chicago Press, 1998) holds that the sense of perceived cultural embattlement and threat is the key to understanding both American evangelical identity and their success. Charles J. Miller, describing the first gather of historians at an AHA meeting, which would later form the CFH, characterized themselves as "a strange conventicle of hesitant Christians meeting almost in secret. . . . [M]ost of us had only a limited expectation that committed Christians could be distinguished historians." See Miller, "The Conference on Faith and History: Reminiscences about Origins and Identity," *Fides et Historia* 9 (1977): 59.

39 This reading of the Christian Right squares with the findings of William Martin, *With God on Our Side: The Rise of the Religious Right in America* (New York: Broadway Books, 1996). See also Darren Dochuk, *From Bible Belt to Sun Belt: Plain-Folk Religion, Grass Roots Politics, and the Rise of Evangelical Conservatism* (New York: Norton, 2011).

40 Even though Mark Noll's *Scandal of the Evangelical Mind* (Grand Rapids: Eerdmans, 1994) functions as a lament for the shortcomings of this "renaissance," he points to some of its important successes. So does George Marsden's *The Outrageous Idea of Christian Scholarship* (New York: Oxford University Press, 1997). The follow-up to these books likewise helped to illustrate the relative health of Christian scholarship and helped to spur a great deal more. See Mark Noll, *Jesus Christ and the Life of the Mind* (Grand Rapids: Eerdmans, 2011), 151–67, for a summary of what had occurred during the ensuing years since the publication of *The Scandal*.

41 One should also pay close attention to the important services rendered by the Institute for the Study of American Evangelicalism at Wheaton College and its monthly *Evangelical Studies Bulletin* as a measure of this development. Even more, a look at some of the ways that the Pew Charitable Trust (whose religion program was, for a time, directed by Christian historian Joel Carpenter) and the Lilly Endowment stood behind some considerable projects that aimed to look at the history of evangelicalism during the 1990s will serve to illustrate a significant sea change in the fortunes of historical scholarship on religion,

especially when produced among Christians. Alan Wolfe places great emphasis on both of these institutions in charting the ascendency of Christian scholarship. See "The Opening of the Evangelical Mind," *Atlantic Monthly* 286, no. 4 (2000): 55–76.

42 A "general overview" of this sort is fraught with dangers. I offer preemptive apologies here because I have surely failed to mention many important names and contributions in this section. A helpful companion to this section of the chapter is a recent roundtable that explores some of the important ways that confessionally oriented historians have contributed to the field of religious history in recent years, especially in cases when the authors are writing from within their own personal confessional traditions. See contributions by William Katerberg, Dana L. Robert, Leslie Woodcock Tentler, and Mark Noll, "Roundtable: Historians, Historiography, and the Confessional Divide," *Fides et Historia* 42, no. 2 (2012): 84–100.

43 Smith students who have likewise made a significant impact on religious historiography as believing historians include D. G. Hart, who has written voluminously on the history of American Protestantism, especially focusing on some of the smaller, more traditional variants associated with J. Gresham Machen and the Orthodox Presbyterian Church, among many other topics; Joel Carpenter, who has played a vital role "behind the scenes" to promote the growth of Christian scholarship, but has also contributed to it in his own right, while also writing an excellent monograph on American fundamentalism that served as a kind of sequel to Marsden's 1980 book; and Margaret Bendroth, whose important *Fundamentalism and Gender: 1875 to the Present* (1993) offers keen insights and refreshing new emphases to the field. Although they all studied with Smith, each of them also has strong ties to Marsden, Noll, and Hatch through, among other things, the Institute for the Study of American Evangelicalism at Wheaton College.

44 *Revivalism and Social Reform: American Protestantism on the Eve of the Civil War* (Nashville: Abingdon, 1957), 10. In a glowing review, Perry Miller praised the book as "so full of new departures that only a few can here be listed." Miller reserved special praise, and delight, for Smith's success in showing that the meager, "plain man's" religion of the heartland—which almost no one had taken the time to study—had proved profoundly more important to understanding social reform and the Civil War than all of the contributions made by Unitarianism, Transcendentalism, and Harvard College combined! See Miller's review in *New England Quarterly* 30, no. 4 (1957): 558–60.

45 Some of these include Catherine Albanese (American religion) at the University of California at Santa Barbara; Edwin Yamauchi (early Christianity) at Miami University (Ohio); Robert Linder (Protestant Reformation) at Kansas State; Jaroslav Pelikan (intellectual history of Christian theology) and Roland Bainton (Protestant Reformation), both at Yale University; Richard Pierard (German church history) at Indiana State University; C. John Sommerville (early modern European religious history) at the University of Florida; Jeffrey Burton Russell (religion in medieval Europe) at the University of California at Santa Barbara; Lewis W. Spitz (Protestant Reformation) at Stanford University;

Robert P. Swierenga (immigration and religion in the United States) at Kent State University; Dale Van Kley (religion and the French Revolution) at Ohio State University; and Robert Kingdon (Protestant Reformation) and Robert Frykenberg (religion in South Asia), both at the University of Wisconsin; and Heiko Oberman (Protestant Reformation) at the University of Arizona. A significant number of second- and third-generation members of the organization sought graduate degrees studying under one or another of these scholars, and many of them likewise produced significant work in religious history.

46 Some of these include John Woodbridge (early modern European religious history) at Trinity Evangelical Divinity School; Richard F. Lovelace (Protestant Reformation) and Garth M. Rosell (American evangelicalism), both at Gordon Conwell Theological Seminary; Kenneth Kinghorn (European historical theology) at Asbury Theological Seminary; William R. Estep (Baptist and Anabaptist history) at Southwestern Baptist Theological Seminary; Donald Dayton (Holiness and Pentecostal traditions) at North Park Theological Seminary; William Hutchison (twentieth-century American Protestantism) at Harvard Divinity School; Martin Marty (American religious history) at the University of Chicago Divinity School; Russell E. Richey (American Methodist history) at the Candler School of Theology; David C. Steinmetz (Protestant Reformation) at Duke Divinity School.

47 See Maxie B. Burch, *The Evangelical Historians: The Historiography of George Marsden, Nathan Hatch, and Mark Noll* (Lanham, Md.: University Press of America, 1996). After his training at Yale, Marsden spent twenty years at Calvin College, left for a brief stint at Duke Divinity School, and concluded his career with a much longer tenure at the University of Notre Dame. Though not his first monograph, *Fundamentalism and American Culture* (1980), his new interpretation of American Protestant evangelicalism's origins, catapulted Marsden to fame. He later also made an immense contribution to the history of Protestantism's presence and decline in the history of American higher education and won the esteemed Bancroft Prize for his brilliant biography of Jonathan Edwards. Along the way, Marsden also trained a host of graduate students, many of them practicing Christians. Mark Noll has had an even more prodigious writing career in number of volumes published. He spent over thirty years on the faculty of Wheaton College, and then filled the same chair Marsden vacated upon his retirement in 2006. Noll early added to the scholarship about Christianity and the American Revolution, and followed with some significant scholarship on the history of Protestant theology in the nineteenth century and the significance of Christian theology in both the American Civil War and the struggle over racial issues in the United States. Nathan Hatch began teaching at the University of Notre Dame in the mid-1970s after completing his doctoral studies at Washington University in St. Louis. Hatch's two seminal contributions to American religious history are his published doctoral dissertation, *The Sacred Cause of Liberty: Republican Thought and the Millennium in Revolutionary New England* (1977) and his highly original *Democratization of American Christianity* (1989).

48 Several members of the Marsden/Noll/Hatch circle should be mentioned. Grant Wacker of Duke Divinity School has written a comprehensive survey of early American Pentecostalism and is at work on a critical biography of Billy Graham. And Harry S. Stout, the Jonathan Edwards Chair of the History of Christianity at Yale University, defined his career with an award-winning assessment of colonial New England Christianity that dramatically challenged standing assumptions about Puritan life by reading and assessing thousands (literally) of sermons that had not been carefully considered up until that time. Stout would later make waves within the evangelical world with a controversial biography of George Whitefield in 1991, which placed great emphasis on the Great Awakening preacher's unfulfilled longings for the stage. Outside the United States, two historians associated with this group (especially Noll) bear special mention. David Bebbington at the University of Stirling has played a vital role in interpreting nineteenth-century British evangelicalism and, with Noll, helping to understand a larger transatlantic communion. He has also been a keen defender of history done in a Christian manner. David Livingstone at Queen's University, Belfast, and the late George Rawlyk of Queen's University (Canada) played similar roles in the study of their respective country's evangelicals.

49 David Edwin Harrell Jr. has long been affiliated with the Church of Christ, which helps to explain his identification with spiritual outsiders. He made a career at Auburn University writing with heart-felt empathy about a diverse group of marginal characters and movements—many of them impoverished—within Christianity in the American South. An appropriate tribute to his career is a Feschrift titled, *Recovering the Margins of American Religious History: The Legacy of David Edwin Harrell, Jr.*, ed. B. Dwain Waldrep and Scott Billingsley (Tuscaloosa: University of Alabama Press, 2012). One of those paying tribute to Harrell was one of his longtime colleagues at Auburn, Wayne Flynt. The Baptist scholar was similarly inclined toward the "underside" of Southern religious and social history, exploring many dimensions to the region's impoverishment, racial exploitation, and social depravation in eleven books. This interest wasn't simply due to progressive politics. According to his memoir, the transformation of Flynt's social consciousness as a college student was due to his encounter with a variety of Christian theologians and pastors who placed social justice at the heart of biblical faith. See Flynt, *Keeping the Faith—Ordinary People, Extraordinary Lives: A Memoir* (Tuscaloosa: University of Alabama Press, 2011), 209–39. Samuel S. Hill served in the University of Florida's department of religion for nearly forty years and is where he wrote and edited many books that gain perspective on the Southern religious experience as a whole, including *The Encyclopedia of Religion in the South* (Macon, Ga.: Mercer University Press, 1984). "If there was a church for the study of southern religion," wrote one chronicler of the Florida religion department's history, "Sam Hill would have his own chapel." David Hackett, "On the Occasion of our 60th Anniversary," University of Florida department of religion website, http://religion.ufl.edu/a-history-of-ufs-religion-department, accessed August 12, 2014.

50   This mix of seasoned scholars and rising young scholars include James Bratt
       (Dutch Calvinism in America) at Calvin College; Timothy Larsen (nineteenth-
       century British Christianity) at Wheaton College; Jay Case (American evan-
       gelicals and world mission) at Malone University; John Fea (religion in
       Colonial America) and Richard Hughes (American religious history), both at
       Messiah College; Bradley Gundlach (intellectual history of American Protes-
       tantism) at Trinity International University; Gillis Harp (intellectual history
       of nineteenth-century Protestantism) at Grove City College; Thomas Albert
       Howard (German Christianity) at Gordon College; Steven M. Nolt (American
       Anabaptist history) at Goshen College; Richard Pointer (nineteenth-century
       American evangelicalism) at Westmont College; Gary Scott Smith (American
       Christianity and politics) at Grove City College; and David Swartz (the Amer-
       ican Evangelical Left) at Asbury University.

51   An incomplete list of these includes Darren Dochuk (twentieth-century evan-
       gelicals and politics) at Washington University (St. Louis); Eamon Duffy (medi-
       eval Catholicism) at the University of Cambridge; Allen Guelzo (Civil War
       and religion) at Gettysburg College; Eugene McCarraher (twentieth-century
       religious social thought) at Villanova University; Robert Orsi (twentieth-
       century American Catholicism) at Northwestern University; James O'Toole
       (American Catholicism) at Boston College; Dana Robert (world religions and
       Christian mission) at Boston University; William Vance Trollinger (twentieth-
       century evangelicalism) at the University of Dayton; Leslie Woodcock Tentler
       (twentieth-century American Catholicism) at Catholic University; and John
       G. Turner (American religion) at George Mason University.

52   Some of these include Elesha Coffman (twentieth-century American Prot-
       estantism) at the University of Dubuque Theological Seminary; Charles
       Hambrick-Stowe (Christian spirituality in America) at Pittsburgh Theological
       Seminary; David Hempton (world Methodism) at Harvard Divinity School;
       Bruce Hindmarsh (British evangelicalism) at Regent College; Lamin Sanneh
       (world Christianity) at Yale Divinity School; Douglas Sweeney (nineteenth-
       century American theology and evangelicalism) at Trinity Evangelical Divinity
       School; Carl Trueman (Protestant Reformation) at Westminster Theological
       Seminary; Mark Valeri (American Puritanism) at Union Presbyterian Semi-
       nary; and Lauren Winner (colonial religious history) at Duke Divinity School.

53   An incomplete list of those in this category includes Christopher Atwood
       (Central Asian religion) at Indiana University; George Rable (religion in the
       American Civil War) at the University of Alabama; Beth Barton Schweiger
       (nineteenth-century Southern religion in the United States) at the University
       of Arkansas; Randall J. Stephens (twentieth-century American Christianity)
       at Northumbria University; and John Wigger (nineteenth-century Methodism
       and American popular religion) at the University of Missouri.

54   The question of "taking religion seriously" has been fiercely debated among
       scholars of various stripes. Elizabeth Pritchard has attempted to put her finger
       on what various scholars might mean by this term in "Seriously, What Does
       'Taking Religion Seriously' Mean?" *Journal of the American Academy of Religion*
       78, no. 4 (2010): 1087–1111.

55 See especially Michael Kammen, "Personal Identity and the Historian's Voca-
tion," in *In the Past Lane: Historical Perspectives on American Culture* (New York:
Oxford University Press, 1997), 3–74. See also Paul A. Cimbala and Robert
F. Himmelberg, eds., *Historians and Race: Autobiography and the Writing of History* (Bloomington: Indiana University Press, 1996); Eileen Borris and Nupur
Chaudhuri, *Voices of Women's History: The Personal, the Political, the Professional*
(Bloomington: Indiana University Press, 1999); Joan Wallach Scott, *Gender
and the Politics of History* (New York: Columbia University Press, 1988); Henry
Abelove, "The Queering of Lesbian/Gay History," *Radical History Review* 62
(1995): 45–57; and Ghislaine Lydon, "Writing Trans-Saharan History: Methods, Sources and Interpretations across the African Divide," *Journal of North
African Studies* 10, nos. 3–4 (2005): 293–324.

56 Collingwood wrote that since "all that the historian has before him are documents and relics from which he has somehow to reconstruct facts . . . the only
thing that enables the historian to reconstruct it is the fact that he himself is a
spirit and a personality." See *The Idea of History* (New York: Oxford University
Press, 1946), 170.

57 Henry F. May, "Religion and American Intellectual History, 1945–1985:
Reflections on an Uneasy Relationship," in *Religion and Twentieth-Century
American Intellectual Life*, ed. Michael J. Lacey (New York: Cambridge Univer-
sity Press, 1989), 22.

58 The "noble dream" of history has become shorthand for the quest for objectivity since the phrase was first used by Theodore Clarke Smith's 1934 presidential
address at the American Historical Association, "The Writing of American
History in America from 1884 to 1934," *American Historical Review* 40, no. 3
(1935): 439–49; or, more famously, Charles Beard's rebuttal of that same address
some months later. See Beard, "That Noble Dream," *American Historical Review*
41, no. 1 (1935): 74–87. On the larger issue of objectivity as it has developed in
historiography within the American academy, see Novick, *That Noble Dream*.

59 McClay, "Teaching Religion," 13–17.

60 McClay, "Teaching Religion."

61 Lewis W. Spitz, "History: Sacred and Secular," *Church History* 47 (1978): 20–21.

62 Martin Marty, "The Difference in Being a Christian and the Difference it
Makes—for History," in *History and Historical Understanding*, ed. C. T. McIntire
(Grand Rapids: Eerdmans, 1984), 41–43.

63 Marty, "Difference in Being a Christian," 46–49.

64 Stout, "Theological Commitment," 44–49. For Stout's own contribution to
early American religious history, see *The New England Soul: Preaching and Religious Culture in Colonial New England* (New York: Oxford University Press,
1986). A very select bibliography of the works of Miller and Morgan: Perry
Miller, *The New England Mind: The Seventeeth Century* (New York: Macmillan,
1939); Perry Miller, *The New England Mind: From Colony to Province* (Cambridge,
Mass.: Harvard University Press, 1953); Perry Miller, *Errand into the Wilderness*
(Cambridge, Mass.: Harvard University Press, 1956); Perry Miller, *Orthodoxy
in Massachusetts, 1630–1650* (New York: Harper & Row, 1970); Edmund Morgan, *The Puritan Dilemma: The Story of John Winthrop* (Boston: Little, Brown,

1958); Edmund Morgan, *The Gentle Puritan: A Life of Ezra Stiles, 1727–1795* (New Haven, Conn.: Yale University Press, 1962); Edmund Morgan, *Visible Saints: The History of a Puritan Idea* (New York: New York University Press, 1963); Edmund Morgan, *Puritan Political Ideas, 1558–1794* (Indianapolis: Bobbs-Merrill, 1965); Edmund Morgan, *Roger Williams: The Church and the State* (New York: Harcourt, Brace & World, 1967).

65 See George Marsden, "Perry Miller's Rehabilitation of the Puritans: A Critique," in *Reckoning with the Past: Historical Essays on American Evangelicalism from the Institute for the Study of American Evangelicals*, ed. D. G. Hart (Grand Rapids: Baker, 1995), 23–38. Here Marsden makes some parallel observations to the ones Stout makes in this essay. While appreciative in many respects, Marsden sees a host of ways where Miller's lack of religious sensibility shines through. In assessing Miller's magisterial *New England Mind* (2 vols.), and its sophisticated and dense intellectual assessments, Marsden thought Miller had needlessly scrubbed Puritan thinking of much of its Christian content. Marsden writes, "By minimizing Scripture, systematic doctrine, and the role of Christ, Miller in effect seems to be engaging in a kind of demythologizing, or more properly 'de-Christianizing,' of Puritanism" (29).

66 Stout, "Theological Commitment," 41.

67 These concepts are more completely explored in H. Richard Niebuhr, *The Meaning of Revelation* (Louisville, Ky.: Westminster John Knox, 2006), 23–48. Drawing from the scholarship of Robert Berkhofer, Grant Wacker makes some comparable observations about writing (especially religious) history, distinguishing between an "internal, actor-oriented approach" and an "external, observer-oriented approach." The former of these endeavors to "enter into the actor's experience and then to gaze back out upon the world exactly as the actor did," whereas the latter attempts to "set aside actors' perceptions of themselves and seek to implicate them in larger frameworks of meaning." He recognizes the value in each, and urges historians to strive to employ some of both. See Wacker, "Understanding the Past, Using the Past: Reflections on Two Approaches to History," in *Religious Advocacy and American History* (Grand Rapids: Eerdmans, 1997), 165.

68 Stout, "Theological Commitment," 48.

69 Stout, "Theological Commitment," 54–57.

70 Writing for what appears to be a largely Christian audience, Stout in this essay makes an impassioned plea to fellow believers that takes the form of a uniquely Christian vocation for the religious historian. He writes, "Christians must eschew the secular tendency to treat religion simply as the outward manifestation of deeper, more fundamental realities that can be defined and understood solely in naturalistic terms. Certainly there are secular themes that condition the church and require our observation and critique. But the story cannot stop there. It must also include spiritual themes that are hidden from non-believing scholars and that ultimately control our narrative. The church is not dealt a bottomless treasury of memory and faith which, once recorded, lives on automatically from generation to generation. Through our stories we must keep the memories alive" (58). A few years after Stout wrote these words, he had his own

commitment to doing history "Christianly" challenged. Upon the publication of *The Divine Dramatist: George Whitefield and the Rise of Modern Evangelicalism* (Grand Rapids: Eerdmans, 1991), some began to complain that his treatment of the great itinerant was overly secularized. The *Banner of Truth*'s David White expressed outrage that Stout would compare the highly charged atmosphere of contemporary revivalism to "the straightforward proclamation of a Whitefield who stood in the best of the tradition of the Puritans." See "Review of *The Divine Dramatist*," *Banner of Truth* 366 (1994): 29. The editorial director of the Banner of Truth Trust and historian, Iain Murray despaired over work like Stout's and others like him who refused to evaluate evangelical history from "the standpoint of supernaturalism." See "Explaining Evangelical History," *Banner of Truth* 370 (1994): 13. Stout replied in the pages of *Banner of Truth* that he believed Christian historians who study the past must be satisfied "to settle for something less than ultimate explanations," and that the ordinary forces in human life warrant careful consideration. "The Reviewers Reviewed," *Banner of Truth* 378 (1995): 7–10.

71 Philip Gleason, "Becoming (and Being) a Catholic Historian," in *Faith and the Historian: Catholic Perspectives*, ed. Nick Salvatore (Urbana: University of Illinois Press, 2007), 14. For another reflection on some of the ways Catholic faith and practice helpfully inform Catholic historiography, see Eric Cochrane, "What is Catholic Historiography?" *Catholic Historical Review* 61 (1975): 169–90.

72 Gleason, "Becoming (and Being) a Catholic Historian," 26.

73 David Emmons, "Homecoming: Finding a Catholic Hermeneutic," in *Faith and the Historian: Catholic Perspectives*, ed. Nick Salvatore (Urbana: University of Illinois Press, 2007), 67–68; emphasis in original. Emmons uses the word "outrageous" as a not-so-oblique reference to George Marsden's book, *Outrageous Idea of Christian Scholarship*. In a footnote, Emmons explicitly references Marsden's book, distancing himself from its proposals.

74 See David Emmons, *The Butte Irish: Class and Ethnicity in an American Mining Town, 1875–1925* (Urbana: University of Illinois Press, 1989).

75 Beth Barton Schweiger thoughtfully reflects on themes parallel to Emmons' observations in "Seeing Things: Knowledge and Love in History," in *Confessing History: Explorations in Christian Faith and the Historian's Vocation*, ed. John Fea, Jay Green, and Eric Miller (Notre Dame, Ind.: University of Notre Dame Press, 2010), 60–80. She considers what she, as a historian, owes the dead, and she frames the problem she faces in this as a historian through the lens of her obligation to love her neighbor. Similarly thoughtful on the same subject is Robert Wennberg, "The Moral Standing of the Dead and the Writing of History," *Fides et Historia* 30, no. 2 (1998): 51–63; Brad S. Gregory also writes with sophistication and nuance about the moral importance (as well as the challenges) of honoring the cosmologies of people in the past. See "Can We 'See Things Their Way'? Should We Try?" in *Seeing Things Their Way: Intellectual History and the Return of Religion*, ed. Alister Chapman, John Coffey, and Brad S. Gregory (Notre Dame, Ind.: University of Notre Dame Press, 2009), 24–45. Historian Robert Orsi studies Catholic devotional life in working-class urban America, which closely approximates his own upbringing. Though his adult

relationship to the tradition has, in his words, grown "unsettled and tenuous," he remains deeply interested in the culture and what its various feast days and saint veneration mean to those who are devoted to them. In "Have You Ever Prayed to Saint Jude?" in *Between Heaven and Earth: The Religious Worlds People Make and the Scholars Who Study Them* (Princeton, N.J.: Princeton University Press, 2005), Orsi writes with feeling about the significant angst he experienced when he came to realize the limits of his empathy for these devoted believers. "There had been a break between me and the world I studied, and the rupture had occurred on the most intimate levels, involving deep intellectual, emotional, spiritual, and existential questions. I was no longer confident that I could find my way to anything like a second naïveté, the revived sense of mystery and awe on the other side of critical inquiry" (150).

76 Emmons, "Finding a Catholic Hermeneutic," 69; emphasis in original.

77 Stephen E. Berk, *Calvinism Versus Democracy: Timothy Dwight and the Origins of American Evangelical Orthodoxy* (Hamden, Conn.: Archon, 1974), vii-xii.

Chapter 2

1 See Brian J. Walsh and J. Richard Middleton, *The Transforming Vision: Shaping a Christian World View* (Downers Grove, Ill.: InterVarsity, 1984).

2 There is no doubt that much of what may be said of Christianity as a worldview orientation applies to discussions of providentialism in that historians who aim to trace the hand of God among humankind often (though not always) invoke their overriding commitment to God's providence as a presuppositional commitment that informs their conception of the past. However, for reasons that will become plain, the majority of those discussed in this chapter do not include "God's hand" within what they see when they peer through the lens of Christianity to assess the past.

3 Wheaton College's Arthur Holmes played a leading role in helping other Christian colleges to think about their task in these terms. See his classic text, *The Idea of a Christian College* (Grand Rapids: Eerdmans, 1975), 3–36.

4 This renaissance has been described in many different venues, but very helpfully so in Wolfe, "Opening of the Evangelical Mind."

5 Joel A. Carpenter, *Revive Us Again: The Reawakening of American Fundamentalism* (New York: Oxford University Press, 1997), 16–22.

6 Douglas Jacobsen and Rhonda Hustedt Jacobsen, *Scholarship and Christian Faith: Enlarging the Conversation* (New York: Oxford University Press, 2004), 18.

7 In addition to Holmes' *Idea of a Christian College*, see also Walsh and Middleton, *Transforming Vision*; James Sire, *The Universe Next Door: A Basic World View Catalog* (Downers Grove, Ill.: InterVarsity, 1976); Nicholas Wolterstorff, *Reason within the Bounds of Religion* (Grand Rapids: Eerdmans, 1976). See also Andrew Sloane, *On Being a Christian in the Academy: Nicholas Wolterstorff and the Practice of Christian Scholarship* (Carlisle, UK: Paternoster, 2003).

8 Jacobsen and Jacobsen, *Scholarship and Christian Faith*, 26.

9 Quoted in Richard J. Mouw, *Uncommon Decency: Christian Civility in an Uncivil World* (Downers Grove, Ill.: InterVarsity, 1992), 147.

10 George Marsden, "The Collapse of American Evangelical Academia," in *Faith and Rationality: Reason and Belief in God*, ed. Alvin Plantinga and Nicholas Wolterstorff (Notre Dame, Ind.: University of Notre Dame Press, 1983), 230.

11 Marsden, "Collapse of American Evangelical Academia," 241–42.

12 Marsden, "Collapse of American Evangelical Academia," 247.

13 Marsden, "Collapse of American Evangelical Academia," 251.

14 Hart, "History in Search of Meaning," 76–82.

15 George Marsden and Frank Roberts, eds., *A Christian View of History?* (Grand Rapids: Eerdmans, 1975); C. T. McIntire and Ronald Wells, eds., *History and Historical Understanding*, (Grand Rapids: Eerdmans, 1984).

16 McIntire, "Ongoing Task of Christian Historiography," 52.

17 McIntire, "Ongoing Task of Christian Historiography," 53.

18 Janette Bohi, "The Relevance of Faith and History: A Mandate from God," *Fides et Historia* 6 (1973): 46, 49.

19 W. Stanford Reid, "The Problem of the Christian Interpretation of History," *Fides et Historia* 5 (1973): 97.

20 W. Stanford Reid, "The Present State of Research in Early Modern European History," *Fides et Historia* 11 (1978): 5.

21 M. Howard Rienstra, "History, Objectivity, and the Christian Scholar," in *History and Historical Understanding*, ed. C. T. McIntire and Ronald A. Wells (Grand Rapids: Eerdmans, 1984), 74.

22 John Warwick Montgomery and James R. Moore, "The Speck in Butterfield's Eye: A Reply to William A. Speck," *Fides et Historia* 4 (1971): 71–77; Kennedy, "John Warwick Montgomery."

23 Steven A. Hein, "The Christian Historian: Apologist or Seeker—A Reply to Ronald J. VanderMolen," *Fides et Historia* 4 (1972): 86.

24 See Herman Dooyeweerd, *A New Critique of Theoretical Thought*, 4 vols. (Philadelphia: Presbyterian and Reformed, 1953–1958); and *In the Twilight of Western Thought: Studies on the Pretended Autonomy of Philosophical Thought* (Nutley, N.J.: Craig Press, 1960). See also Earl W. Kennedy, "Herman Dooyeweerd on History: An Attempt to Understand Him," *Fides et Historia* 4 (1973): 1–21.

25 Dale Van Kley, "Dooyeweerd as Historian," in *A Christian View of History?* ed. George Marsden and Frank Roberts (Grand Rapids: Eerdmans, 1975), 179.

26 See, e.g., Azusa Pacific University's eighty-one-page faculty guide for doing faith-learning integration, along with guidelines and tenure requirements for producing a substantial integration paper. *Faith Integration Faculty Guide Book*, 2012–2013, http://www.apu.edu/live_data/files/219/fi_faculty_guidebook_1213.pdf, August 7, 2014. See also William Hasker, "Faith-Learning Integration: An Overview," *Christian Scholar's Review* 21, no. 3 (1992): 231–48.

27 For some examples of these papers, see Aaron Hutchison, "The Redeemed Scientist," Cedarville University, (n.d.), https://www.cedarville.edu/~/media/Files/PDF/Center-for-Biblical-Integration/Faculty-Integration-Paper-Aaron-Hutchison-Chemistry.pdf; Angela Gaddis, "Integration of Christian Faith and Social Work Practice," Belhaven University, September 15, 2011, http://www.belhaven.edu/pdfs/worldview-papers/Gaddis-Angela.pdf, August 7, 2014; and David W. McEowen, "Teaching Business at a Christian University:

Issues, Challenges, and Practices," Huntington University, (n.d.), https://www.yumpu.com/en/document/view/22379488/faith-integration-essay-huntington-university.

28   An incomplete list of Christian worldview-oriented guides for historians: Roland H. Bainton, *Yesterday, Today, and What Next?: Reflections on History and Hope* (Minneapolis: Augsburg, 1978); David Bebbington, *Patterns in History* (Downers Grove, Ill.: InterVarsity, 1979); Roy Swanstrom, *History in the Making: An Introduction to the Study of the Past* (Downers Grove, Ill.: InterVarsity, 1979); Ronald A. Wells, *History through the Eyes of Faith* (New York: Harper & Row, 1989); Colin Brown, *History and Faith: A Personal Exploration* (Grand Rapids: Zondervan, 1987); Earle E. Cairns, *God and Man in Time: A Christian Approach to Historiography* (Grand Rapids: Baker, 1979); Louis J. Voskuil, "History: Sound and Fury Signifying Nothing?" *Pro Rege* 16, no. 3 (1988): 2–12; Louis J. Voskuil, "History as Process: Meaning in Change," *Pro Rege* 16, no. 4 (1988): 22–31; Paul Waibel, "History," in *Opening the Evangelical Mind: The Integration of Biblical Truth in the Curriculum of the University*, ed. W. David Beck (Grand Rapids: Baker, 1991), 117–34; Robert Eric Frykenberg, *History and Belief: The Foundations of Historical Understanding* (Grand Rapids: Eerdmans, 1996); Gary Land, "A Biblical-Christian Approach to the Study of History," in *Christ in the Classroom: Adventist Approaches to the Integration of Faith and Learning*, vol. 21, ed. Humberto M. Rasi (Silver Spring, Md.: Institute for Christian Teaching, 1999), 455–72; and James Patterson, "The Study of History," in *Faith and Learning: A Handbook for Christian Higher Education*, ed. David S. Dockery (Nashville: Broadman & Holman, 2012), 217–38.

29   Donald A. MacPhee, "The Muse Meets the Master: Clio and Christ," in *A Christian View of History?* ed. George Marsden and Frank Roberts (Grand Rapids: Eerdmans, 1975), 85–86.

30   This is one of the central complaints of intellectual historian David Hollinger in his essay, "Enough Already: Universities Do Not Need More Christianity," in *Religion, Scholarship, and Higher Education: Perspectives, Models, and Future Prospects*, ed. Andrea Sterk (Notre Dame, Ind.: University of Notre Dame Press, 2002), 40–49.

31   John-Charles Duffy explores the work and ideas of Marsden, Noll, and Hatch, and, for the sake of argument, treats their writings as "constituting a unitary school of thought." However, he concludes that evangelical historiography is "incoherent, fractured by contradictions, pressing theological categories to do work they are not equipped to do—an attempt by these historians to have their cake and eat it too." See "Mark Noll's God: The Theology and Politics of Evangelical Historiography," Southeastern Commission for the Study of Religion Regional Meeting, Winston-Salem, N.C., March 12, 2005, 2–3.

32   While their longtime friend Nathan Hatch is often linked with them as part of "a triumvirate" or, more sinisterly, "the Reformed mafia," Hatch has written much less on the topic of integration and hasn't produced nearly as many scholarly books and articles. See Maxie B. Burch, *The Evangelical Historians: The Historiography of George Marsden, Nathan Hatch, and Mark Noll* (Lanham, Md.: University Press of America, 1996).

33 Noll's sensibilities in this way are carefully explored and explained in a variety of places in his writing, but most fully in *Jesus Christ and the Life of the Mind.*

34 Noll, *Scandal of the Evangelical Mind.*

35 Mark A. Noll, "The Conference on Faith and History and the Study of Early American History," *Fides et Historia* 11, no. 1 (1978): 8–11.

36 Noll, "Conference on Faith and History," 14–15.

37 Noll, "Conference on Faith and History," 17.

38 Mark A. Noll, "Teaching History as a Christian," in *Religion, Scholarship, and Higher Education: Perspectives, Models, and Future Prospects,* ed. Andrea Sterk (Notre Dame, Ind.: University of Notre Dame Press, 2002), 163.

39 Mark A. Noll, "Traditional Christianity and the Possibility of Historical Knowledge," *Christian Scholar's Review* 19 (1990): 388–406.

40 Noll, "Traditional Christianity," 398.

41 Noll, "Teaching History as a Christian," 165–66.

42 Mark A. Noll, "The Potential of Missiology for the Crises of History," in *History and the Christian Historian* ed. Ronald A. Wells (Grand Rapids: Eerdmans, 1998), 111–12.

43 Noll, "Potential of Missiology," 122.

44 George M. Marsden, "A Christian Perspective for the Teaching of History," in *A Christian View of History?* ed. George Marsden and Frank Roberts (Grand Rapids: Eerdmans, 1975), 37.

45 Marsden, "Christian Perspective," 36.

46 George M. Marsden, "Common Sense and the Spiritual Vision of History," in *History and Historical Understanding,* eds. C. T. McIntire and Ronald Wells (Grand Rapids: Eerdmans, 1984), 58.

47 Marsden, "Collapse of American Evangelical Academia," 224–28.

48 Marsden, "Common Sense," 59.

49 Marsden, "Common Sense," 63.

50 George M. Marsden, "Concluding Unscientific Postscript," in *Soul of the American University,* 429–44.

51 Quoted in Marsden, *Outrageous Idea of Christian Scholarship,* 7.

52 Marsden, *Outrageous Idea of Christian Scholarship,* 25–43.

53 Marsden, *Outrageous Idea of Christian Scholarship,* 45–46.

54 See Nicholas Wolterstorff, "Scholarship Grounded in Religion," in *Religion, Scholarship, and Higher Education: Perspectives, Models, and Future Prospects,* ed. Andrea Sterk (Notre Dame, Ind.: University of Notre Dame Press, 2002), 3–15. A helpful example of Marsden's attempt to unpack one such control belief is his thoughtful essay, "Human Depravity: A Neglected Explanatory Category," in *Figures in the Carpet: Finding the Human Person in the American Past,* ed. Wilfred M. McClay (Grand Rapids: Eerdmans, 2007), 15–32.

55 Bruce Kuklick, review of George Marsden, *The Soul of the American University,* in *Method and Theory in the Study of Religion* 8, no. 1 (1996): 82.

56 Kuklick, "On Critical History," 61.

57 Randall Balmer, a Christian scholar who has held endowed chairs at both Columbia and Dartmouth, makes essentially the same point. Quoting Marsden, he believes that if Christian scholars feel "deterred from attempting

critical and self critical history shaped by their religious commitments," the real source of deterrence is more apt to be authoritarian religious bodies rather than the university. In fact, given the astounding success that Marsden and other believers—Balmer included—have achieved in the most prestigious parts of the academy, he believes Marsden's complaints register as hollow and disingenuous. He believes Christian believers have unprecedented freedom to speak *as Christians*, and are among the greatest beneficiaries of multiculturalism. See Balmer, "Response to Marsden," (unpublished paper from the 155th Annual Conference of the American Society of Church History, San Francisco, Calif., January 6–9, 1994), 1–7.

58 Hollinger, "Enough Already," 41.

59 Hollinger, "Enough Already," 43.

60 D. G. Hart spent much of his scholarly career working in the company of Mark Noll and George Marsden, very often participating in some of the same projects on the history of American evangelicalism. He has written extensively on the history of American Protestantism, among other related topics, always with a fairly clear admission of his own partisanship as a conservative Reformed Christian. In 1997 he edited a volume with Bruce Kuklick that contained a discussion of what they called "religious advocacy" in the study of history among a wide variety of scholars, including both Noll and Marsden. Hart's contribution to that discussion was relatively muted in its critique, but he turned decisively against the Marsden proposal in subsequent years. See D. G. Hart, "What's So Special about the University, Anyway?" in *Religious Advocacy and American History*, ed. Bruce Kuklick and D. G. Hart (Grand Rapids: Eerdmans, 1997), 137–58.

61 Hart has subsequently developed these ideas further, and, drawing on the scholarship of theologian David VanDrunen, argues that the two-kingdom paradigm constitutes a more historically mainstream Reformed approach rather than being uniquely Lutheran. See VanDrunen's *Natural Law and the Two Kingdoms: A Study in the Development of Reformed Social Thought* (Grand Rapids: Eerdmans, 2010); and *Living in God's Two Kingdoms: A Biblical Vision for Christianity and Culture* (Wheaton, Ill.: Crossway, 2010).

62 D. G. Hart, "Christian Scholars, Secular Universities," 401.

63 Michael S. Hamilton, "The Elusive Idea of Christian Scholarship," *Christian Scholar's Review* 31 (2001): 13.

64 Hamilton, "Elusive Idea of Christian Scholarship," 21.

65 Stanley Fish, "Why We Can't All Just Get Along," *First Things* 64 (1996): 25.

66 Roger Schultz, "The Evangelical Meltdown: The Trouble with Evangel*historie*," *Contra Mundum* (Winter 1992): 42.

67 Michael J. Baxter, "Not Outrageous Enough," *First Things*, May 2001, http://www.firstthings.com/article/2001/05/not-outrageous-enough, accessed January 10, 2014.

68 Christopher Shannon, "Between Outrage and Respectability: Taking Christian History Beyond the Logic of Modernization," *Fides et Historia* 31, no. 1 (2002): 3–13.

69 Christopher Shannon, "After Monographs: A Critique of Christian Scholarship as Professional Practice," in *Confessing History: Explorations in Christian Faith and the Historian's Vocation*, ed. John Fea, Jay Green, and Eric Miller (Notre Dame, Ind.: University of Notre Dame Press, 2010), 169–77.

Chapter 3

1 Ernst Breisach, *Historiography: Ancient, Medieval, and Modern* (Chicago: University of Chicago Press, 1983), 14, 16, 18, 20, 24, 25, 32, 35, 49, 50, 53, 50–51, 53–54, 57–58, 66.

2 Quoted in Gertrude Himmelfarb, "Lord Acton: The Historian as Moralist," in *Victorian Minds* (New York: Knopf, 1968), 179.

3 Georg Iggers, "The Image of Ranke in American and German Historical Thought," *History and Theory* 2, no. 1 (1962): 17–40. Iggers explains that the American academy interpreted Ranke's famous dictum in a more strictly scientific way than those within Germany, and perhaps more so than Ranke had intended. The result was an American historiographic tradition much more enthralled to a wooden scientism (and deadly dull prose) than it should have been. Within the United States, "Rankean" has come to mean "strict factualism" in a way that is hard to square with much Ranke actually wrote.

4 Breisach, *Historiography*, 233.

5 Herbert Butterfield, *The Whig Interpretation of History* (New York: Norton, 1931), 22.

6 Butterfield, *Whig Interpretation of History*, 114.

7 E. Harris Harbison, "The Marks of a Christian Historian," in *God, History and Historians: Modern Christian Views of History*, ed. C. T. McIntire (New York: Oxford University Press, 1977), 347–51.

8 Breisach, *Historiography*, 333.

9 Peter Charles Hoffer, *Past Imperfect: Facts, Fictions, Fraud—American History from Bancroft and Parkman to Ambrose, Bellesiles, Ellis, and Goodwin* (New York: Public Affairs, 2004), 63–72. Though hardly a young radical, Gordon Wright reflected many of their concerns in his 1975 presidential address at the American Historical Society when he urged fellow historians to abandon the pretensions of scientific detachment, and instead commit themselves to viewing the past within the frame of deeply held, shared human values. See Wright, "History as a Moral Science," *American Historical Review* 81 (1976): 1–11.

10 See Zinn's *A People's History of the United States* (New York: New Press, 1990).

11 Quoted in Hoffer, *Past Imperfect*, 67.

12 Zinn, "What is Radical History?" in *The Politics of History* (Chicago: University of Chicago Press, 1990), 44, 45.

13 James Davison Hunter, *To Change the World: The Irony, Tragedy, and Possibility of Christianity in the Late Modern World* (New York: Oxford University Press, 2010), 132.

14 Richard Pierard, "Evangelical Christianity and the Radical Right," in *The Cross and the Flag* (Carol Stream, Ill.: InterVarsity, 1972), 103.

15 Pierard, "Evangelical Christianity," 117–18.

16 Donald Dayton, *Discovering an Evangelical Heritage* (New York: Harper & Row, 1976). David Swartz' brilliant book on the Evangelical Left provides a helpful exploration of some of the moral discourse that shaped so much of the thinking among many who were likewise trying to reconcile the deeply conservative politics of most traditional Christians with what they saw as a deeper and deeply historical mandate to join the movement of justice-oriented reform that was changing the political landscape in the 1960s and 1970s. Important points of reference for people like Dayton were Jim Wallis, Ron Sider, David Moberg, and Richard Quebedeaux. See David Swartz, *Moral Minority: The Evangelical Left in an Age of Conservatism* (Philadelphia: University of Pennsylvania Press, 2012).

17 Douglas W. Frank, *Less Than Conquerors: How Evangelicals Entered the Twentieth Century* (Grand Rapids: Eerdmans, 1986), 1–29. Though not formally framed this way, Frank's book picks up the story where Dayton leaves off, and implicitly answers some of the questions Dayton raises.

18 Randall Balmer, *Mine Eyes Have Seen the Glory: A Journey through the Evangelical Subculture in America* (New York: Oxford University Press, 2006), 263–64. Balmer was one of Frank's star undergraduate students, and would go on to achieve more professional prestige than probably any other Christian historian of his generation. After completing a degree at Trinity College (Deerfield) where he studied with Frank, and another across the road at Trinity Evangelical Divinity School, Balmer earned a doctoral degree from Princeton in American colonial history. He would eventually go on to hold endowed chairs at Columbia University and, later, at Dartmouth. While he distinguished himself early in his career with a fine monograph on religion in colonial New York, much of his professional life has been marked by his work as a kind of journalist and commentator of contemporary religious life (including an award winning PBS special based on his book, *Mine Eyes Have Seen the Glory*). In this capacity, as well as in his recent work writing history, Balmer has clearly taken cues from his undergraduate mentor, writing with a sense of moral urgency, even outrage that is reminiscent of *Less Than Conquerers*. And, like Frank, Balmer's moralizing analysis has been leveled pretty squarely at the religious conservatism of his own childhood. Balmer details some of the dynamics of this childhood in his memoir, *Growing Pains: Learning to Love My Father's Faith* (Grand Rapids: Brazos, 2001). See *Thy Kingdom Come: How the Religious Right Distorts the Faith and Threatens America* (New York: Basic Books, 2006); and *The Making of Evangelicalism: From Revivalism to Politics and Beyond* (Waco, Tex.: Baylor University Press, 2010) for only the latest of his less-than-nuanced broadsides on conservative Christianity. After the publication of *Thy Kingdom Come*, the editor of *Books & Culture*, John Wilson, offered a biting critique of Balmer's sanctimonious finger wagging. While recognizing Balmer as a "friend," Wilson expresses deep disappointment that this effort lacked the nuance, depth, and complexity so evident in his earlier work. That he seemed incapable of mustering even the slightest empathy for conservative evangelicals in his latest work, after giving his life to their study, struck Wilson as especially regrettable. See, "The Strange Case of Dr. Balmer and

Mr. Hyde," *Books & Culture*, September/October 2006, http://www.booksand culture.com/articles/2006/sepoct/1.7.html, accessed January 10, 2014.

19 David Edwin Harrell Jr., "Review of *Less Than Conquerors*," *American Historical Review* 93 (1988): 781–82.

20 Joseph A. McCartin, "*Utraque Unum*: Finding My Way as a Catholic and a Historian," in *Faith and the Historian: Catholic Perspectives*, ed. Nick Salvatore (Urbana: University of Illinois Press, 2007), 178–79.

21 Richard T. Hughes, *Myths America Lives By* (Urbana: University of Illinois Press, 2004), 11.

22 Hughes, *Myths*, 9.

23 Hughes, *Myths*, 195.

24 Richard T. Hughes, *Christian America and the Kingdom of God* (Urbana: University of Illinois Press, 2009), 236–86.

25 James Juhnke and Carol M. Hunter, *The Missing Peace: The Search for Nonviolent Alternatives in United States History* (Kitchener, Ont.: Pandora, 2001), 11.

26 Juhnke and Hunter, *Missing Peace*, 13.

27 Hunter, *To Change the World*, 132.

28 One might legitimately ask if some of the "historians" discussed in this chapter actually deserve the label. In his recent book, *Why Study History? Reflections on the Importance of the Past* (Grand Rapids: Baker Academic, 2013), historian John Fea argues that they don't. In this excellent primer designed to help Christian undergraduate students grapple with what it means to "think historically," Fea challenges them to develop some of the sensibilities and methodologies that have helped develop the modern historical profession. In Fea's desire to maintain a high standard for historical thinking, he rules out-of-bounds a lot that calls itself "history" and would, on this basis, not recognize as historians many authors included in this book. While I recognize the need to maintain high standards for credible and quality history (Fea and I would agree on most of these, I think), I don't think it's necessary to deny the label "history" to those who fall outside those boundaries.

29 See David Barton, "Revisionism: A Willing Accomplice," in *Original Intent: The Courts, The Constitution, and Religion* (Aledo, Tex.: WallBuilders, 2010), 285. Fears of "historical revisionism" not infrequently devolve into conspiracy-theory-laden fears that the liberal agenda of the academy is a part of a grander strategy to annihilate the American republic. Such fears are fully present in Catherine Millard, *The Rewriting of America's History* (Camp Hill, Pa.: Horizon House, 1991). "Rewriting a nation's history is frequently one of the first strategies taken by a conquering nation. Why? Because a people who do not know from where they came also do not know where they are going. Thus they become easy prey for a conquering nation. While this phenomenon has occurred repeatedly throughout history and thoughout the world, today it is happening to our beloved United States. It's happening through the rewriting and/or reinterpretation of American historical records" (iii).

30 Roger Schultz, "Historical Revisionism: Why All the Fuss," *Faith for All of Life*, March/April 2007, 7–10. Schultz is supporter of the Christian Reconstructionist Rousas J. Rushdoony, and his convictions about Christian historiography

reflect those views. Schultz laments that most historians working at Christian colleges have sadly fallen prey to the academy's liberal agenda. See Schultz, "Evangelical Meltdown," 41–47.

31 Roger Schultz, "Judgments in History," *Chalcedon Report*, February 2003, 21–22.

32 Christian biography remains a fixture in the devotional reading habits of contemporary (especially conservative) Christians, and the role it plays for its readers today has not changed markedly from the time of Einhard's Charlemagne or from that of the biblical writers, for that matter. This present study does not give sufficient attention to this literature. For contemporary works written in this older hagiographic tradition, see David Aikman, *Great Souls: Six Who Changed the Century* (Nashville: Word, 1998); Jonathan Aitken, *John Newton: From Disgrace to Amazing Grace* (Wheaton, Ill.: Crossway, 2007); George Grant, *The Last Crusader: The Untold Story of Christopher Columbus* (Wheaton, Ill.: Crossway, 1992); Os Guiness, ed., *Character Counts: Leadership Qualities in Washington, Wilberforce, Lincoln, and Solzhenitzyn* (Grand Rapids: Baker, 1999); Richard M. Hannula, *Trials and Triumph: Stories from Church History* (Moscow, Idaho: Canon, 1999); Helen Kooiman Hosier, *100 Christian Women Who Changed the 20th Century* (Grand Rapids: Revell, 2000); Eric Metaxas, *Bonhoeffer: Pastor, Martyr, Prophet, Spy* (Nashville: Thomas Nelson, 2010); also by Metaxas, see *Seven Men and the Secret of their Greatness* (Nashville: Thomas Nelson, 2013); and *Amazing Grace: William Wilberforce and the Heroic Campaign to End Slavery* (New York: HarperOne, 2007); John Piper, *The Hidden Smile of God: The Fruit of Affliction in the Lives of John Bunyan, William Cowper, and David Brainerd* (Wheaton, Ill.: Crossway, 2001); John Woodbridge, ed., *More than Conquerors: Portraits of Believers from All Walks of Life* (Chicago: Moody, 1992). In the wake of a dustup over a biography he had written about George Whitefield that was not sufficiently laudatory and bore none of the devotional elements so many Christians expect from biography of Christian "heroes," Stout wrote an essay that helpfully distinguished this kind of biography from the ways the Bible *actually* deals with biography. He concluded that the Bible is much more forthright in laying out the foibles and failures of its "heroes" than have subsequent Christian writers. See Stout, "Biography as Battleground: The Competing Legacies of the Religious Historian," *Books & Culture*, June/July 1996, 9–10.

33 For a taste of some of the ways this approach to history is appropriated at the level of secondary education, consider the "History of the World Mega-Conference" sponsored by Vision Forum Ministries. The very conservative Christian homeschooling network and curriculum publisher hosted families from around the country to help them better prepare for teaching history to their children. If conference speakers were not warning families against the dangers of rampant secularism, they were inviting them to look back on the past to learn enduring moral lessons. The many seminars at its 2006 gathering included, among many others, the following topics: "How Families Changed the World"; "The Influence of Marxist Thinking on Modern Textbooks and Historiography"; "The Lessons of the Pagan World and their Ongoing

Influence on the West"; "A Terrifying Beauty: The Message of the Mayans"; "The Remarkable Life of Oliver Cromwell"; and "A Brief History of Martyrdom." "A Historic Conference on Providential History," http://www.workforceministries.com/issues/news_and_reports/hwmc_recap.html, accessed January 10, 2014.

34 A prime example of writing in this vein is Gary DeMar, *America's Christian History: The Untold Story* (Atlanta, Ga.: American Vision, 1995). For an excellent general survey of this question, along with a much more expansive discussion of the various kinds of writings that have advanced this argument, see John Fea, *Was America Founded as a Christian Nation?: A Historical Introduction* (Louisville, Ky.: Westminster John Knox, 2011). There is a great deal of overlap between these studies and the ones surveyed in the following two chapters: history as Christian apologetic and historical study as search for God. The prime difference is that histories covered in this chapter are primarily interested in using Christian moral categories to restore American virtue, while those in subsequent chapters aspire to vindicate the Christian faith itself.

35 The name WallBuilders is taken from the Old Testament story of Nehemiah, who, after the Babylonian Captivity, was sent ahead to Jerusalem to rebuild the city walls. In the same way, Barton views himself as doing the work of rebuilding the structures of American civilization.

36 Most of Barton's writings, positions, and arguments are available at the WallBuilder's website, wallbuilders.com. One of his books that pretty well spells out most of what he has to say about American history and its potential role in restoring God to his proper place in American society is *Original Intent*.

37 For a fairly thorough survey of Barton and his standing in the evangelical world, see Randall J. Stephens and Karl W. Giberson, *The Anointed: Evangelical Truth in a Secular Age* (Cambridge, Mass.: Harvard University Press, 2011), 83–96. For a similar account, see also Molly Worthen, *Apostles of Reason: The Crisis of Authority in American Evangelicalism* (New York: Oxford University Press, 2014), 251–52.

38 Siddhartha Mahanta, "The GOP's Favorite Fringe Historian," *Mother Jones*, April 28, 2011, http://www.motherjones.com/politics/2011/04/david-barton-gingrich-bachmann-huckabee, accessed August 12, 2014.

39 Worthen, *Apostles of Reason*, 251–52.

40 Marvin Olasky, *The Tragedy of American Compassion* (New York: Regnery, 1992), 5.

41 Marvin Olasky, *Fighting for Liberty and Virtue: Political and Cultural Wars in Eighteenth-Century America* (New York: Regnery, 1995).

42 Marvin Olasky, *The American Leadership Tradition: Moral Vision from Washington to Clinton* (New York: Free Press, 1999), xvii–xviii.

43 Marvin Olasky, *Abortion Rites: A Social History of Abortion in America* (Wheaton, Ill.: Crossway, 1992), xiv. See James Mohr, *Abortion in America* (New York: Oxford University Press, 1978).

44 See especially Olasky's final chapter, "The Uses of History," in *Abortion Rites*, 283–306.

45 The Catholic writer and historian, Paul Johnson, wrote an early conservative counterpoint to Zinn's *People's History*. His mammoth *A History of the American People* (New York: HarperCollins, 1997), weighing in at over a thousand pages, does not mention Zinn's book directly. But its decidedly conservative interpretation of American history is often used as a counterpoint to Zinn's.

46 Larry Schweikart and Michael Allen, *A Patriot's History of the United States: From Columbus's Great Discovery to the War on Terror* (New York: Sentinel, 2004), xi.

47 See a transcript of Schweikart's interview with Virgil Vaduva, "An Interview with Dr. Larry Schweikart," Planet Preterist, July 17, 2006, http://planet preterist.com/content/interview-dr-larry-schweikart, accessed August 4, 2014.

48 To cite only one example, see William Appleman Williams, *The Contours of American History* (Cleveland, Ohio: World Publishing, 1961). Williams served as a kind of guiding light for many early New Left scholars. Irwin Unger writes that Williams' book "is saturated with old-fashioned philosophical idealism. Ideas, not interests, are what count in history, for mercantilism, at least, is no mere rationalization of individual or class advantage. Derived from Biblical moralism, it is tough and autonomous with the power to blunt and tame the acquisitive instincts." See Unger, "The 'New Left,' " 1246.

49 Richard Wightman Fox and Robert B. Westbrook, eds., *In Face of Facts: Moral Inquiry and American Scholarship* (New York: Cambridge University Press, 1998), 4. Another more recent entre into the world of history as moral inquiry is the thoughtful collection of essays in Donald A. Yerxa, ed. *British Abolitionism and the Question of Moral Progress in History* (Columbia: University of South Carolina Press, 2012). Here, the authors—nearly half of them Christian writers—aspire to weigh the relative merits of assessing developments surrounding the early nineteenth-century debate over abolishing the slave trade by appealing to fairly normative moral categories of good and evil. See especially Yerxa's introduction, "Historians, Moral Progress, and the Limits of History," 1–12.

50 Eugene McCarraher, "The Enchantments of Mammon: Notes toward a Theological History of Capitalism," *Modern Theology* 21 (2005): 432–33.

51 Charles Marsh, *God's Long Summer: Stories of Faith and Civil Rights* (Princeton, N.J.: Princeton University Press, 1997), 4–8. For another example of history written in this vein, see Peter Slade, one of Marsh's students, *Open Friendship in a Closed Society: Mission Mississippi and a Theology of Friendship* (New York: Oxford University Press, 2009).

52 Charles Marsh, *The Beloved Community: How Faith Shapes Social Justice, From the Civil Rights Movement to Today* (New York: Basic Books, 2005), 5.

53 Marsh, *Beloved Community*, 128.

54 Marsh, *Beloved Community*, 138.

55 Harry S. Stout, *Upon the Altar of the Nation: A Moral History of the American Civil War* (New York: Viking, 2006).

56 Harry S. Stout, *Upon the Altar of the Nation*, xi.

57 Harry S. Stout, *Upon the Altar of the Nation*, xii.

58 Douglas A. Sweeney, "On the Vocation of Historians to the Priesthood of Believers: A Plea to Christians in the Academy," in *Confessing History:*

Explorations in Christian Faith and the Historian's Vocation, ed. John Fea, Jay Green, and Eric Miller (Notre Dame, Ind.: University of Notre Dame Press, 2010), 308.

59 William Katerberg, "The 'Objectivity Question' and the Historian's Vocation," in *Confessing History: Explorations in Christian Faith and the Historian's Vocation*, ed. John Fea, Jay Green, and Eric Miller (Notre Dame, Ind.: University of Notre Dame Press, 2010), 109, 102.

60 David Harlan, *The Degradation of American History* (Chicago: University of Chicago Press, 1997), xxviii.

61 Michael Kugler, "Enlightenment, Objectivity, and Historical Imagination," in *Confessing History: Explorations in Christian Faith and the Historian's Vocation*, ed. John Fea, Jay Green, and Eric Miller (Notre Dame, Ind.: University of Notre Dame Press, 2010), 141–42, 144.

62 Thomas Albert Howard, "Virtue Ethics and Historical Inquiry: The Case for Prudence," in *Confessing History: Explorations in Christian Faith and the Historian's Vocation*, ed. John Fea, Jay Green, and Eric Miller (Notre Dame, Ind.: University of Notre Dame Press, 2010), 92.

63 Herbert Butterfield, "Moral Judgments in History," in *History and Human Relations* (London: Collins, 1951), 101.

64 Butterfield, "Moral Judgments," 105.

65 Butterfield, "Moral Judgments," 110.

66 Butterfield, "Moral Judgments," 122–23.

67 Butterfield, "Moral Judgments," 123.

68 Iain Murray, *Revival and Revivalism: The Making and Marring of American Evangelicalism, 1750–1858* (Carlisle, Pa.: Banner of Truth Trust, 1994), passim.

69 Carl R. Trueman, "The Sin of Uzzah," The Mortification of Spin, published by the Alliance of Confessing Evangelicals, July 10, 2012, http://www.mortificationofspin.org/mos/postcards-from-palookaville/the-sin-of-uzzah#.VT41eaNViko.

70 James LaGrand, "The Problems of Preaching through History," in *Confessing History: Explorations in Christian Faith and the Historian's Vocation*, ed. John Fea, Jay Green, and Eric Miller (Notre Dame, Ind.: University of Notre Dame Press, 2010), 201.

71 LaGrand, "Problems of Preaching," 209–10.

72 Gordon S. Wood, *Purpose of the Past: Reflections on the Uses of History* (New York: Penguin, 2008), 268–69, 276.

Chapter 4

1 Georges Florovsky, "The Predicament of the Christian Historian," in *Religion and Culture: Essays in Honor of Paul Tillich*, ed. Walter Leibrecht (New York: Harper & Brothers, 1959), 140.

2 See Craig Blomberg, *The Historical Reliability of the Gospels* (Downers Grove, Ill.: IVP Academic, 2007); Gary Habermas, *The Historical Jesus: Ancient Evidence for the Life of Christ* (Joplin, Mo.: College Press, 1996); and William Lane

Craig, *Reasonable Faith: Christian Truth and Apologetics* (Wheaton, Ill.: Crossway, 2004).

3   Edwin M. Yamauchi, "Easter—Myth, Hallucination, or History? Part 1," *Christianity Today*, March 15, 1974, 4–7; Edwin M. Yamauchi, "Easter—Myth, Hallucination, or History? Part 2," *Christianity Today*, March 29, 1974, 12–16. See also Gary R. Habermas, *Ancient Evidence for the Life of Jesus: Historical Records of His Death and Resurrection* (Nashville: Thomas Nelson, 1985); F. F. Bruce, *Jesus and Christian Origins Outside the New Testament* (Grand Rapids: Eerdmans, 1974); and J. N. D. Anderson, *Christianity: The Witness of History* (Downers Grove, Ill.: InterVarsity, 1970).

4   For an early articulation of Montgomery's ideas about history, see his essay, "Toward a Christian Philosophy of History," in *Jesus of Nazareth: Saviour and Lord*, ed. Carl F. H. Henry (Grand Rapids: Eerdmans, 1966), 227–40. For more on Montgomery's apologetic approach to historical study, see Martin Batts, "A Summary and Critique of the Historical Apologetic of John Warwick Montgomery" (Th.M. thesis, Dallas Theological Seminary, 1977); Stephen D. Rook, "Historical Objectivism: The Apologetic Methodology of John Warwick Montgomery" (M.A. thesis, Harding Graduate School of Religion, 1985); Keith Andrew Mascord, "Faith, History and the Morality of Knowledge: The Contrasting Views of J. W. Montgomery and V. A. Harvey" (M.Th. thesis, Australian College of Theology, 1993); and Kerry McRoberts, "Faith Founded on Fact: The Apologetic Theology of John Warwick Montgomery" (M.C.S. thesis, Regent College, 2000). See also debates on Montgomery's approach in *Fides et Historia*: Ronald J. VanderMolen, "The Christian Historian: Apologist or Seeker," *Fides et Historia* 3, no. 1 (1970): 41–56; William A. Speck, "Herbert Butterfield on the Christian and Historical Study," *Fides et Historia* 4, no. 1 (1971): 50–70; Montgomery and Moore, "Speck in Butterfield's Eye"; Hein, "The Christian Historian"; Reid, "Problem of the Christian Interpretation of History"; and Timothy Paul Erdel, "Stigma and Dogma: A Reply to Earl William Kennedy on Behalf of John Warwick Montgomery," *Fides et Historia* 6, no. 1 (1974): 26–32. See also Feinberg, "History: Private or Public?"; and Stephen J. Wykstra, "The Problem of Miracle in the Apologetic from History," *Journal of the American Scientific Affiliation* 30, no. 4 (1978): 154–63.

5   Quoted in Ronald Nash, "The Use and Abuse of History in Christian Apologetics," *Christian Scholar's Review* 1 (1971): 219. Nash largely shares both Montgomery's commitment to evidentialist apologetics and his general conviction that the primary task of the historian's trade is to demonstrate the historicity of events that lay at the foundations of Christian faith. See Nash, *Christian Faith and Historical Understanding* (Grand Rapids: Zondervan, 1984).

6   Nash, "Use and Abuse of History," 219.

7   John Warwick Montgomery, *Where Is History Going? Essays in Support of the Historical Truth of Christian Revelation* (Grand Rapids: Zondervan, 1969), 31.

8   John Warwick Montgomery, *History and Christianity* (Downers Grove, Ill.: InterVarsity, 1972), 80. It is remarkable today to recall the attention that Montgomery's style of historical apologetics drew among Christian historians during the late 1960s and early 1970s. Any suggestion that history—in its complexity—or

the historian—in her frailty—is capable of returning anything short of crystal clear reconstructions of the past, Montgomery met with passionate indignation. The first several years *Fides et Historia*, the journal of the CFH, was in print were dominated by Montgomery's and his students' irate replies to various pieces published in its pages. For an account of some of this discourse, see D. G. Hart, "History in Search of Meaning," 76–77.

9 Dinesh D'Souza, *What's So Great About Christianity?* (Wheaton, Ill.: Tyndale House, 2008), 42.

10 D'Souza, *What's So Great About Christianity?* 43–44. In Alan Roebuck's review in *American Thinker*, he compares D'Souza's strategy to that of the Christian apologist Francis Schaeffer. He writes, D'Souza "mostly engages in what the late Christian theologian and apologist Francis Schaeffer called 'pre-evangelism,' that is, clearing away false ideas so that the unbeliever actually has a chance to hear the arguments for Christianity. To do this, D'Souza uses non-biblical arguments drawn from science, philosophy and history to establish both the reasonableness of believing in the God of the Bible (that is, that Christianity could possibly be true if the evidence indicates it), and the positive effect that Christianity has had upon Western Civilization and the entire world. In this way he nullifies the negative arguments of the atheists who contend that religion in general is patently absurd even before the evidence is examined, and that religion causes more evil than good." See Alan Roebuck, "D'Souza's Comeback," *American Thinker*, December 25, 2007, http://www.americanthinker .com/2007/12/dsouzas_comeback.html, accessed 10 January 2014.

11 D'Souza, *What's So Great About Christianity?* 53.

12 See Breisach, *Historiography*, 217. Breisach adds that this view of Christianity, and this general interpretation of its decline, was regularly put forward by residents of the late Roman Empire.

13 D'Souza's book was largely written as a response to Hitchens' book. See Christopher Hitchens, *God Is Not Great: How Religion Poisons Everything* (New York: Twelve, 2007).

14 John Howard Yoder, "The Constantinian Sources of Western Social Ethics," in *The Priestly Kingdom: Social Ethics as Gospel* (Notre Dame, Ind.: University of Notre Dame Press, 1984), 135. See also Yoder, *The Politics of Jesus* (Grand Rapids: Eerdmans, 1994).

15 See Hauerwas, *After Christendom? How the Church Is to Behave If Freedom, Justice, and a Christian Nation Are Bad Ideas* (Nashville: Abingdon, 1991); Hauerwas and William Willimon, *Resident Aliens: A Provocative Christian Assessment of Culture and Ministry for People Who Know that Something Is Wrong* (Nashville: Abingdon, 1989); Hauerwas, *Unleashing the Scripture: Freeing the Bible from Captivity to America* (Nashville: Abingdon, 1993); Hauerwas, *A Community of Character: Toward a Constructive Christian Social Ethic* (Notre Dame, Ind.: University of Notre Dame Press, 1991).

16 Gregory A. Boyd, *Myth of a Christian Nation: How the Quest for Political Power Is Destroying the Church* (Grand Rapids: Zondervan, 2007); Brian McLaren, *A New Kind of Christianity: Ten Questions that Are Transforming the Faith* (New York: HarperOne, 2011); and Lee C. Camp, *Mere Discipleship: Radical*

Christianity in a Rebellious Age (Grand Rapids: Brazos, 2008). For an interesting rebuttal to books like these that revisits the actual world of Constantine, see Peter Leithart, *Defending Constantine: The Twilight of an Empire and the Dawn of Christendom* (Downers Grove, Ill.: IVP Academic, 2010). For an even more interesting look at this discussion, see Stanley Hauerwas' surprisingly sympathetic review of Leithart's book, "A Review of *Defending Constantine*," *Christian Century*, October 13, 2010, http://www.christiancentury.org/reviews/2010-09/nonfiction-1, accessed January 10, 2014. Here Hauerwas writes, "Asking me to write a review of Peter Leithart's defense of Emperor Constantine may seem like asking the fox to inspect the henhouse." But, remarkably, Hauerwas concedes the central thrust of Leithart's book, even as it did little to change his own understanding of social ethics.

17 Marvin Olasky, "The History of Compassion," *World Magazine*, June 18, 2011, http://www.worldmag.com/articles/18137, accessed October 7, 2011. Some of Olasky's own historical writings are considered elsewhere in this book.

18 D. James Kennedy and Jerry Newcombe, *What If Jesus Had Never Been Born?* (Nashville: Thomas Nelson, 1994), 3.

19 Kennedy and Newcombe, *What If Jesus Had Never Been Born?* 205.

20 Jonathan Hill, *What Has Christianity Ever Done for Us? How It Shaped the Modern World* (Downers Grove, Ill.: InterVarsity, 2005), 6–7.

21 Hill, *What Has Christianity Ever Done for Us?* 111.

22 Alvin J. Schmidt, *How Christianity Changed the World* (Grand Rapids: Zondervan, 2001), 7–8.

23 Schmidt, *How Christianity Changed the World*, 9; emphasis in original.

24 See Roger Finke and Rodney Stark, *The Churching of America, 1776–1990: Winners and Losers in Our Religious Economy* (New Brunswick, N.J.: Rutgers University Press, 1992); Stark, *The Rise of Christianity: How the Obscure, Marginal Jesus Movement Became the Dominant Force in the Western World* (San Francisco: HarperSanFrancisco, 1997); Stark, *For the Glory of God: How Monotheism Led to Reformations, Science, Witch-Hunts, and the End of Slavery* (Princeton, N.J.: Princeton University Press, 2004); Stark, *The Victory of Reason: How Christianity Led to Freedom, Capitalism, and Western Success* (New York: Random House, 2005); Stark, *Cities of God: The Real Story of How Christianity Became an Urban Movement and Conquered Rome* (New York: HarperOne, 2007); Stark, *God's Battalions: The Case for the Crusades* (New York: HarperOne, 2010); Stark, *The Triumph of Christianity: How the Jesus Movement Became the World's Largest Religion* (New York: HarperOne, 2012); Stark, *America's Blessings: How Religion Benefits Everyone, Including Atheists* (West Conshohocken, Pa.: Templeton Press, 2012); Stark, *How the West Won: The Neglected Story of the Triumph of Modernity* (Wilmington, Del.: ISI Books, 2014).

25 William Grimes, "Capitalism, Brought to You by Religion," *New York Times*, December 30, 2005.

26 Stark, *Victory of Reason*, x.

27 Stark, *Victory of Reason*, 233.

28 Mike Aquilina, "A Double Take on Early Christianity: An Interview with Rodney Stark," *Touchstone*, January/February 2000, http://touchstonemag .com/archives/article.php?id=13-01-044-i, accessed November 4, 2011.

29 James Hannam, *God's Philosophers: How the Medieval World Laid the Foundations of Modern Science* (London: Icon, 2009).

30 Douglas F. Kelly, *The Emergence of Liberty in the Modern World* (Phillipsburg, N.J.: Presbyterian and Reformed, 1992), 142.

31 Benjamin Hart, *Faith and Freedom: The Christian Roots of American Liberty* (Dallas, Tex.: Stanley & Lewis, 1988), 19.

32 Hart, *Faith and Freedom*, 19.

33 Gary T. Amos, *Defending the Declaration: How the Bible and Christianity Influenced the Writing of the Declaration of Independence* (Charlottesville, Va.: Providence Foundation, 1996), 20.

34 Steven J. Keillor, *This Rebellious House: American History and the Truth of Christianity* (Downers Grove, Ill.: InterVarsity, 1996).

35 C. Gregg Singer, *A Theological Interpretation of American History* (Phillipsburg, N.J.: Presbyterian and Reformed, 1964), 19.

36 Singer, *Theological Interpretation of American History*, 21.

37 Singer, *Theological Interpretation of American History*, 285.

38 Singer, *Theological Interpretation of American History*, 294.

39 Singer, *Theological Interpretation of American History*, 300.

40 Christian scholars, overall, extended a lot of goodwill to Schaeffer due to his effectiveness in speaking to young people and his overarching willingness to take ideas seriously. But this goodwill was tested regularly as Schaeffer didn't exhibit the patience or the nuance needed to engage scholarship in a serious way. "While Schaeffer had inspired a generation of Christian young people to become scholars," writes his biographer, Barry Hankins, "he had little idea of what scholars actually do." See " 'I'm Just Making a Point': Francis Schaeffer and the Irony of Faithful Christian Scholarship," *Fides et Historia* 39, no. 1 (2007): 15.

41 Francis Schaeffer, *How Should We Then Live: The Rise and Decline of Western Thought and Culture* (Old Tappan, N.J.: Revell, 1976). The reception of Schaeffer's book among Christian scholars is noteworthy. Reviewers George Giacumakis and Gerald C. Tiffin begin their review, straining to make it clear that they consider Schaeffer a "friend" and Christian brother and "laud him for his attempt to communicate the truths of the Christian faith to a secularistic thinking world." They are intent on assuring him and anyone who supports him that the criticisms that follow are "friendly." But the reviewers, in the end, don't think the book is very good as a work of history and express concern that Christians might consume it as if it were intended as a complete chronology of Western history. It is not. The reviewers walk through a series of sometimes devastating criticisms, but with each turn, deliver them with kid gloves. They want desperately to see Schaeffer's project succeed, but it's apparent that they have a hard time imagining how it can. "Persons convinced that evangelical Christians find it difficult to be both historians and believers, may find that impression confirmed." See "Francis

Schaeffer's New Intellectual Enterprise: Some Friendly Criticisms," *Fides et Historia* 9 (1977): 52–58.

42 Barry Hankins, *Francis Schaeffer and the Shaping of Evangelical America* (Grand Rapids: Eerdmans, 2008), 169.

43 Schaeffer, *How Should We Then Live*, 134.

44 Robert L. Waggoner, "Why Genuine Christianity Improves the World," Biblical Theism, http://www.thebible.net/biblicaltheism/0402christianityimproves.pdf, accessed January 10, 2014.

45 J. H. Hexter, "The Historical Method of Christopher Hill," in *On Historians: Reappraisals of Some of the Masters of Modern History* (Cambridge, Mass.: Harvard University Press, 1979), 241.

46 Noll, "Potential of Missiology," 113.

47 Noll, "Potential of Missiology," 114.

48 Tackett quoted in Randal Rauser, "Learning in a Time of (Culture) War: Indoctrination in Focus on the Family's *Truth Project*," *Christian Scholar's Review* 39, no. 1 (2009): 80.

49 Edward Gibbon, *The Decline and Fall of the Roman Empire* (London: Wordsworth, 1999), 244. Historian George Marsden echoes Gibbon's sentiments in the afterword to his classic study, *Fundamentalism and American Culture*. "The theologian's task is to try to establish from Scripture criteria for determining what in the history of the church is truly the work of the Spirit. The Christian historian takes an opposite, although complimentary, approach. While he must keep in mind certain theological criteria, he may refrain from explicit judgments on what is properly Christian while he concentrates on observable cultural forces" (230).

Chapter 5

1 Jacob Viner, *The Role of Providence in the Social Order: An Essay in Intellectual History* (Philadelphia: American Philosophical Society, 1972), 4–5.

2 Saint Augustine, *City of God* (New York: Modern Library, 1993), 158, 4.

3 John Cumming, *God in History: Or, Facts Illustrative of the Presence and Providence of God in the Affairs of Men* (New York: Lane & Scott, 1852), 74.

4 Cumming, *God in History*, 15.

5 David Fisher, "A Biblical Pattern for Teaching God's Providence in History," in *The Providence of God in History*, ed. Edward M. Panosian, David Fisher, and Mark Sidwell (Greenville, S.C.: Bob Jones University Press, 1996), 26.

6 Edward M. Panosian, "A Case for History in the Christian School," in *The Providence of God in History*, ed. Edward M. Panosian, David Fisher, and Mark Sidwell (Greenville, S.C.: Bob Jones University Press, 1996), 3.

7 Garrett Heyns and Garritt E. Roelofs, *Christian Interpretation of American History* (Chicago: National Union of Christian Schools, 1928), 50; James Rose makes a similar argument in his *Guide to American Christian Education for Home and School: The Principle Approach* (Camarillo, Calif.: American Christian Institute, 1987): "If they do not know the Hand of God in our nation's past, how can they be sure of it in the present, or the future? As a consequence, they would

not know *how important they are to God in respect to His government of men and nations, nor would they know what a responsibility they have, not only to those sacrificing Christians who have gone before, but to themselves and to their own posterity.* Most young Christians want to have a goal toward which they can work with God's help; they want to have a purpose and a hope. But if they have not been taught the Hand of God in history, they enter the work-a-day world *not realizing their importance as Christians in directing the course of human events.* They will not think it important to make decisions predicated upon Biblical principles of government in *all* fields of endeavor, for they will assume they are Christians in a secular world governed by secular rules and concepts. . . . The Providential view of history is important because it is true, because it is Biblical, and because it challenges and supplants the prevailing secular social studies approaches to history and government. The curricula of most schools and colleges omit this emphasis. Furthermore, understanding the Hand of God makes the lessons of history immediately individual and implants *hope* into the daily life of the teacher and student in the home, church, or school" (28; emphasis in original).

8 Heyns and Roelofs, *Christian Interpretation of American History*, 7.

9 Wilkins quoted in Phillip G. Kayser, *Seeing History with New Eyes: A Guide to Presenting Providential History* (Omaha, Neb.: Providence History Festival, 2008), 20.

10 Peter Marshall and David Manuel, *The Light and the Glory: Did God Have a Plan for America?* (Grand Rapids: Revell, 1977), 22. Based on the success of this first volume, Marshall and Manuel followed this effort with others, including *From Sea to Shining Sea: God's Plan for America 1787–1837* (Grand Rapids: Revell, 1993); and *Sounding Forth the Trumpet: God's Plan for America 1837–1860* (Grand Rapids: Revell, 1999).

11 Marshall and Manuel, *Light and the Glory*, 68.

12 Marshall and Manuel, *Light and the Glory*, 110.

13 Marshall and Manuel, *Light and the Glory*, 245.

14 Kayser, *Seeing History with New Eyes*, 4; emphasis in original.

15 Kayser, *Seeing History with New Eyes*, passim.

16 Mark A. Beliles and Stephen K. McDowell, *America's Providential History* (Charlottesville, Va.: Providence Foundation, 1989), 1.

17 Beliles and McDowell, *America's Providential History*, viii.

18 Steve Wilkins quoted in Kayser, *Seeing History with New Eyes*, 20.

19 Keillor, *This Rebellious House.*

20 Steven J. Keillor, *God's Judgments: Interpreting History and the Christian Faith* (Downers Grove, Ill.: IVP Academic, 2007), 13–18.

21 Keillor, *God's Judgments*, 189–204.

22 See Craig M. Gay, *The Way of the (Modern) World: Or, Why It's Tempting to Live as If God Doesn't Exist* (Grand Rapids: Eerdmans, 1998).

23 Herbert Butterfield, "God in History," in *God, History, and Historians: An Anthology of Modern Christian Views of History*, ed. C. T. McIntire (New York: Oxford University Press, 1977), 93.

24 Fisher, "Biblical Pattern," 25.

25 Shannon, "After Monographs," 174–75.

26   Tim Stafford, "Whatever Happened to Christian History?" *Christianity Today* 45, no. 5 (2001): 42–49.

27   Novick, *That Noble Dream*, passim.

28   Sam Wineburg, *Historical Thinking and Other Unnatural Acts* (Philadelphia: Temple University Press, 2001), 11.

29   Jonathan Tucker Boyd put the matter plainly when he observed, "Logically, providence makes a lousy category for analysis. If God's rule extends over all and his providence comprises all events . . . it makes little sense to name some events as more providential than others." See "If We Ever Needed the Lord Before," *Books & Culture* 5 (1999): 40.

30   C. T. McIntire, "God's Work in History: The Post-Biblical Epoch," (unpublished paper presented at the Public Colloquium of the Institute for Christian Studies, Toronto, and Regent College, Vancouver, at York University, May 16, 1975), 2.

31   C. S. Lewis, "Historicism," in *God, History, and Historians: An Anthology of Modern Christian Views of History*, ed. C. T. McIntire (New York: Oxford University Press, 1977), 230.

32   Herbert Butterfield, *Christianity and History* (London: G. Bell & Sons, 1949), 94.

33   Smith, *American Evangelicalism*, 120–53.

34   R. Scott Appleby, "History in the Fundamentalist Imagination," *Journal of American History* 89 (2002): 499–500.

Conclusion

1   Mark Schwehn and Dorothy Bass were heavily involved in consulting with Lilly in the creation of this project. Helpful background on the program can be found in a book they edited together, *Leading Lives that Matter: What We Should Do and Who We Should Be* (Grand Rapids: Eerdmans, 2006). Two examples of the excellent scholarship published in the spirit of this turn toward vocation include Richard T. Hughes, *The Vocation of a Christian Scholar: How Christian Faith Can Sustain the Life of the Mind* (Grand Rapids: Eerdmans, 2005); and Douglas V. Henry and Bob R. Agee, eds., *Faithful Learning and the Christian Scholarly Vocation* (Grand Rapids: Eerdmans, 2003).

2   Douglas Jacobsen and Rhonda Hustedt Jacobsen were especially vocal in their concerns about the ways the Reformed paradigm had overwhelmed the conversation about Christian scholarship. The idea of vocation gave them and others a bigger canvas to think about their work. See *Scholarship and Christian Faith: Enlarging the Conversation* (New York: Oxford University Press, 2004).

3   A collection of essays I coedited with John Fea and Eric Miller in 2010 obviously flows out of these conversations about vocation. All three of us teach at institutions that were recipients of Lilly funds, and we all became involved with Lilly initiatives on our respective campuses. Lilly funds were instrumental in allowing us to complete that project. See John Fea, Jay Green, and Eric Miller, eds., *Confessing History: Explorations in Christian Faith and the Historian's Vocation* (Notre Dame, Ind.: University of Notre Dame Press, 2010).

4 J. I. Packer, "Call, Called, Calling," in *Baker's Dictionary of Theology*, ed. Everett F. Harrison (Grand Rapids: Baker, 1960), 108.

5 Paul Marshall, *A Kind of Life Imposed on Man: Vocation and the Social Order from Tyndale to Locke* (Toronto: University of Toronto Press, 1996), 13; emphasis in original.

6 Packer, "Call, Called, Calling," 108.

7 Quoted in Douglas Schuurman, *Vocation: Discerning our Callings in Life* (Grand Rapids: Eerdmans, 2004), 78.

8 Marshall, *Kind of Life*, 3.

9 Marshall, *Kind of Life*, 3.

10 Schuurman, *Vocation*, 1–16.

11 Schuurman, *Vocation*, 5.

12 Karlfried Froehlich, "Luther on Vocation," *Lutheran Quarterly* 13 (1999): 196.

13 Morgan, *Puritan Political Ideas*, xvii.

14 Schuurman, *Vocation*, 6–7.

15 Quoted in Morgan, *Puritan Political Ideas*, 36.

16 Quoted in Marshall, *Kind of Life*, 41.

17 Lee Hardy, *The Fabric of this World: Inquiries into Calling, Career Choice, and the Design of Human Work* (Grand Rapids: Eerdmans, 1990), 60.

18 Cornelius Plantinga, *Engaging God's World: A Christian Vision of Faith, Learning, and Living* (Grand Rapids: Eerdmans, 2002), 113.

19 Plantinga, *Engaging God's World*, 117.

20 John McGreevy, "Faith Histories," in *Religion, Scholarship, and Higher Education: Perspectives, Models, and Future Prospects*, ed. Andrea Sterk (Notre Dame, Ind.: University of Notre Dame Press, 2002), 63.

21 Hamilton, "Elusive Idea of Christian Scholarship," 21.

22 Richard Horner, "Paradoxes of Christian Scholarship," *Reconsiderations* 1, no. 4 (2002): 1.

23 Hart, "Christian Scholars, Secular Universities," 401–2.

24 Hart draws an important analogy between the ways the Apostle Paul talks about the Christian duty to submit to "the governing authorities" in Rom 13 to parallel responsibilities of the Christian to accept the powers that be in other spheres of the kingdom of humanity. This realist, Lutheran sense of the powers and their authority over human life shapes, among other things, the practices of much of Lutheran higher education. See Hart, "Christian Scholars, Secular Universities," 400; and Ernest L. Simmons, *Lutheran Higher Education: An Introduction for Faculty* (Minneapolis: Augsburg, 1998).

25 Sweeney, "On the Vocation of Historians," 306, 309; emphasis in original. For similar, even more radical invitations to this manner of calling, see Richard C. Goode, "The Radical Idea of Christian Scholarship: Plea for a Scandalous Historiography," in *Restoring the First-Century Church in the Twenty-First Century: Essays on the Stone-Campbell Restoration Movement in Honor of Don Haymes*, ed. Warren Lewis and Hans Rollmann, Studies in the History and Culture of World Christianities (Eugene, Ore.: Wipf & Stock, 2005), 238–39; and Perry Bush, "Economic Justice and the Evangelical Historian," *Fides et Historia* 33 (2001): 11–27.

26 Schweiger reflects thoughtfully on themes parallel to Emmons' observations in "Seeing Things," 75. Mark Schwehn is much more sanguine about the continuity between the virtues cultivated in the Christian life and those required for good historical scholarship. Academic virtues of charity and humility are resident with nonbelieving historians and necessary for good work, but Schwehn believes he personally learned them first and most enduringly through his faith development as a Christian. See "Faith Seeking Historical Understanding," in *Confessing History: Explorations in Christian Faith and the Historian's Vocation*, ed. John Fea, Jay Green, and Eric Miller (Notre Dame, Ind.: University of Notre Dame Press, 2010), 23–38; also Mark R. Schwehn, *Exiles from Eden: Religion and the Academic Vocation in America* (New York: Oxford University Press, 1993).

27 Robert Tracy McKenzie, "Christian Faith and the Study of History: A View from the Classroom," *Fides et Historia* 32, no. 2 (2000): 5; emphasis added. See also "The Vocation of the Christian Historian: Re-envisioning Our Calling, Reconnecting to the Church," *Fides et Historia* 45, no. 1 (2013): 1–13. The latter essay was McKenzie's presidential address at the 2012 biennial meeting of the CFH.

28 Robert Tracy McKenzie, "Don't Forget the Church: Reflections on the Forgotten Dimension of Our Dual Calling," in *Confessing History: Explorations in Christian Faith and the Historian's Vocation*, ed. John Fea, Jay Green, and Eric Miller (Notre Dame, Ind.: University of Notre Dame Press, 2010), 289.

29 McKenzie, "Don't Forget the Church," 285. McKenzie put his money where his mouth is with a fine narrative history about the Pilgrim settlement of 1620 at Plymouth Plantation, pitched to a popular Christian audience with an aim to instruct in both historical thinking and piety. See *The First Thanksgiving: What the Real Story Tells Us about Loving God and Learning from History* (Downers Grove, Ill.: InterVarsity, 2013).

30 Quoted in Georges Florovsky, "The Predicament of the Christian Historian," in *Religion and Culture: Essays in Honor of Paul Tillich*, ed. Walter Leibrecht (New York: Harper & Brothers, 1959), 140.

31 This is precisely the conviction that animates James K. Hoffmeier and Dennis R. Magary, eds., *Do Historical Matters Matter to Faith? A Critical Appraisal of Modern and Postmodern Approaches to Scripture* (Wheaton, Ill.: Crossway, 2012).

32 Arthur S. Link, "The Historian's Vocation," *Theology Today* 19 (1962): 77–79.

33 Link, "Historian's Vocation," 80–82.

WORKS CITED

Abelove, Henry. "The Queering of Lesbian/Gay History." *Radical History Review* 62 (1995): 45–57.

Aikman, David. *Great Souls: Six Who Changed the Century.* Nashville: Word, 1998.

Aitken, Jonathan. *John Newton: From Disgrace to Amazing Grace.* Wheaton, Ill.: Crossway, 2007.

Amos, Gary T. *Defending the Declaration: How the Bible and Christianity Influenced the Writing of the Declaration of Independence.* Charlottesville, Va.: Providence Foundation, 1996.

Anderson, J. N. D. *Christianity: The Witness of History.* Downers Grove, Ill.: InterVarsity, 1970.

Appleby, Joyce, Lynn Hunt, and Margaret Jacob. *Telling the Truth about History.* New York: Norton, 1995.

Appleby, R. Scott. "History in the Fundamentalist Imagination." *Journal of American History* 89 (2002): 498–511.

Aquilina, Mike. "A Double Take on Early Christianity: An Interview with Rodney Stark." *Touchstone*, January/February 2000. http://touchstonemag.com/archives/article.php?id=13-01-044-i, accessed November 4, 2011.

Augustine. *City of God.* New York: Modern Library, 1993.

Bailyn, Bernard. "The Problem of the Working Historian: A Comment." In *Philosophy and History,* edited by Sidney Hook, 92–101. New York: New York University Press, 1990.

Bainton, Roland H. *Yesterday, Today, and What Next? Reflections on History and Hope.* Minneapolis: Augsburg, 1978.

Balmer, Randall. *Growing Pains: Learning to Love My Father's Faith.* Grand Rapids: Brazos, 2001.

————. *The Making of Evangelicalism: From Revivalism to Politics and Beyond.* Waco, Tex.: Baylor University Press, 2010.

————. *Mine Eyes Have Seen the Glory: A Journey through the Evangelical Subculture in America.* New York: Oxford University Press, 2006.

————. "Response to Marsden." Unpublished paper from the 155th Annual Conference of the American Society of Church History. San Francisco, Calif., January 6–9, 1994.

————. *Thy Kingdom Come: How the Religious Right Distorts the Faith and Threatens America.* New York: Basic Books, 2006.

Barnes, Harry Elmer. *The Twilight of Christianity.* New York: Vanguard, 1929.

Barton, David. *Original Intent: The Courts, the Constitution, and Religion.* Aledo, Tex.: WallBuilders, 2010.

Batts, Martin. "A Summary and Critique of the Historical Apologetic of John Warwick Montgomery." Th.M. thesis, Dallas Theological Seminary, 1977.

Baxter, Michael J. "Not Outrageous Enough." *First Things*, May 2001. http://www.firstthings.com/article/2001/05/not-outrageous-enough, accessed January 10, 2014.

Beard, Charles. "That Noble Dream." *American Historical Review* 41, no. 1 (1935): 74–87.

Bebbington, David. *Patterns in History: A Christian Perspective on Historical Thought.* Downers Grove, Ill.: InterVarsity, 1979.

————. "Response: The History of Ideas and the Study of Religion." In *Seeing Things Their Way: Intellectual History and the Return of Religion,* edited by Alister Chapman, John Coffey, and Brad S. Gregory, 240–57. Notre Dame, Ind.: University of Notre Dame Press, 2009.

Beliles, Mark A. and Stephen K. McDowell. *America's Providential History.* Charlottesville, Va.: The Providence Foundation, 1989.

Bendroth, Margaret. *Fundamentalism and Gender: 1875 to the Present.* New Haven: Yale University Press, 1996.

Berdyaev, Nicholas. *The Meaning of History.* New York: Scribner's, 1936.

Berk, Stephen E. *Calvinism Versus Democracy: Timothy Dwight and the Origins of American Evangelical Orthodoxy.* Hamden, Conn.: Archon, 1974.

Berkhof, Hendrikus. *Christ and the Meaning of History.* Richmond, Va.: John Knox, 1966.

Birzer, Bradley J. *Sanctifying the World: The Augustinian Life and Mind of Christopher Dawson.* Front Royal, Va.: Christendom, 2007.

Blomberg, Craig. *The Historical Reliability of the Gospels.* Downers Grove, Ill.: IVP Academic, 2007.

Bohi, Janette. "The Relevance of Faith and History: A Mandate from God." *Fides et Historia* 6 (1973): 44–51.

Borris, Eileen, and Nupur Chaudhuri. *Voices of Women's History: The Personal, the Political, the Professional.* Bloomington: Indiana University Press, 1999.

Boyd, Gregory A. *Myth of a Christian Nation: How the Quest for Political Power Is Destroying the Church.* Grand Rapids: Zondervan, 2007.

Boyd, Jonathan. "Faith & Scholarship: A Bibliography for Christian Historians." http://gfm.intervarsity.org/resources/bibliography-for-christian -historians, accessed November 8, 2012.

———. "If We Ever Needed the Lord Before." *Books & Culture* 5 (1999): 40.

Breisach, Ernst. *Historiography: Ancient, Medieval, and Modern.* Chicago: University of Chicago Press, 1983.

Brown, Colin. *History and Faith: A Personal Exploration.* Grand Rapids: Zondervan, 1987.

Bruce, F. F. *Jesus and Christian Origins outside the New Testament.* Grand Rapids: Eerdmans, 1974.

Brundage, Burr C. "The Crisis of Modern Historiography." *Christian Scholar* 37 (1954): 385–95.

Brunner, Emil. *Christianity and Civilization.* New York: Scribner's, 1948.

Burch, Maxie B. *The Evangelical Historians: The Historiography of George Marsden, Nathan Hatch, and Mark Noll.* Lanham, Md.: University Press of America, 1996.

Bush, Perry. "Economic Justice and the Evangelical Historian." *Fides et Historia* 33 (2001): 11–27.

Bushman, Richard. *Believing History: Latter-Day Saint Essays.* New York: Columbia University Press, 2004.

Butterfield, Herbert. *Christianity and History.* London: G. Bell & Sons, 1949.

———. "God in History." In *God, History, and Historians: An Anthology of Modern Christian Views of History,* edited by C. T. McIntire, 192–204. New York: Oxford University Press, 1977.

———. *History and Human Relations.* London: Collins, 1951.

———. *The Whig Interpretation of History.* New York: Norton Library, 1931.

Cairns, Earle E. *God and Man in Time: A Christian Approach to Historiography.* Grand Rapids: Baker, 1979.

Caldecott, Stratford, and John Morrill, eds. *Eternity in Time: Christopher Dawson and the Catholic Idea of History.* Edinburgh: T&T Clark, 1997.

Camp, Lee C. *Mere Discipleship: Radical Christianity in a Rebellious Age.* Grand Rapids: Brazos, 2008.

Carpenter, Joel A. *Revive Us Again: The Reawakening of American Fundamentalism*. New York: Oxford University Press, 1997.

Case, Shirley Jackson. *The Christian Philosophy of History*. Chicago: University of Chicago Press, 1943.

Cimbala, Paul A., and Robert F. Himmelberg, eds. *Historians and Race: Autobiography and the Writing of History*. Bloomington: Indiana University Press, 1996.

Cochrane, Eric. "What is Catholic Historiography?" *Catholic Historical Review* 61 (1975): 169–90.

Coffey, John, and Alister Chapman. "Intellectual History and the Return of Religion." In *Seeing Things Their Way: Intellectual History and the Return of Religion*, edited by Alister Chapman, John Coffey, and Brad S. Gregory, 1–23. Notre Dame, Ind.: University of Notre Dame Press, 2009.

Coffman, Elesha. "The Historian as Latter-Day Saint." *Books & Culture*, November/December 2004. http://www.booksandculture.com/articles/2004/novdec/18.38.html, accessed February 1, 2014.

Collingwood, R. G. *The Idea of History*. New York: Oxford University Press, 1946.

Craig, William Lane. *Reasonable Faith: Christian Truth and Apologetics*. Wheaton, Ill.: Crossway, 2004.

Cumming, John. *God in History: Or, Facts Illustrative of the Presence and Providence of God in the Affairs of Men*. New York: Lane & Scott, 1852.

Daniélou, Jean. *The Lord of History*. Chicago: Regnery, 1958.

Dawson, Christopher. *The Gods of Revolution*. New York: New York University Press, 1972.

———. *The Movement of World Revolution*. Washington, D.C.: Catholic University Press, 2013.

———. "Prevision in Religion." In *The Dynamics of World History*, edited by John Mulloy, 90–102. Wilmington, Del.: ISI Books, 2002.

———. *Religion and Culture*. New York: Wade & Sheen, 1948.

Dayton, Donald. *Discovering an Evangelical Heritage*. New York: Harper & Row, 1976.

DeMar, Gary. *America's Christian History: The Untold Story*. Atlanta: American Vision, 1995.

Dochuk, Darren. *From Bible Belt to Sun Belt: Plain-Folk Religion, Grass Roots Politics, and the Rise of Evangelical Conservatism*. New York: Norton, 2011.

Dooyeweerd, Herman. *In the Twilight of Western Thought: Studies on the Pretended Autonomy of Philosophical Thought*. Nutley, N.J.: Craig Press, 1960.

———. *A New Critique of Theoretical Thought*. 4 vols. Philadelphia: Presbyterian & Reformed, 1953–1958.

D'Souza, Dinesh. *What's So Great about Christianity?* Wheaton, Ill.: Tyndale House, 2008.

Duffy, John-Charles. "Mark Noll's God: The Theology and Politics of Evangelical Historiography." Southeastern Commission for the Study of Religion Regional Meeting, Winston-Salem, N.C., March 12, 2005.

Durkheim, Emile. *The Division of Labor in Society.* New York: Free Press, 1964.

Emmons, David. "Homecoming: Finding a Catholic Hermeneutic." In *Faith and the Historian: Catholic Perspectives*, edited by Nick Salvatore, 49–81. Urbana: University of Illinois Press, 2007.

———. *The Butte Irish: Class and Ethnicity in an American Mining Town, 1875–1925.* Urbana: University of Illinois Press, 1989.

Erdel, Timothy Paul. "Stigma and Dogma: A Reply to Earl William Kennedy on Behalf of John Warwick Montgomery." *Fides et Historia* 6, no. 1 (1974): 26–32.

Fea, John. *Was America Founded as a Christian Nation? A Historical Introduction.* Louisville, Ky.: Westminster John Knox, 2011.

———. *Why Study History? Reflections on the Importance of the Past.* Grand Rapids: Baker Academic, 2013.

Fea, John, Jay Green, and Eric Miller, eds. *Confessing History: Explorations in Christian Faith and the Historian's Vocation.* Notre Dame, Ind.: University of Notre Dame Press, 2010.

Feinberg, Paul D. "History: Private or Public? A Defense of John Warwick Montgomery's Philosophy of History." *Christian Scholar's Review* 1, no. 4 (1971): 325–31.

Finke, Roger, and Rodney Stark. *The Churching of America, 1776–1990: Winners and Losers in Our Religious Economy.* New Brunswick, N.J.: Rutgers University Press, 1992.

Fish, Stanley. "Why We Can't All Just Get Along." *First Things* 64 (1996): 18–26.

Fisher, David. "A Biblical Pattern for Teaching God's Providence in History." In *The Providence of God in History*, edited by Edward M. Panosian, David Fisher, and Mark Sidwell. Greenville, S.C.: Bob Jones University Press, 1996.

Florovsky, Georges. "The Predicament of the Christian Historian." In *Religion and Culture: Essays in Honor of Paul Tillich*, edited by Walter Leibrecht, 140–66. New York: Harper & Brothers, 1959.

Flynt, Wayne. *Keeping the Faith—Ordinary People, Extraordinary Lives: A Memoir.* Tuscaloosa: University of Alabama Press, 2011.

Fox, Richard Wightman. "The Niebuhrs and the Liberal Protestant Heritage." In *Religion and Twentieth-Century American Intellectual Life*, edited by Michael J. Lacey, 94–115. New York: Cambridge University Press, 1989.

Fox, Richard Wightman, and Robert B. Westbrook, eds. *In Face of Facts: Moral Inquiry and American Scholarship*. New York: Cambridge University Press, 1998.

Frank, Douglas W. *Less Than Conquerors: How Evangelicals Entered the Twentieth Century*. Grand Rapids: Eerdmans, 1986.

Froehlich, Karlfried. "Luther on Vocation." *Lutheran Quarterly* 13 (1999): 195–207.

Frykenberg, Robert Eric. *History and Belief: The Foundations of Historical Understanding*. Grand Rapids: Eerdmans, 1996.

Gaddis, Angela. "Integration of Christian Faith and Social Work Practice." Belhaven University, September 15, 2011. http://www.belhaven.edu/pdfs/worldview-papers/Gaddis-Angela.pdf. Accessed August 4, 2014.

Gay, Craig M. *The Way of the (Modern) World: Or, Why It's Tempting to Live as If God Doesn't Exist*. Grand Rapids: Eerdmans, 1998.

Giacumakis, George, and Gerald C. Tiffin. "Francis Schaeffer's New Intellectual Enterprise: Some Friendly Criticisms." *Fides et Historia* 9 (1977): 52–58.

Gibbon, Edward. *The Decline and Fall of the Roman Empire*. London: Wordsworth, 1999.

Gilkey, Langdon. *Reaping the Whirlwind: A Christian Interpretation of History*. New York: Seabury, 1976.

Gleason, Philip. "Becoming (and Being) a Catholic Historian." In *Faith and the Historian: Catholic Perspectives*, edited by Nick Salvatore, 7–30. Urbana: University of Illinois Press, 2007.

Good, Richard C. "The Radical Idea of Christian Scholarship: Plea for a Scandalous Historiography." In *Restoring the First-Century Church in the Twenty-First Century: Essays on the Stone-Campbell Restoration Movement in Honor of Don Haymes*, edited by Warren Lewis and Hans Rollmann, 226–42. Eugene, Ore.: Wipf & Stock, 2005.

Grant, George. *The Last Crusader: The Untold Story of Christopher Columbus*. Wheaton, Ill.: Crossway, 1992.

Gregory, Brad S. "Can We 'See Things Their Way'? Should We Try?" In *Seeing Things Their Way: Intellectual History and the Return of Religion*, edited by Alister Chapman, John Coffey, and Brad S. Gregory, 24–45. Notre Dame, Ind.: University of Notre Dame Press, 2009.

————. "The Other Confessional History: On Secular Bias in the Study of Religion." *History and Theory* 45 (2006): 132–49.

Grimes, William. "Capitalism, Brought to You by Religion." *New York Times*, December 30, 2005.

Guiness, Os. *Character Counts: Leadership Qualities in Washington, Wilberforce, Lincoln, and Solzhenitzyn*. Grand Rapids: Baker, 1999.

Habermas, Gary R. *Ancient Evidence for the Life of Jesus: Historical Records of His Death and Resurrection*. Nashville: Thomas Nelson, 1985.

————. *The Historical Jesus: Ancient Evidence for the Life of Christ*. Joplin, Mo.: College Press, 1996.

Hamilton, Michael S. "The Elusive Idea of Christian Scholarship." *Christian Scholar's Review* 31 (2001): 13–21.

Handy, Robert. "Christian Faith and the Historical Method." In *History and Historical Understanding*, edited by C. T. McIntire and Ronald A. Wells, 83–92. Grand Rapids: Eerdmans, 1984.

Hankins, Barry. *Francis Schaeffer and the Shaping of Evangelical America*. Grand Rapids: Eerdmans, 2008.

————. "'I'm Just Making a Point': Francis Schaeffer and the Irony of Faithful Christian Scholarship." *Fides et Historia* 39, no. 1 (2007): 15–34.

Hannam, James. *God's Philosophers: How the Medieval World Laid the Foundations of Modern Science*. London: Icon, 2009.

Hannula, Richard M. *Trial and Triumph: Stories from Church History*. Moscow, Idaho: Canon, 1999.

Harbison, E. Harris. *Christianity and History*. Princeton, N.J.: Princeton University Press, 1964.

————. "The Marks of a Christian Historian." In *God, History, and Historians: Modern Christian Views of History*, edited by C. T. McIntire, 330–56. New York: Oxford University Press, 1977.

Hardy, Lee. *The Fabric of this World: Inquiries into Calling, Career Choice, and the Design of Human Work*. Grand Rapids: Eerdmans, 1990.

Harlan, David. *The Degradation of American History*. Chicago: University of Chicago Press, 1997.

Harrell, David Edwin, Jr. "Review of *Less Than Conquerors*." *American Historical Review* 93 (1988): 781–82.

Hart, Benjamin. *Faith and Freedom: The Christian Roots of American Liberty*. Dallas, Tex.: Stanley & Lewis, 1988.

Hart, D. G. "Christian Scholars, Secular Universities, and the Problem with the Antithesis." *Christian Scholar's Review* 30 (2001): 383–402.

————. "History in Search of Meaning: The Conference on Faith and History." In *History and the Christian Historian*, edited by Ronald Wells, 68–90. Grand Rapids: Eerdmans, 1998.

————. *The University Gets Religion: Religious Studies in American Higher Education.* Baltimore, Md.: Johns Hopkins University Press, 1999.

————. "What's So Special about the University, Anyway?" In *Religious Advocacy and American History*, edited by Bruce Kuklick and D. G. Hart, 137–58. Grand Rapids: Eerdmans, 1997.

Harvey, Van A. *The Historian and the Believer: The Morality of Historical Knowledge and Christian Belief.* Philadelphia: Westminster, 1966.

Hasker, William. "Faith-Learning Integration: An Overview." *Christian Scholar's Review* 21, no. 3 (1992): 231–48.

Hatch, Nathan O. *Democratization of American Christianity.* New Haven, Conn.: Yale University Press, 1989.

————. *The Sacred Cause of Liberty: Republican Thought and the Millennium in Revolutionary New England.* New Haven, Conn.: Yale University Press, 1977.

Hauerwas, Stanley. *After Christendom? How the Church Is to Behave If Freedom, Justice, and a Christian Nation Are Bad Ideas.* Nashville: Abingdon, 1991.

————. *A Community of Character: Toward a Constructive Christian Social Ethic.* Notre Dame, Ind.: University of Notre Dame Press, 1991.

————. "A Review of *Defending Constantine.*" *Christian Century*, October 13, 2010. http://www.christiancentury.org/reviews/2010-09/nonfiction-1, accessed January 10, 2014.

————. *Unleashing the Scripture: Freeing the Bible from Captivity to America.* Nashville: Abingdon, 1993.

Hauerwas, Stanley, and William Willimon. *Resident Aliens: A Provocative Christian Assessment of Culture and Ministry for People Who Know That Something Is Wrong.* Nashville: Abingdon, 1989.

Hein, Steven A. "The Christian Historian: Apologist or Seeker?—A Reply to Ronald J. VanderMolen." *Fides et Historia* 4, no. 2 (1972): 85–93.

Henry, Douglas V., and Bob R. Agee, eds. *Faithful Learning and the Christian Scholarly Vocation.* Grand Rapids: Eerdmans, 2003.

Hexter, J. H. *On Historians: Reappraisals of Some of the Masters of Modern History.* Cambridge, Mass.: Harvard University Press, 1979.

Heyns, Garrett, and Garritt E. Roelofs. *Christian Interpretation of American History.* Chicago: National Union of Christian Schools, 1928.

Hill, Jonathan. *What Has Christianity Ever Done for Us? How It Shaped the Modern World.* Downers Grove, Ill.: InterVarsity, 2005.

Hill, Samuel S., ed. *The Encyclopedia of Religion in the South*. Macon, Ga.: Mercer University Press, 1984.

Himmelfarb, Gertrude. *Victorian Minds: A Study of Ideologies in Crisis and Ideologies in Transition*. New York: Knopf, 1968.

Hitchens, Christopher. *God Is Not Great: How Religion Poisons Everything*. New York: Twelve, 2007.

Hoffer, Peter Charles. *Past Imperfect: Facts, Fictions, Fraud—American History from Bancroft and Parkman to Ambrose, Bellesiles, Ellis, and Goodwin*. New York: Public Affairs, 2004.

Hoffmeier, James K., and Dennis R. Magary, eds. *Do Historical Matters Matter to Faith? A Critical Appraisal of Modern and Postmodern Approaches to Scripture*. Wheaton, Ill.: Crossway, 2012.

Hollinger, David. "Enough Already: Universities Do Not Need More Christianity." In *Religion, Scholarship, and Higher Education: Perspectives, Models, and Future Prospects*, edited by Andrea Sterk, 40–49. Notre Dame, Ind.: University of Notre Dame Press, 2002.

Holmes, Arthur. *The Idea of a Christian College*. Grand Rapids: Eerdmans, 1975.

Horner, Richard. "Paradoxes of Christian Scholarship." *Reconsiderations* 1, no. 4 (2002): 1–4.

Hosier, Helen Kooiman. *100 Christian Women Who Changed the 20th Century*. Grand Rapids: Revell, 2000.

Howard, Thomas Albert. "Virtue Ethics and Historical Inquiry: The Case for Prudence." In *Confessing History: Explorations in Christian Faith and the Historian's Vocation*, ed. John Fea, Jay Green, and Eric Miller. Notre Dame, Ind.: University of Notre Dame Press, 2010), 83-100.

Hughes, Richard T. *Christian America and the Kingdom of God*. Urbana: University of Illinois Press, 2009.

———. *Myths America Lives By*. Urbana: University of Illinois Press, 2004.

———. *The Vocation of a Christian Scholar: How Christian Faith Can Sustain the Life of the Mind*. Grand Rapids: Eerdmans, 2005.

Hume, David. *The Natural History of Religion*. Stanford, Calif.: Stanford University Press, 1956.

Hunter, James Davison. *To Change the World: The Irony, Tragedy, and Possibility of Christianity in the Late Modern World*. New York: Oxford University Press, 2010.

Hutchison, Aaron. "The Redeemed Scientist." Cedarville University, n.d. https://www.cedarville.edu/~/media/Files/PDF/Center-for-Biblical-Integration/Faculty-Integration-Paper-Aaron-Hutchison-Chemistry.pdf. Accessed August 7, 2014.

Hutchison, William R. *The Modernist Impulse of American Protestantism.* Cambridge, Mass.: Harvard University Press, 1976.

Iggers, Georg. "The Image of Ranke in American and German Historical Thought." *History and Theory* 2, no. 1 (1962): 17–40.

Jacobsen, Douglas, and Rhonda Hustedt Jacobsen. *Scholarship and Christian Faith: Enlarging the Conversation.* New York: Oxford University Press, 2004.

Johnson, Paul. *A History of the American People.* New York: HarperCollins, 1997.

Juhnke, James, and Carol Hunter. *The Missing Peace: The Search for Nonviolent Alternatives in United States History.* Kitchener, Ont.: Pandora, 2001.

Kammen, Michael. *In the Past Lane: Historical Perspectives on American Culture.* New York: Oxford University Press, 1997.

Katerberg, William. "The 'Objectivity Question' and the Historian's Vocation." In *Confessing History: Explorations in Christian Faith and the Historian's Vocation,* edited by John Fea, Jay Green, and Eric Miller, 101–27. Notre Dame, Ind.: University of Notre Dame Press, 2010.

Katerberg, William, Dana L. Robert, Leslie Woodcock Tentler, and Mark Noll. "Roundtable: Historians, Historiography, and the Confessional Divide." *Fides et Historia* 42, no. 2 (2012): 84–100.

Kayser, Phillip G. *Seeing History with New Eyes: A Guide to Presenting Providential History.* Omaha, Neb.: Providence History Festival, 2008.

Keillor, Steven J. *God's Judgments: Interpreting History and the Christian Faith.* Downers Grove, Ill.: IVP Academic, 2007.

———. *This Rebellious House: American History and the Truth of Christianity.* Downers Grove, Ill.: InterVarsity, 1996.

Kelly, Douglas F. *The Emergence of Liberty in the Modern World.* Phillipsburg, N.J.: Presbyterian & Reformed, 1992.

Kennedy, D. James, and Jerry Newcombe. *What If Jesus Had Never Been Born?* Nashville: Thomas Nelson, 1994.

Kennedy, Earl W. "Herman Dooyeweerd on History: An Attempt to Understand Him." *Fides et Historia* 4 (1973): 1–21.

———. "John Warwick Montgomery and the Objectivist Apologetics Movement." *Fides et Historia* 5 (1973): 117–21.

King, William McGuire. "An Enthusiasm for Humanity: The Social Emphasis in Religion and Its Accommodation in Protestant Theology." In *Religion and Twentieth-Century American Intellectual Life,* edited by Michael J. Lacey, 49–77. New York: Cambridge University Press, 1989.

Kugler, Michael. "Enlightenment, Objectivity, and Historical Imagination." In *Confessing History: Explorations in Christian Faith and the Historian's*

Vocation, edited by John Fea, Jay Green, and Eric Miller, 128–52. Notre Dame, Ind.: University of Notre Dame Press, 2010.

Kuklick, Bruce. "On Critical History." In *Religious Advocacy and American History*, edited by Bruce Kuklick and D. G. Hart, 54–64. Grand Rapids: Eerdmans, 1997.

———. "Review of George Marsden, *The Soul of the American University*." *Method and Theory in the Study of Religion* 8, no. 1 (1996): 79–84.

Kuklick, Bruce, Richard Bushman, and Mark Noll. "Believing History." *Books & Culture*, March/April 2005. http://www.booksandculture.com/articles/2005/marapr/4.06.html, accessed February 1, 2014.

LaGrand, James. "The Problems of Preaching through History." In *Confessing History: Explorations in Christian Faith and the Historian's Vocation*, edited by John Fea, Jay Green, and Eric Miller, 187–216. Notre Dame, Ind.: University of Notre Dame Press, 2010.

Land, Gary. "A Biblical-Christian Approach to the Study of History." In *Christ in the Classroom: Adventist Approaches to the Integration of Faith and Learning*, vol. 21, edited by Humberto M. Rasi, 455–72. Silver Spring, Md.: Institute for Christian Teaching, 1998.

Latourette, Kenneth Scott. "The Christian Understanding of History." *American Historical Review* 54 (1949): 259–76.

Leithart, Peter. *Defending Constantine: The Twilight of an Empire and the Dawn of Christendom*. Downers Grove, Ill.: IVP Academic, 2010.

Lewis, C. S. "Historicism." In *God, History, and Historians: An Anthology of Modern Christian Views of History*, edited by C. T. McIntire, 224–38. New York: Oxford University Press, 1977.

Linenthal, Edward T., and Tom Engelhardt, eds. *History Wars: The Enola Gay and Other Battles for the American Past*. New York: Henry Holt, 1996.

Link, Arthur S. "The Historian's Vocation." *Theology Today* 19 (1962): 75–89.

Loveland, Anne C. "Later Stages of the Recovery of American Religious History." In *New Directions in American Religious History*, edited by Harry S. Stout and D. G. Hart, 487–502. New York: Oxford University Press, 1996.

Löwith, Karl. *Meaning in History: The Theological Implications of the Philosophy of History*. Chicago: University of Chicago Press, 1950.

Lydon, Ghislaine. "Writing Trans-Saharan History: Methods, Sources and Interpretations across the African Divide." *Journal of North African Studies* 10, nos. 3–4 (2005): 293–324.

MacPhee, Donald A. "The Muse Meets the Master: Clio and Christ." In *A Christian View of History?* edited by George Marsden and Frank Roberts, 75–88. Grand Rapids: Eerdmans, 1975.

Mahanta, Siddhartha. "The GOP's Favorite Fringe Historian." *Mother Jones,* April 11, 2011. http://www.motherjones.com/politics/2011/04/david -barton-gingrich-bachmann-huckabee, accessed August 12, 2014.

Marsden, George M. "A Christian Perspective for the Teaching of History." In *A Christian View of History?* edited by George Marsden and Frank Roberts, 31–50. Grand Rapids: Eerdmans, 1975.

———. "The Collapse of American Evangelical Academia." In *Faith and Rationality: Reason and Belief in God,* edited by Alvin Plantinga and Nicholas Wolterstorff, 219–64. Notre Dame, Ind.: University of Notre Dame Press, 1983.

———. "Common Sense and the Spiritual Vision of History." In *History and Historical Understanding,* edited by C. T. McIntire and Ronald A. Wells, 55–68. Grand Rapids: Eerdmans, 1984.

———. *Fundamentalism and American Culture.* New York: Oxford University Press, 1980.

———. "Human Depravity: A Neglected Explanatory Category." In *Figures in the Carpet: Finding the Human Person in the American Past,* edited by Wilfred M. McClay, 15–32. Grand Rapids: Eerdmans, 2007.

———. *The Outrageous Idea of Christian Scholarship.* New York: Oxford University Press, 1997.

———. "Perry Miller's Rehabilitation of the Puritans: A Critique." In *Reckoning with the Past: Historical Essays on American Evangelicalism from the Institute for the Study of American Evangelicals,* edited by D. G. Hart, 23–38. Grand Rapids: Baker, 1995.

———. *The Soul of the American University: From Protestant Establishment to Established Nonbelief.* New York: Oxford University Press, 1992.

Marsden, George M., and Frank Roberts, eds. *A Christian View of History?* Grand Rapids: Eerdmans, 1975.

Marsh, Charles. *The Beloved Community: How Faith Shapes Social Justice, From the Civil Rights Movement to Today.* New York: Basic Books, 2005.

———. *God's Long Summer: Stories of Faith and Civil Rights.* Princeton, N.J.: Princeton University Press, 1997.

Marshall, Paul. *A Kind of Life Imposed on Man: Vocation and the Social Order from Tyndale to Locke.* Toronto: University of Toronto Press, 1996.

Marshall, Peter, and David Manuel. *From Sea to Shining Sea: God's Plan for America 1787–1837.* Grand Rapids: Revell, 1993.

———. *The Light and the Glory: Did God Have a Plan for America?* Grand Rapids: Revell, 1977.

———. *Sounding Forth the Trumpet: God's Plan for America 1837–1860.* Grand Rapids: Revell, 1999.

Martin, William. *With God on Our Side: The Rise of the Religious Right in America.* New York: Broadway Books, 1996.

Marty, Martin E. "The Difference in Being a Christian and the Difference It Makes—for History." In *History and Historical Understanding,* edited by C. T. McIntire and Ronald A. Wells, 41–54. Grand Rapids: Eerdmans, 1984.

Mascord, Keith Andrew. "Faith, History and the Morality of Knowledge: The Contrasting Views of J. W. Montgomery and V. A. Harvey." M.Th. thesis, Australian College of Theology, 1993.

May, Henry F. "The Recovery of American Religious History." *American Historical Review* 70 (1964): 79–92.

———. "Religion and American Intellectual History, 1945–1985: Reflections on an Uneasy Relationship." In *Religion and Twentieth-Century American Intellectual Life,* edited by Michael J. Lacey, 12–22. New York: Cambridge University Press, 1989.

McCarraher, Eugene. "The Enchantments of Mammon: Notes toward a Theological History of Capitalism." *Modern Theology* 21 (2005): 429–61.

McCartin, Joseph A. "*Utraque Unum:* Finding My Way as a Catholic and a Historian." In *Faith and the Historian: Catholic Perspectives,* edited by Nick Salvatore, 165–86. Urbana: University of Illinois Press, 2007.

McClay, Wilfred M. "Teaching Religion in American Schools and Colleges: Some Thoughts for the 21st Century." *Historically Speaking* 3, no. 2 (2001): 13–17.

McEowen, David W. "Teaching Business at a Christian University: Issues, Challenges, and Practices." Huntington University, n.d. http://www.huntington.edu/uploadedFiles/Dean/Faith_Integration/McEowen.pdf. Accessed August 7, 2014.

McGreevy, John. "Faith Histories." In *Religion, Scholarship, and Higher Education: Perspectives, Models, and Future Prospects,* edited by Andrea Sterk, 63–75. Notre Dame, Ind.: University of Notre Dame Press, 2002.

McIntire, C. T. "God's Work in History: The Post-Biblical Epoch." Public colloquium of the Institute for Christian Studies, Toronto, and Regent College, Vancouver, York University, May 16, 1975.

———. "Kenneth Scott Latourette." In *God, History, and Historians: Modern Christian Views of History,* edited by C. T. McIntire, 46. New York: Oxford University Press, 1977.

————. "The Ongoing Task of Christian Historiography." In *A Christian View of History?* edited by George Marsden and Frank Roberts, 51–74. Grand Rapids: Eerdmans, 1975.

McIntire, C. T., and Ronald Wells, eds. *History and Historical Understanding.* Grand Rapids: Eerdmans, 1984.

McKenzie, Robert Tracy. "Christian Faith and the Study of History: A View from the Classroom." *Fides et Historia* 36 (2000): 1–15.

————. "Don't Forget the Church: Reflections on the Forgotten Dimension of Our Dual Calling." In *Confessing History: Explorations in Christian Faith and the Historian's Vocation,* edited by John Fea, Jay Green, and Eric Miller, 280–98. Notre Dame, Ind.: University of Notre Dame Press, 2010.

————. *The First Thanksgiving: What the Real Story Tells Us about Loving God and Learning from History.* Downers Grove, Ill.: InterVarsity, 2013.

————. "The Vocation of the Christian Historian: Re-envisioning Our Calling, Reconnecting to the Church." *Fides et Historia* 45, no. 1 (2013): 1–13.

McLaren, Brian. *A New Kind of Christianity: Ten Questions that Are Transforming the Faith.* New York: HarperOne, 2011.

McRoberts, Kerry. "Faith Founded on Fact: The Apologetic Theology of John Warwick Montgomery." M.C.S. thesis, Regent College, 2000.

Metaxas, Eric. *Amazing Grace: William Wilberforce and the Heroic Campaign to End Slavery.* New York: HarperOne, 2007.

————. *Bonhoeffer: Pastor, Martyr, Prophet, Spy.* Nashville: Thomas Nelson, 2010.

————. *Seven Men and the Secret of their Greatness.* Nashville: Thomas Nelson, 2013.

Millard, Catherine. *The Rewriting of America's History.* Camp Hill, Pa.: Horizon House, 1991.

Miller, Charles J. "The Conference on Faith and History: Reminiscences about Origins and Identity." *Fides et Historia* 9 (1977): 59–63.

Miller, Perry. *Errand into the Wilderness.* Cambridge, Mass.: Harvard University Press, 1956.

————. *The New England Mind: From Colony to Province.* Cambridge, Mass.: Harvard University Press, 1953.

————. *The New England Mind: The Seventeenth Century.* New York: Macmillan, 1939.

————. *Orthodoxy in Massachusetts, 1630–1650.* New York: Harper & Row, 1970.

————. "Review of Timothy Smith's *Revivalism and Social Reform: American Protestantism on the Eve of the Civil War.*" *New England Quarterly* 30, no. 4 (1957): 558–60.

Mohr, James. *Abortion in America.* New York: Oxford University Press, 1978.

Moltmann, Jürgen. *Religion, Revolution, and the Future.* New York: Scribner's, 1966.

Montgomery, John Warwick. *History and Christianity.* Downers Grove, Ill.: InterVarsity, 1972.

————. "Toward a Christian Philosophy of History." In *Jesus of Nazareth: Saviour and Lord,* edited by Carl F. H. Henry, 227–40. Grand Rapids: Eerdmans, 1966.

————. *Where Is History Going? Essays in Support of the Historical Truth of Christian Revelation.* Grand Rapids: Zondervan, 1969.

Montgomery, John Warwick, and James R. Moore. "The Speck in Butterfield's Eye: A Reply to William A. Speck." *Fides et Historia* 4 (1971): 71–77.

Morgan, Edmund. *The Gentle Puritan: A Life of Ezra Stiles, 1727–1795.* New Haven, Conn.: Yale University Press, 1962.

————. *The Puritan Dilemma: The Story of John Winthrop.* Boston: Little, Brown, 1958.

————. *Puritan Political Ideas, 1558–1794.* Indianapolis, Ind.: Bobbs-Merrill, 1965.

————. *Roger Williams: The Church and the State.* New York: Harcourt, Brace & World, 1967.

————. *Visible Saints: The History of a Puritan Idea.* New York: New York University Press, 1963.

Mouw, Richard J. *Uncommon Decency: Christian Civility in an Uncivil World.* Downers Grove, Ill.: InterVarsity, 1992.

Murphey, Murray G. "On the Scientific Study of Religion in the United States, 1870–1980." In *Religion and Twentieth Century American Intellectual Life,* edited by Michael J. Lacey, 136–71. New York: Cambridge University Press, 1989.

Murray, Iain. "Explaining Evangelical History." *Banner of Truth* 370 (1994): 8–14.

————. *Revival and Revivalism: The Making and Marring of American Evangelicalism, 1750–1858.* Carlisle, Pa.: Banner of Truth Trust, 1994.

Nash, Ronald. "The Use and Abuse of History in Christian Apologetics." *Christian Scholar's Review* 1 (1971): 217–26.

————. *Christian Faith and Historical Understanding.* Grand Rapids: Zondervan, 1984.

Niebuhr, H. Richard. *The Meaning of Revelation*. Louisville, Ky.: Westminster John Knox, 2006.

———. *The Social Sources of Denominationalism*. New York: Henry Holt, 1929.

Niebuhr, Reinhold. *Faith and History: A Comparison of Christian and Modern Views of History*. New York: Scribner's, 1949.

Noll, Mark A. "The Conference on Faith and History and the Study of Early American History." *Fides et Historia* 11, no. 1 (1978): 8–18.

———. *Jesus Christ and the Life of the Mind*. Grand Rapids: Eerdmans, 2011.

———. "The Potential of Missiology for the Crises of History." In *History and the Christian Historian*, edited by Ronald A. Wells, 106–23. Grand Rapids: Eerdmans, 1998.

———. *The Scandal of the Evangelical Mind*. Grand Rapids: Eerdmans, 1994.

———. "Teaching History as a Christian." In *Religion, Scholarship, and Higher Education: Perspectives, Models, and Future Prospects*, edited by Andrea Sterk, 161–71. Notre Dame, Ind.: University of Notre Dame Press, 2002.

———. "Traditional Christianity and the Possibility of Historical Knowledge." *Christian Scholar's Review* 19 (1990): 388–406.

Novick, Peter. *That Noble Dream: The "Objectivity Question" and the American Historical Profession*. New York: Cambridge University Press, 1988.

Numbers, Ronald. "In Defense of Secular History." *Spectrum* 1 (1969): 64–68.

Olasky, Marvin. *Abortion Rites: A Social History of Abortion in America*. Wheaton, Ill.: Crossway, 1992.

———. *The American Leadership Tradition: Moral Vision from Washington to Clinton*. New York: Free Press, 1999.

———. *Fighting for Liberty and Virtue: Political and Cultural Wars in Eighteenth-Century America*. New York: Regnery, 1995.

———. "The History of Compassion." *World Magazine*, June 18, 2011. http://www.worldmag.com/articles/18137, accessed October 7, 2011.

———. *The Tragedy of American Compassion*. New York: Regnery, 1992.

Olson, Carl E. "Rediscovering Christopher Dawson: An Interview with Bradley Birzer." *Ignatius Insight*, February 4, 2008. http://www.ignatiusinsight.com/features2008/bbirzer_interview_feb08.asp, accessed January 10, 2014.

Orsi, Robert. *Between Heaven and Earth: The Religious Worlds People Make and the Scholars Who Study Them*. Princeton, N.J.: Princeton University Press, 2005.

Packer, J. I. "Call, Called, Calling." In *Baker's Dictionary of Theology*, edited by Everett F. Harrison, Geoffrey W. Bromiley, and Carl F. H. Henry, 108. Grand Rapids: Baker, 1960.

Pannenberg, Wolfhart. *Revelation as History*. New York: Macmillan, 1968.

Panosian, Edward M., David Fisher, and Mark Sidwell, eds. *The Providence of God in History*. Greenville, S.C.: Bob Jones University Press, 1996.

Patterson, James. "The Study of History." In *Faith and Learning: A Handbook for Christian Higher Education*, edited by David S. Dockery, 217–38. Nashville: Broadman & Holman, 2012.

Pierard, Richard. *The Cross and the Flag*. Carol Stream, Ill.: InterVarsity, 1972.

Piper, John. *The Hidden Smile of God: The Fruit of Affliction in the Lives of John Bunyan, William Cowper, and David Brainerd*. Wheaton, Ill.: Crossway, 2001.

Plantinga, Cornelius. *Engaging God's World: A Christian Vision of Faith, Learning, and Living*. Grand Rapids: Eerdmans, 2002.

Pointer, Richard. "Kenneth Scott Latourette." In *Historians of the Christian Tradition: Their Methodology and Influence on Western Thought*, edited by Michael Bauman and Martin I. Klauber, 411–30. Nashville: Broadman & Holman, 1995.

Pritchard, Elizabeth. "Seriously, What Does 'Taking Religion Seriously' Mean?" *Journal of the American Academy of Religion* 78, no. 4 (2010): 1087–1111.

Purcell, Edward G. *The Crisis of Democratic Theory*. Lexington: University of Kentucky Press, 1973.

Rauser, Randal. "Learning in a Time of (Culture) War: Indoctrination in Focus on the Family's *Truth Project*." *Christian Scholar's Review* 39, no. 1 (2009): 75–89.

Reid, W. Stanford. "The Present State of Research in Early Modern European History." *Fides et Historia* 11, no. 1 (1978): 19–27.

———. "The Problem of the Christian Interpretation of History." *Fides et Historia* 5 (1973): 96–106.

Ridderbos, Herman N. *The Coming of the Kingdom*. Philadelphia: Presbyterian & Reformed, 1962.

Rienstra, M. Howard. "Christianity and History: A Bibliographical Essay." In *A Christian View of History?* edited by George Marsden and Frank Roberts, 181–96. Grand Rapids: Eerdmans, 1975.

———. "History, Objectivity, and the Christian Scholar." In *History and Historical Understanding*, edited by C. T. McIntire and Ronald A. Wells, 69–82. Grand Rapids: Eerdmans, 1984.

Rietveld, Ronald. "The Christian Historian as Activist." *Fides et Historia* 9 (1977): 25–38.

Roberts, Jon H. "In Defense of Methodological Naturalism." *Fides et Historia* 44, no. 1 (2012): 61–64.

Roebuck, Alan. "D'Souza's Comeback." *American Thinker*, December 25, 2007. http://www.americanthinker.com/2007/12/dsouzas_comeback.html, accessed January 10, 2014.

Rook, Stephen D. "Historical Objectivism: The Apologetic Methodology of John Warwick Montgomery." M.A. thesis, Harding Graduate School of Religion, 1985.

Rose, James. *Guide to American Christian Education for Home and School: The Principle Approach.* Camarillo, Calif.: American Christian Institute, 1987.

Russell, Jeffrey. "Religious Commitment and Historical Writing." *Christian Scholar* 45 (1962): 18–19.

Schaeffer, Francis. *How Should We Then Live: The Rise and Decline of Western Thought and Culture.* Old Tappan, N.J.: Revell, 1976.

Schmidt, Alvin J. *How Christianity Changed the World.* Grand Rapids: Zondervan, 2001.

Schultz, Roger. "Evangelical Meltdown: The Trouble with Evangel*histoire*." *Contra Mundum* 2 (1992): 41–47.

———. "Historical Revisionism: Why All the Fuss?" *Faith for All of Life*, March/April 2007, 7–10.

———. "Judgments in History." *Chalcedon Report*, February 2003, 21–22.

Schuurman, Douglas. *Vocation: Discerning our Callings in Life.* Grand Rapids: Eerdmans, 2004.

Schwehn, Mark R. *Exiles from Eden: Religion and the Academic Vocation in America.* New York: Oxford University Press, 1993.

———. "Faith Seeking Historical Understanding." In *Confessing History: Explorations in Christian Faith and the Historian's Vocation*, edited by John Fea, Jay Green, and Eric Miller, 23–38. Notre Dame, Ind.: University of Notre Dame Press, 2010.

Schwehn, Mark R., and Dorothy Bass. *Leading Lives that Matter: What We Should Do and Who We Should Be.* Grand Rapids: Eerdmans, 2006.

Schweiger, Beth Barton. "Seeing Things: Knowledge and Love in History." In *Confessing History: Explorations in Christian Faith and the Historian's Vocation*, edited by John Fea, Jay Green, and Eric Miller, 60–80. Notre Dame, Ind.: University of Notre Dame Press, 2010.

Schweikart, Larry, and Michael Allen. *A Patriot's History of the United States: From Columbus's Great Discovery to the War on Terror.* New York: Sentinel, 2004.

Scott, Joan Wallach. *Gender and the Politics of History.* New York: Columbia University Press, 1988.

Shankel, George Edgar. *God and Man in History.* Nashville: Southern Association, 1967.

Shannon, Christopher. "After Monographs: A Critique of Christian Scholarship as Professional Practice." In *Confessing History: Explorations in Christian Faith and the Historian's Vocation,* edited by John Fea, Jay Green, and Eric Miller, 168–86. Notre Dame, Ind.: University of Notre Dame Press, 2010.

———. "Between Outrage and Respectability: Taking Christian History Beyond the Logic of Modernization." *Fides et Historia* 34, no. 1 (2002): 3–13.

Shinn, Roger. *Christianity and the Problem of History.* New York: Scribner's, 1953.

Simmons, Ernest L. *Lutheran Higher Education: An Introduction for Faculty.* Minneapolis: Augsburg, 1998.

Singer, C. Gregg. *A Theological Interpretation of American History.* Phillipsburg, N.J.: Presbyterian & Reformed, 1964.

Sire, James. *The Universe Next Door: A Basic World View Catalog.* Downers Grove, Ill.: InterVarsity, 1976.

Skotheim, Robert. *American Intellectual Histories and Historians.* Princeton, N.J.: Princeton University Press, 1966.

Slade, Peter. *Open Friendship in a Closed Society: Mission Mississippi and a Theology of Friendship.* New York: Oxford University Press, 2009.

Sloane, Andrew. *On Being a Christian in the Academy: Nicholas Wolterstorff and the Practice of Christian Scholarship.* Carlisle, UK: Paternoster, 2003.

Smith, Christian. *American Evangelicalism: Embattled and Thriving.* Chicago: University of Chicago Press, 1998.

Smith, Theodore Clarke. "The Writing of American History in America from 1884 to 1934." *American Historical Review* 40, no. 3 (1935): 439–49.

Smith, Timothy. *Revivalism and Social Reform: American Protestantism on the Eve of the Civil War.* Nashville: Abingdon, 1957.

Speck, William A. "Herbert Butterfield on the Christian and Historical Study." *Fides et Historia* 4, no. 1 (1971): 50–70.

Spitz, Lewis W. "History: Sacred and Secular." *Church History* 47 (1978): 5–22.

Stafford, Tim. "Whatever Happened to Christian History?" *Christianity Today* 45, no. 5 (2001): 42–49.

Stark, Rodney. *America's Blessings: How Religion Benefits Everyone, Including Atheists.* West Conshohocken, Pa.: Templeton, 2012.

———. *Cities of God: The Real Story of How Christianity Became an Urban Movement and Conquered Rome.* New York: HarperOne, 2007.

———. *For the Glory of God: How Monotheism Led to Reformations, Science, Witch-Hunts, and the End of Slavery.* Princeton, N.J.: Princeton University Press, 2004.

———. *God's Battalions: The Case for the Crusades.* New York: HarperOne, 2010.

———. *How the West Won: The Neglected Story of the Triumph of Modernity.* Wilmington, Del.: ISI Books, 2014.

———. *The Rise of Christianity: How the Obscure, Marginal Jesus Movement Became the Dominant Force in the Western World.* San Francisco: HarperSanFrancisco, 1997.

———. *The Triumph of Christianity: How the Jesus Movement Became the World's Largest Religion.* New York: HarperOne, 2012.

———. *The Victory of Reason: How Christianity Led to Freedom, Capitalism, and Western Success.* New York: Random House, 2005.

Stephens, Randall J., and Karl W. Giberson. *The Anointed: Evangelical Truth in a Secular Age.* Cambridge, Mass.: Harvard University Press, 2011.

Sterk, Andrea, and Nina Caputo. "The Challenge of Religion in History." In *Faithful Narratives: Historians, Religion, and the Challenge of Objectivity,* edited by Andrea Sterk and Nina Caputo, 1–14. Ithaca, N.Y.: Cornell University Press, 2014.

Stout, Harry S. "Biography as Battleground: The Competing Legacies of the Religious Historian." *Books & Culture,* June/July 1996, 9–10.

———. *The Divine Dramatist: George Whitefield and the Rise of Modern Evangelicalism.* Grand Rapids: Eerdmans, 1991.

———. *The New England Soul: Preaching and Religious Culture in Colonial New England.* New York: Oxford University Press, 1986.

———. "The Reviewers Reviewed." *Banner of Truth* 378 (1995): 7–10.

———. "Theological Commitment and American Religious History." *Theological Education* 25 (1989): 44–59.

———. *Upon the Altar of the Nation: A Moral History of the American Civil War.* New York: Viking, 2006.

Swanstrom, Roy. *History in the Making: An Introduction to the Study of the Past.* Downers Grove, Ill.: InterVarsity, 1979.

Swartz, David. *Moral Minority: The Evangelical Left in an Age of Conservatism.* Philadelphia: University of Pennsylvania Press, 2012.

Sweeney, Douglas A. "On the Vocation of Historians to the Priesthood of Believers: A Plea to Christians in the Academy." In *Confessing History: Explorations in Christian Faith and the Historian's Vocation,* edited by John Fea, Jay Green, and Eric Miller, 299–315. Notre Dame, Ind.: University of Notre Dame Press, 2010.

Tentler, Leslie Woodcock. "One Historian's Sundays." In *Religious Advocacy and American History,* edited by D. G. Hart and Bruce Kuklick, 209–20. Grand Rapids: Eerdmans, 1997.

Trollinger, William Vance. "Faith, History, and the Conference on Faith and History." *Fides et Historia* 32, no. 1 (2001): 1–10.

Trueman, Carl R. *Histories and Fallacies: Problems Faced in the Writing of History.* Wheaton, Ill.: Crossway, 2010.

———. "The Sin of Uzzah." The Mortification of Spin. Published by the Alliance of Confessing Evangelicals. July 10, 2012. http://www.mortificationofspin.org/mos/postcards-from-palookaville/the-sin-of-uzzah#.VT41eaNViko. Accessed January 10, 2014.

Unger, Irwin. "The 'New Left' and American History: Some Recent Trends in United States Historiography." *American Historical Review* 72, no. 4 (1967): 1238–39.

Vaduva, Virgil. "An Interview with Dr. Larry Schweikart." Planet Preterist website, July 17, 2006, http://planetpreterist.com/content/interview-dr-larry-schweikart, accessed August 4, 2014.

Van Kley, Dale. "Dooyeweerd as Historian." In *A Christian View of History?* edited by George Marsden and Frank Roberts, 89–98. Grand Rapids: Eerdmans, 1975.

VanderMolen, Ronald J. "The Christian Historian: Apologist or Seeker." *Fides et Historia* 3, no. 1 (1970): 41–56.

VanDrunen, David. *Living in God's Two Kingdoms: A Biblical Vision for Christianity and Culture.* Wheaton, Ill.: Crossway, 2010.

———. *Natural Law and the Two Kingdoms: A Study in the Development of Reformed Social Thought.* Grand Rapids: Eerdmans, 2010.

Viner, Jacob. *The Role of Providence in the Social Order: An Essay in Intellectual History.* Philadelphia: American Philosophical Society, 1972.

Voskuil, Louis J. "History as Process: Meaning in Change." *Pro Rege* 16, no. 4 (1988): 22–31.

———. "History: Sound and Fury Signifying Nothing?" *Pro Rege* 16, no. 3 (1988): 2–12.

Wacker, Grant. "Understanding the Past, Using the Past: Reflections on Two Approaches to History." In *Religious Advocacy and American History*, edited by Bruce Kuklick and D. G. Hart, 159–78. Grand Rapids: Eerdmans, 1997.

Waggoner, Robert L. "Why Genuine Christianity Improves the World." Biblical Theism. http://www.thebible.net/biblicaltheism/0402 christianityimproves.pdf, accessed January 10, 2014.

Waibel, Paul. "History." In *Opening the Evangelical Mind: The Integration of Biblical Truth in the Curriculum of the University*, edited by W. David Beck, 117–34. Grand Rapids: Baker, 1991.

Waldrep, B. Dwain, and Scott Billingsley, eds. *Recovering the Margins of American Religious History: The Legacy of David Edwin Harrell, Jr.* Tuscaloosa: University of Alabama Press, 2012.

Walsh, Brian J., and J. Richard Middleton. *The Transforming Vision: Shaping a Christian World View.* Downers Grove, Ill.: InterVarsity, 1984.

Wells, Ronald A. *History through the Eyes of Faith.* New York: Harper & Row, 1989.

Wennberg, Robert. "The Moral Standing of the Dead and the Writing of History." *Fides et Historia* 30, no. 2 (1998): 51–63.

White, David. "Review of *The Divine Dramatist*." *Banner of Truth* 366 (1994): 29.

Williams, William Appleman. *The Contours of American History.* Cleveland, Ohio: World, 1961.

Wilson, John. "The Strange Case of Dr. Balmer and Mr. Hyde." *Books & Culture*, September/October 2006. http://www.booksandculture.com/articles/2006/sepoct/1.7.html, accessed January 10, 2014.

Wineburg, Sam. *Historical Thinking and Other Unnatural Acts.* Philadelphia: Temple University Press, 2001.

Wolfe, Alan. "The Opening of the Evangelical Mind." *The Atlantic Monthly* 286, no. 4 (2000): 55–76.

Wolterstorff, Nicholas. *Reason within the Bounds of Religion.* Grand Rapids: Eerdmans, 1976.

———. "Scholarship Grounded in Religion." In *Religion, Scholarship, and Higher Education: Perspectives, Models, and Future Prospects*, edited by Andrea Sterk, 3–15. Notre Dame, Ind.: University of Notre Dame Press, 2002.

Wood, Gordon S. *Purpose of the Past: Reflections on the Uses of History.* New York: Penguin, 2008.

Woodbridge, John, ed. *More Than Conquerors: Portraits of Believers from All Walks of Life.* Chicago: Moody, 1992.

Worthen, Molly. *Apostles of Reason: The Crisis of Authority in American Evangelicalism.* New York: Oxford University Press, 2014.

Wright, Gordon. "History as a Moral Science." *American Historical Review* 81 (1976): 1–11.

Wykstra, Stephen J. "The Problem of Miracle in the Apologetic from History." *Journal of the American Scientific Affiliation* 30, no. 4 (1978): 154–63.

Yamauchi, Edwin M. "Easter—Myth, Hallucination, or History? Part 1." *Christianity Today*, March 15, 1974, 4–7.

———. "Easter—Myth, Hallucination, or History? Part 2." *Christianity Today*, March 29, 1974, 12–16.

Yerxa, Donald A., ed. *British Abolitionism and the Question of Moral Progress in History.* Columbia: University of South Carolina Press, 2012.

Yoder, John Howard. *The Politics of Jesus.* Grand Rapids: Eerdmans, 1994.

———. *The Priestly Kingdom: Social Ethics as Gospel.* Notre Dame, Ind.: University of Notre Dame Press, 1984.

Zinn, Howard. *A People's History of the United States.* New York: New Press, 1990.

———. *The Politics of History.* Chicago: University of Chicago Press, 1990.

INDEX

MacPhee, Donald A., 49

Mahanta, Siddhartha, 188n38

Maier, Paul, 109

Marsden, George, 26, 41–43, 49–50, 52, 54, 59–65, 167n9, 177n65, 181n31, 183n57, 183n60, 195n49; at Calvin College, 50, 54, 173n47; "A Christian Perspective for the Teaching of History," 55; "Common Sense and the Spiritual Vision of History," 55; at Duke Divinity School, 50, 173n47; on evangelicals and epistemology of naïve realism, 41–42; with Hatch, 26, 27, 181n31 181n32; on Kuyper's "two sciences," 42; on Kuyperianism, 54, 55, 56; with Noll, 50, 52, 54, 181n31 181n32; *The Outrageous Idea of Christian Scholarship*, 57, 171n40; on reformed epistemology, 42; *The Soul of the American University: From Protestant Establishment to Established Nonbelief*, 173n47; at The University of Notre Dame, 27, 50, 173n47; at Westminster Theological Seminary, 54; at Yale University, 54, 173n47

"Marsden Settlement," 59–65; Michael Baxter on, 64; Michael Hamilton on, 62–63; D. G. Hart on, 62, 63; David Hollinger on, 60–62; Bruce Kuklick on, 60; Roger Schultz on, 63–64; Christopher Shannon on, 64–65

Marsh, Charles, 88–89

Marshall, Paul, 151–52, 153

Marshall, Peter, and David Manuel, 132–33, 196n10

Martin, William, 171n39

Marty, Martin E., 30–31, 32, 173n46

Marx, Karl, 12, 102

Marxism, 16–17, 31, 33, 42, 44, 50, 57, 87; *see also* historiography, Marxist; Marx, Karl

Mathews, Shailer, 15

May, Henry F., 22, 29

McCarraher, Eugene, 87–88, 175n51

McCartin, Joseph A., 77

McClay, Wilfred M., 17, 30

McEowen, David W., 180–81n27

McGreevy, John, 28, 156

McIntire, C. T., 44–45, 145; on Kenneth Scott Latourette, 20

McKenzie, Robert Tracy, 159–60, 199n29

McLaren, Brian, 107

Mead, Sidney, 35

Metaxas, Eric, 187n32

methodological atheism, 138; *see also* methodological naturalism; practical deism

methodological naturalism, 5–6, 12–17

Middleton, J. Richard, 39

Millard, Catherine, 186n29

Miller, Charles J., 171n38

Miller, Perry: George Marsden on, 177n65; on Timothy L. Smith, 172n44; Harry Stout on, 32–33, 177n65

Moberg, David, 185n16

Mohr, James, 84–85

Moltmann, Jürgen, 165n2

Montgomery, John Warwick, 47, 101–3, 191n4, 191n5, 191–92n8; with James R. Moore and William A. Speck, 191n4

moral judgments in writing history, 67–70, 73, 80–81, 87–96, 136–37, 195n49; *see also* historical moralizing

morality and historical study: *see* moral judgments in writing

Printed in the USA
CPSIA information can be obtained
at www.ICGtesting.com
CBHW031408110824
13000CB00004B/234

9 781481 302630